MONSTERLAND

Nicholas Jubber is an award-winning travel writer. Fascinated by history and its relationship with the present, he explores connections — and misconnections — across the centuries. In his book, *The Fairy Tellers*, this fascination carries him from Kashmir to Lapland to find out the history behind some of the world's most beloved, and many long-forgotten, fairy tales. He has been shortlisted three times for the Stanford Dolman Award, and won it for his debut *The Prester Quest*. He has spoken at literary festivals including Hay-on-Wye and Edinburgh, and has written articles for *The Guardian*, *The Telegraph*, and *The Irish Times*, among others.

MONSTERLAND

A JOURNEY AROUND THE WORLD'S DARK IMAGINATION

NICHOLAS JUBBER

SCRIBE
Melbourne | London | Minneapolis

This one's for the booksellers

Scribe Publications
18–20 Edward St, Brunswick, Victoria 3056, Australia
2 John St, Clerkenwell, London, WC1N 2ES, United Kingdom
3754 Pleasant Ave, Suite 223w, Minneapolis, Minnesota 55409, USA

Published by Scribe 2025

Copyright © Nicholas Jubber 2025

All rights reserved. Without limiting the rights under copyright reserved above, no part of this publication may be reproduced, stored in or introduced into a retrieval system, or transmitted, in any form or by any means (electronic, mechanical, photocopying, recording or otherwise) without the prior written permission of the publishers of this book.

The moral rights of the author have been asserted.

Internal illustrations by Joe McLaren.

Typeset in Fournier by the publishers

Printed and bound in the UK by CPI Group (UK) Ltd, Croydon CR0 4YY

Scribe is committed to the sustainable use of natural resources and the use of paper products made responsibly from those resources.

978 1 761380 29 7 (Australian edition)
978 1 915590 29 9 (UK edition)
978 1 964992 11 2 (US edition)
978 1 761386 05 3 (ebook)

Catalogue records for this book are available from the National Library of Australia and the British Library.

scribepublications.com.au
scribepublications.co.uk
scribepublications.com

CONTENTS

Prologue   1

PART ONE: WHEN THE WILD ROARS
Chapter One: The Giant Who Fell in Love   15
Chapter Two: City of the Dragon   38
Chapter Three: The Ogre on the Purple Mountain   59

PART TWO: WHEN THEY BECOME US
Chapter Four: Shapeshifters at Sea   85
Chapter Five: The Realm of the Unseen   106
Chapter Six: Who's Afraid of the Rougarou?   131

PART THREE: WHEN THE DEAD RISE
Chapter Seven: The Conquistador and the Ghost   161
Chapter Eight: The Age of Vampires   190
Chapter Nine: Revolution of the Undead   216

PART FOUR: WHEN THE FUTURE BECKONS
Chapter Ten: Mary Shelley's Monster-Making Circle   241
Chapter Eleven: The Humans Must Die   265
Chapter Twelve: King of the Monsters   286

Epilogue   309
Acknowledgements   316
Bibliography   319
Endnotes   330

Prologue

Snow was falling over the mountains. It shrouded the trees and hooded the rocks; it smeared the roofs in the village below and speckled the river like the spots on a wild beast's pelt. It was just the kind of weather you'd expect on the day when the monsters are coming.

There they were, stomping down the stony, snow-laden path towards me. Some were fanned by feathers, others obscured by fleece. Under pinhole eyes rimmed with colour, bear-like snouts bulged and bony fangs curled out of mouths as red as the horns on their heads.

Spring comes late to the Rhodope Mountains. The streets were still rinky, the log piles capped with snow. The monsters were better at negotiating the slopes than me, so I flattened myself against the stone walls of my host Ilia's house and watched them go by. Cow-bells tinkled from their horns. Bronze clappers rattled on their knees, the sort of clanging you'd expect to hear if a metal gate had been flung open.

'We call them *kukeri*. It goes back to the ancient Thracians.' Ilia's eyes flashed in his broad, beaming face. 'Dionysus and all his parties. That's what it is, it's celebration — the kukeri are about life!'

Behind him, a mask hung from a nail, over an old saddle and a woodpile. A beard of silky black goat hair spilled from a face tessellated with pieces of bone. Apotropaic: an image of evil, warding off the evil outside. A lesson in the ambiguity of folk monsters and the stories we tell about them.

The square of Shiroka Laka was their destination, the heart of a Bulgarian mountain village. Count all the eyes fixed on the monsters: a thousand and rising. The kukeri swung around each other, leaped, and tumbled. Like animals taking over the farm, they yoked themselves to a wooden plough and drove it around the square. Others held up a wooden spindle, a stump of wood painted red.

Their name remains a mystery. Some derive it from *kuka*, proto-Slavic for 'evil spirit', others from the Latin for 'hood'. But the longer I watched them, the less they seemed like 'evil spirits'; more like distorted mirrors for humanity.

Guided by their leader, who had antler-like horns and went by the tongue-twisting title of 'Byulyukbashiya', they were acting out a cosmic drama handed down from generation to generation. It plays out like some burlesque variation on a Greek tragedy. Over here, the kukeri roll on the ground, conical hoods swaying like sheaves of corn in the breeze, a chorus in mime to the scattering of grain. Over there, an old groom is girded in a three-feet-long strap-on. He lowers his red wooden phallus over the bride (a man in a burlap dress), instigating a fast-forward pregnancy. Life swells on one side, sinks on the other: the bride's belly balloons, and at the same time, the leader is stabbed by a spindle. While the bride's legs are parted and a ragged doll presented to the crowd, the kukeri surround the slain leader and will him back to life. This is Kukerovden, the day of the kuker: a spell without words, dramatising the cycle of life and death, rapture and pain.

*

'Of course it brings us together. This is the purpose!'

Late in the evening, one of the kukeri faced me in the village bar. Poor man: he was having to field questions from the gangly, pasty-faced fellow from way-out-of-town. With his mask on the table between us, he took a swig from a bottle of Krušovice beer: 'It is in our blood. My father did it also, and my grandfather. The best thing is not what you can see. For us, it is the time we are practising.'

'What does it feel like?' I asked. 'When you're in the mask, when you become a kuker — do you feel different?'

He shrugged. Took a sip of his beer, while I was rephrasing the question. But another kuker leaned across his shoulder:

'I know what you say. Something — when we put the mask on — something happens to us. In life, even when everything is ...' — he screwed his fists together, showing how dark things can get — '... still, when the mask is on, then we are ...' One hand grasped at the air, as if the word was hiding in the rafters, and his eyes lit up when he found it: 'free!'

MONSTERS THROUGH MILLENNIA

As far back as we can go, they are there, waiting for us. 40,000 years ago, or so, a figure known today as the 'Löwenmensch', or 'lion-man', was carved from a mammoth's tusk in the Swabian Jura, a bipedal theriomorph combining features of human and beast. In the oldest written tale, the 4,000-year-old Sumerian *Epic of Gilgamesh*, the eponymous hero confronts the forest guardian Humbaba the Terrible, a tusked giant born from a mountain, whose 'speech is fire, and his breath is death!' The Bible tells of Behemoth, the chaos-monster at the beginning of creation. Browse the pages of *The Tibetan Book of the Dead* and you'll come across Wrathful Deities with the heads of wild beasts, garlands of snakes, and corpses over their shoulders, stirring the cycle of existence with their lions' manes and bulging eyes.

The stories of the ancient world can be so boggy, with their arcane rites and auguries, baffling hierarchies and obsession with honour; it's a challenge to find an accessible entry point. What guides us in, again and again, are the monsters: Odysseus and his crew trying not to get eaten by the Cyclops, the Hindu hero Rama and his monkey army battling demonic Rakshasas, the great northern strongman Beowulf ripping the clawed arm from the fen beast Grendel's shoulder. A few things may have changed over the millennia, but our fascination for monsters isn't one of them.

What is different, however, is the way that we perceive the monsters. For the people who told those long-ago tales, they were more than mere fodder for heroic deeds. They were palpable threats to life and (even more worryingly) the afterlife, liable at any moment to tear through the flimsy barrier between our world and theirs. The earliest monsters were scarcely distinguishable from the gods — terrifying beings that decided when avalanches fell and thunder roared and floods drowned the early settlements.

Four thousand years ago, pregnant women in Mesopotamia feared a visit from Lamashtu, a skull-breasted figure with a donkey's ears, a bird's talons, and a mantle of coarse black hair, whose companions included a hound with red and green eyes and a fourteen-foot jackal. Lamashtu was the daughter of the Sun God, not some wily outcast but a representative of the powers-that-be, and if she took against you, she would tear your newborn baby out of your arms, to suck its blood and chew on its bones. Like many of the gods that emerged across the Red Sea in ancient Egypt — jackal-headed, lion-headed, falcon-headed, guardians of mummies, night spirits, or deities of disease — Lamashtu was a god *and* a monster, appeased with ritual sacrifices and prayers.

But time slowly prised gods and monsters apart. Animism (the belief that spirits reside in all things) gave way to theism (the belief that power over all is the preserve of a few divine beings, or a single deity in the case of monotheism). Monster-gods were shunned in favour of gods made (to flip the biblical line) in humanity's image. Even where the monster-gods were retained, they tended to slip down the hierarchy. The leading gods became ever more human-like, reflecting the soaring confidence of human societies. As for those fanged, clawed, beast-like gods, they tended to fall out of the pantheons, doomed to prowl the earth, demoted and decayed but retaining something of their old mystique, repurposed as vanquishable monsters for human heroes to hunt.

It was the gods that had changed. The monsters had always reflected our uneasy relationship with the wild places around us, our fear of what might lurk in the dark. When a retired warrior called Guthlac decided to devote his life to prayer in seventh-century Lincolnshire, he knew he would have to reckon with the 'multitude of fiends'. Kneeling in his hermitage, he was ransacked by 'the loathsome clutches of spirits, wretched and wracking ... fierce to rush upon him with greedy grasp'. The monsters were existential torments, the old deities that men and women used to worship, but they were also physical. Mired in dirty water and swarming with insects, the fens of Lincolnshire were no place for the healthy. Dark stories hovered, incessant as the midges.

Roaring out of hostile environments as well as our own agitated psyches, monsters embody what unsettles us. Which is why they are so easily projected onto 'others': other races, other belief systems, other ways of living. Mediaeval writers and illustrators filled vast tracts of terra incognita, the yet-to-be-discovered world, with monstrous races — dog-headed Cynocephali, Blemmyes with their heads in their chests, Sciapods lying in the sun under a single clubbed foot; dragons, mer-people, wave-sweeping leviathans. *Here be monsters:* kicked out of the heavens, they were roiling around us on earth, and if we pointed our spears at them, we had a decent chance of laying them low. They represented the fringes, wherever civilisation had yet to assert control. And they represented other civilisations too — the ones our own had yet to conquer.

But if the wild places harboured many of the monsters of folk belief, others poured out of an even more unsettling realm. In 1642, the residents of Edgehill in Warwickshire reported a spectre of 'incorporeall souldiers', and so many testified to these apparitions that a report was commissioned by King Charles I. Visions of the dead have been cited throughout history, manifesting as ghosts, vampires, and other eerie apparitions. They feature in many of the most troubling tales ever told, evoking our apprehension as well as our curiosity about the Great Hereafter.

Wild places and the realm of the dead: most folk monsters can be assigned to one or the other. But another, even more disturbing category, is required. Back in biblical times, King Nebuchadnezzar of Babylon suffered from a curse: 'his hair grew like the feathers of an eagle and his nails like the claws of a bird'. He was a theriomorph, like the werewolves and other shapeshifters of more recent tales. There's nothing freakier than the fear of turning into a monster. Except, perhaps, when the monsters turn into us.

Monsters flourished for millennia, pressing against the psyches of every stratum of society, from rulers like Nebuchadnezzar to the shepherds of Edgehill. But time caught up with them at last. The Age of Discovery revealed a lot, but it didn't produce any dog-headed men or sunbathing Sciapods. Instead of nations of weird beings, monsters were reduced to isolated individuals with genetic anomalies: sufferers of elephantiasis, Proteus syndrome, hypertrichosis. Crowds may have gawked, but fear shrank as humanity's knowledge and power increased.

With the Age of Science, the traditional monsters found themselves against an insuperable barrier, dismissed from reality and excluded from scientific taxonomies. They were confined to the zone of storytelling, glamorous after-images of dying or disempowered cultures. As we shall see, some of the most powerful manifestations of monsters exist in this limbo state, representing historical memories of times long past, emotional connections with periods of seismic change and traumatic loss.

But the world keeps turning, and in the industrialised world, a new perception of monsters emerged. In a world less and less convinced of their existence, they became monetised spectacles, marshalled for a rapidly increasing range of mass media. From macabre bloodsuckers in penny dreadfuls to stop-motion, rubber-suited, or (latterly) CGI movie behemoths, monsters have taken pride of place in commercial storytelling. This doesn't mean the old fears have been fully suppressed (or, at least, in being suppressed, they still have a knack for finding outlets). In an irony that says much about the twisty path of the monster story, science — which had done so much to smother the old beliefs — became the most fertile source of our modern fears, and inspiration for new hordes.

Now, instead of being spawned by gods or magic spells, monsters draw their power from electrolysis, poisonous chemicals, neutron radiation, fossil-fuel extraction, cloning technology; or they travel across the stars, alerted to our planet by the signals we're relentlessly broadcasting. Punishments for human hubris, these new monsters transform our scientific achievements into visions of the apocalypse that will eventually engulf us.

METAMORPHOSIS: A BOY'S LIFE

This is how you turn into a monster.

You go down to the woods, over a threshold of nettles, under canopies of hawthorn and beech. Dive in and climb the oak trees, scrape your knees on the bark, wedge yourself against the scaffold branches. It helps if you're under the age of twelve, but I don't think that's a deal breaker.

Now for the important bit: you sit down on a cracked and moss-covered log. Give it some time. Wait until it feels as if a subterranean goblin has thrust out a venomous claw and pierced your flesh. Now the poison's inside you, coursing through your veins, and it's just a matter of counting down.

... ninety-nine,
ninety-eight,
ninety-seven ...

I came back from the wood that day with a sting in my thigh. Once

I was inside the house, I rolled up my shorts. The pain had subsided, so I was able to study the wound with the morbid curiosity that comes easily when you're eight-and-a-half. A pair of puncture marks and a patch of itchy redness spreading around it. Within a few hours, the patch had turned to a sallow, ogreish green. Blisters bubbled, the size of sucker-pads, expanding in a relentless march of body horror that was starting to threaten my groin.

My grandmother was looking after us that day. I tried to keep it from her, at first. Some unconscious part of me suspected my incipient metamorphosis wouldn't meet with the approval of Jesus or the rows of sombre-looking saints that gazed across the pews at Sunday Mass. My favourite TV show involved a time-travelling hero in a police box who fended off monsters on a weekly basis; my hobbies included drawing my own beasties. Sure, my education might not have extended to the classical motto 'Be careful what you wish for or the gods might grant it', but I understood there was a certain poetic justice to what was happening.

My grandmother saw the spreading discolouration when I was putting on my pyjamas and did her best for me. By which I mean: she slapped on some baby lotion and recited a decade of the rosary.

By day three, the blisters covered an area the circumference of a jam jar, but my imagination was racing ahead, mapping the transformation across my entire body (would I develop glowing buboes, would my eyes shoot up on stalks, and — most important of all — how sharp would my teeth become?).

As soon as my parents came home, my mother took me to the GP. The doctor's solution was less incantatory than my grandmother's, his bland expression and long white coat downgrading my condition. I was singularly unimpressed: all those mutterings about an adder bite, the scribbled prescription for antihistamine. Oh, sure, the green patch might have shrunk the next day, but I already had my own diagnosis, and I was sticking with it. Over the years, it became a family myth, shaped by countless retellings. The time I started turning into a monster.

Once the genie's out of its bottle, as they say. The kind of boy who imagines he's becoming a monster is the kind of boy who's always looking for them. I hid myself in huts made out of blankets and sofa cushions, waiting for the claws to break through; I traced shaggy heads and spiky spines on reams of paper; I scripted my own monster movie and mobilised a gang of fellow eleven-year-olds to film it on a borrowed Betamax. A quarter-century after my abortive transformation, my wife and I named the tables at our wedding after our favourite monsters (which made the seating plan a challenge — do you put your father-in-law with the gorgons or the goblins, and which monster's the best fit for that prickly distant cousin?).

Monsters bled into my working life as well. Over the years, researching books about travel and history, I puzzled my way around different forms of storytelling, and monsters crept through the cracks in my journeys: standing in a butcher's shop in the Zagros Mountains of Iran, listening to the tale of a hero's wrestle with a horned, spotted demon known as a 'div'; clambering around Icelandic rock formations named after trolls; interviewing Sicilian puppeteers who staged a marionette's battle with a papier-mâché dragon.

Monsters were always skulking at the edge of my vision. But now it was time to tackle them head on. It was time to seek them out, all around the world.

MAPPING THE MONSTER TRAIL

Monster — from the Latin 'monstrare', to show: something that reveals itself, makes itself manifest. 'Mostro' in Italian, 'mostre' in French, 'Monster' in German. With echoes of 'monere', to warn. But if we peer beyond Western Europe, different shades of meaning can be incorporated. The Arabic term is 'wahsh', cognate with words for barrenness and desolation. In China, 'guaiwu' is used, literally translating as 'weird creatures' but connected to the word for a shaman, underscoring the association between monsters and the spirit world. The traditional Japanese term, 'bakemono', refers to something that 'changes shape', reflecting a rich folklore around shapeshifting as well as the instability of monster definitions, which have morphed to 'yokai' and more recently the English-derived 'monsuta'. Such a range of definitions, overlapping rather than contradictory: mix them together and we have a worldwide hybrid, a lumbering conglomeration of words, reflecting the many angles through which monsters have been perceived by different cultures.

The more I thought about monsters, the more I found myself turning the pages of my atlas, indulging an old habit for trailing my fingers along possible route lines. It would never be enough to delve into this subject from the comfort of a library. I wanted to hear different perspectives, to encounter different voices; and I knew from experience this could only be done through travel. If I wanted to learn about ogres, I needed to climb a mountain where ogres are said to dwell; if I wanted to understand dragons, I needed to go to the place where they've been parading a dragon for hundreds of years. By visiting a selection of these monster locations, moving from ancient to more recent imaginings, I hoped to feel the stories for myself. In the process, I would weave my own story, a monster tapestry narrating our knotty relationship with the creatures of our imaginings.

I'm no cryptozoologist: this book isn't a search for Big Foot or the Loch Ness Monster. I had no intention of scaling the Himalayas in search of the Yeti (there are better reasons to go mountain-trekking). But if I could explore the monsters we've invented, meet people who still cherish the stories, if I could find a way to peer inside the blurry portal between past and present ...

To witness the ogres of Kyoto, bombarded by soya beans on the eve of spring, tramp to an eighteenth-century Balkan vampire's forest dwelling, paddle among the folk-beasts of the Louisiana bayous — these and other adventures inscribed themselves across the dotted lines on my map. A dozen monsters, divided across the four monster categories I had chosen: the wild, the shapeshifters, the undead, and the monsters of the modern imagination. Four categories with one thing in common: their ability to terrify.

*

Monsters aren't real ... I remember telling myself that, fingers curling around the rim of my duvet, at the age of six or seven, when the lights were out and the door to the bedroom cupboard was swinging wide. Monsters aren't real ...

But that isn't how the imagination works.

The monsters recounted in this book all stalked the land, and continue to do so, forever and ever. They aren't biological species, huffing for oxygen under the menace of extinction. They don't need specific vegetation or a thousand-hectare habitat range. They just need somebody with imagination enough to whisper them to life.

This book is a journey into story time, not real time: where everything is possible, and all our fears have tangible form. Where there are ghosts in the closet, werewolves howling under every full moon and a monster under every child's bed.

But stories don't come blasting out of a void. They trail the texture of lived experience, like the spoor by which an unlikely beast is tracked. Which brings us to a gnarly hill at the edge of England. A brisk south-easterly tickles the heather and slides over slabs of granite. A giant lurks round here, a real brute. And yet ... for all his monstrous size, his goggly eyes, his habit of smashing down farmers' crofts, he has one endearing feature that makes it really hard to hate him: he's in love with a human, who is about to give him the challenge of his life.

PART ONE

When the Wild Roars

'Appear, O Bacchus, to our eyes as a bull
or serpent with a hundred heads,
or take the shape of a lion breathing flame!'

Euripides, *The Bacchae*, 405 BC

CHAPTER ONE

The Giant Who Fell in Love

THE FIRST TALE

Ever since the people of Cornwall can remember, giants have prowled their hills. Some are fierce, a few are friendly, but surely there has never been one like Bolster. His head is as hard as granite, his forehead as cracked as the cliffs where he roams. Spikes of hair poke out of his ears like bars of iron, and his beard is so big and dirty that the sea-fowl nest in it while he's sleeping. He has a huge stride: he can stand with one foot on Carn Brea, and another on Carn Bryanack, a pair of hills six miles apart, looking over the heather and gorse towards the crashing waves of the ocean. If he were a more contemplative sort of giant, he might see the water as a mirror to his own salty temper.

The people live in terror of Bolster. He rolls boulders onto their homes and smelting houses, and sometimes he snatches up children and takes them home for his supper. He has a wife, nearly as big as him. But love curdles quickly with giants. Bolster won't stop pushing her about, telling her to move a boulder for a new cairn or seek out children to eat. She carries the stones in her apron, hauling them on her back. Sometimes the apron-strings snap and the stones tumble down the hillside.

The old beliefs have held fast for a long time in Cornwall, but now the saints are wandering between the villages. One of them is called Saint Agnes, and she spreads the word of God in song — her voice so pure, so angelic, even the giant on the hilltop can't resist.

'Come and live with me on my stronghold,' he begs. 'I'll give you anything you want.'

'Tut tut, don't you have a wife? You should be ashamed of yourself.'

Exasperated by the giant's attention, at last Saint Agnes makes a suggestion:

'You really love me? Then prove it — by filling one of these holes in the ground with your blood.'

She points to a hole on a hillside near the sea. To a giant's eye, it's barely a pin-prick on the ground, so without a second thought he takes a knife to his arm and makes a cut.

What Bolster fails to realise is that the hole has been drilled by wind and water all the way to the sea. So he carries on bleeding, carries on bleeding. When he presses his other arm against the ground to lift himself up, the earth doesn't even quake. He collapses to his knees and topples over, his wounded arm still leaking into the hole.

What a sight that is — the giant lying lifeless on the hillside, his corpse bled dry. The villagers let out a great chorus of whooping — nearly as loud as a giant's roar! No more holes in their walls, no more ruined smelting houses! Bolster's wife looks happy too — she leaps down the hill and darts across the heathland, never to be seen again. The people accept Agnes's teachings, for she has saved them from the giant, and a new world is dawning.

A CORNISH BFG

Thirty miles from my home in Dorset is the Cerne Abbas Giant, a 180-foot club-wielding nude with an erection nearly as long as his head, carved into the chalk of the hillside — England's most beloved flasher, surely. Sixty miles north, I once camped on the outskirts of Bristol by a wood-covered stone divot known for centuries as the footprint of a giant called Goram. But to delve among a range of giants I needed to roam towards the edge: the county where a 'mighty race of Titans dwelt', to quote the nineteenth-century folklorist William Bottrell, 'looked upon as giants'.

Down the Tinners' Way: out of St Ives, past brightly painted artists' doors, garden Buddhas, and long-haired mermaids curling around the side walls of pubs. I was looking for giants — and nowhere has them in spades like Cornwall.

Hedges of gorse ribboned the roadside. The meadows were speckled with stubs of granite, which burst from outcrops like bones breaking out of the earth's skin. Beyond grazing fields, hemmed in by drystone walls and the corrugated roofs of farmhouses, the spiky granite of Gurnard's Head seethed at the waves like the head of a giant lizard.

Another mile west, a red-brick chimney torpedoed over the crumbling grey walls of a pair of nineteenth-century engine houses, the wrack of many generations' worth of tin-mining. Across the road, gleaming on its granite crest, was Carn Galver, the 'outcrop of the lookout'. With its neolithic walls of heaped and delicately balanced granite, it was transmuted over the centuries into the dwelling-place of a giant called Holiburn. A monster, perhaps. But it's hard to imagine a gentler giant this side of Roald Dahl's BFG.

'People of the northern hills have always had a loving regard for this giant,' recorded William Bottrell (who lived with his cat in a hut near St Ives) in 1870, 'because he appears to have passed all his life at the carn in single blessedness, merely to protect his beloved people of Morvah and Zennor from the depredations of the less honest Titans who dwelt on the Lelant hills.' The tale of Holiburn was a gentle one with which to begin my journey, although in the end a tragic one.

Granite boulders strung a zigzagging bridge between the heather and gorse, their cracks glowing with blue squill and yellow wheels of coltsfoot. Leaving my backpack in a low granite chamber, I bounced up the path, fired by excitement. From a simple boulder wall, the crest expanded, swelling to a multilayered construction, like some giants' game of Jenga. An illusion, a trick of the landscape. In places the rock was so sharp it looked as if it had been sawn. Narrow menhirs and slanted granite slabs jabbed at the sky, suggesting direction indicators. A fin-shaped skyline-marker drew the eye towards St Michael's Mount to the south-east, another guided you further towards Lizard Point. Students of ancient geometry have identified Carn Galver on a trajectory that reaches as far as the Scilly Isles, reflecting the site's ancient significance, which in storytelling terms has expressed itself through tales about giants. Without scientific processes to align to these features, how else would you explain them?

The same mythic principle appears around the world. Who built the Mesoamerican pyramid of Cholula? The Quinametzin giants, in the era of the Sun of Rain. How were the sarsens of Stonehenge transported? By giants under the orders of Merlin. They were here before us, goes the universal pattern, and we have inherited a world of their making. Of all the monsters imagined around the world, giants drive us deepest in time.

Up on the tor, I had a giant's eye view across the plains of Morvah and Zennor, the districts that lay under Holiburn's legendary protection. Some 230 metres above the sea, Carn Galver isn't steep or perilous. Mystery oozes from its stony crest, but its contours are gentle, matching the temper of the giant it inspired.

According to the tale, Holiburn had a particular friend, from the village of Choon, who would climb up the carn to play with him. One evening, tapping him on the head, Holiburn invited him to come back and play the next day. No answer came from his friend, however, and for good reason. The giant realised what he'd accidentally done when he saw the crack in the youth's skull. 'Oh my son, why didn't they make the skull of thy noddle stronger?' Holiburn lamented (in Bottrell's transcription, taken from a local storyteller in the 1860s). 'A es as plum as a pie-crust, dough-baked, and made too thin by the half! How shall I ever pass my time without you to play bob and mop-and-heave?'

Even if they want to, the story warns us, man and monster cannot mix. And so, for seven years, the giant pined until at last his broken heart gave way and he was absorbed into the granite and gorse. Like so many giants around the world (such as Atlas, collapsing into the mountain range of North Africa), he *became* the landscape. In mythical terms, human society isn't only standing on the shoulders of giants. It's stamping all over their terraformed corpses.

THE GRANITE FOLK

Gods or monsters: giants embody the overlap. They have the size and destructive capabilities of the former, but they differ in one essential characteristic: they can be vanquished. In folk tales, especially, they are fallible antagonists, like the fee-fi-fo-fummer who tumbles down Jack's beanstalk. Many stories pivot on the giants' clumsiness or stupidity, emphasising the guile of human heroes like Jack (or Saint Agnes against Bolster, or Odysseus against Polyphemus), celebrating human ingenuity against the larger elemental forces around us. But legends attribute great skills and craftsmanship to giants, such as the Jentil of the Basque country, credited with raising the megalithic dolmens of the Pyrenees. In this respect, they are folkloric shorthand for millions of years of geological processes. They bring a certain order to the wild places that humans sought to tame, in the process holding up a mirror to humanity: our ambition and our savagery, amplified to the scale of the big wide world around us.

'Stories of giants feed off the landscape,' as the storyteller Mike O'Connor (author of a popular collection called *Cornish Folk Tales*), put it to me in his home near Padstow. 'Whenever you see a big lump of rock in an unlikely place, such as below Carn Galver, you can persuade yourself it's a giant's bowling ball.' Like so many giants, the Cornish ones are as old as the hills, many of which they are credited with raising. Although the folk tales weren't systematically collected until the nineteenth century, there are earlier written versions. As Mike pointed out, their presence on the Poly-Olbion maps of the early seventeenth century hint at their antiquity, as do the Celtic origins of many giant names (Cormoran, decapitated by Jack the Giant-Killer at St Michael's Mount, for example, means 'great man by the sea'). Often they serve an etiological purpose — folk explanations for features of the landscape. But for all their grandeur, the Cornish giants are closer to the people than most giants in other lands. Holiburn playing with his ill-fated friend; Bolster falling in love with Saint Agnes: like the rocks spilling down the hillsides, leaving their crumbs of granite among the fields, the Cornish giants mingle with the folk below.

Walking the narrow road to Penzance after my climb up Carn Galver, I spotted a few of these mysterious spillages along the way. Near an ancient burial chamber was the Lanyon Quoit, a slab of granite resting on a set of natural buttresses (a decent-sized dining table if you happened to be the height of a house). A mile north, a dirt track wriggled past a quillet, a small field where a doughnut of granite stood between a couple of rocky stumps. Known as the 'Mên-an-Tol', the 'stone of the hole', it was believed to have magical properties. Parents used to pass their sick children through the hole in hope of a cure. It illustrates the mystery associated with Cornish granite and the human desire to interpret these forms, the same instinct that turned the conglomeration on Carn Galver into a giant's fortress.

From the small to the mighty: a few miles east of Penzance, I boarded a boat from a skerry of grass-furred stone. It was put in place, so the legend goes, by the wife of the red-headed giant Cormoran. Now it's a convenient docking point for crossings over the choppy water to St Michael's Mount. Up a cobbled path, I clambered past the so-called 'giant's well' and a heart-shaped cobblestone known as the 'giant's heart'. Beyond the eighteenth-century porringers and tea caddies adorning the turreted castle, I stopped in a chapel where a human skeleton measuring seven feet and eight inches long was found in a cellar in 1725.

'And we still don't know who he was or why he was so tall,' said the docent on duty.

By the time I was ready to walk back to the mainland, the sea level had dropped, revealing the causeway. Limpets on the rocks and snails on the slabs, traces of a fossilised forest suggesting a lusher landscape than we're left with today. *Carrack Looz en Cooz*, as people called St Michael's Mount in Cornish: 'the grey rock in the wood'.

Now it's named for the archangel who brings down a dragon in the Book of Revelation. (The Cornish version has him stabbing the dragon on the mount.) But the most popular folk tale associates the mount with Jack the Giant-Killer. So the tale goes: Cormoran was a curmudgeon who bullied his wife into dragging white granite from the neighbouring hills to build the mount. When she set down the greenstone instead, he knocked her dead. But he was growing old, half-blind with only a single tooth in his mouth. Jack dug a pit at the base of the mount, covered with sticks and skins, the weary giant sank into the trap, and Jack came along with his axe.

In this story, we see the classic giant role as fallen demigod. Jack represents human audacity, and his victory over the giant is a folkloric rendering of the slower process by which the wooded rock was taken over by human inhabitants. But sometimes the giants reign supreme, and at the broodiest of Cornwall's giant lairs, it's said they did the blood-shedding themselves. I made my way there after a damp night camping on the edge of Penzance, boarding the coaster towards Land's End. At Treen, a river chuckled under a mill, past idyllic gardens fenced with Japanese bamboo and debouched near a slipway and a stone hut swagged in buoys, like a film set for *Poldark*. I took inspiration from the giants: long strides suppress the distance. I may not have a pair of seven-league boots, but walk like a giant and you're bound to reach your destination much faster.

The sea ahead was a gorgeous blue, rippling with white foam where the tide was racing. Bursting over the water was one of Cornwall's most dramatic manifestations of granite. Separated by a narrow waist from the mainland, the neolithic rock fort of Treryn Dinas lunged at the sky, rock so spiky that any sentence describing it is overwhelmed by verbs: thrusting, darting, angling its claws to catch unwary gannets. Clambering over heather and sea-beet, I hauled myself over porphyritic slabs where green sprigs of sea ivory fingered out of boulder cracks. At last, I pulled myself onto a curved lump of lichen-patched rock. Arms swung out at the sides and there were divots in the granite in which you could have rested a tankard. This unlikely projection is known as 'The Giant's Chair', and it's matched by a smaller one across the fort: 'The Giant's Lady's Chair'.

This is the story: a giant lived up on Treryn Dinas with his wife. He used to sit on the rock and lour over the sea. But one day another giant scurried up the fort, for he had fallen in love with the giantess. He threw himself on his rival and stabbed him in the belly. The giantess saw it all from her seat, but said nothing. She accepted the assassin as her lover. For many happy years after, they lived together on the fort.

Now I was the one in the Giant's Chair. No sign of any blade-wielding assassin, unless you counted the razorbills wheeling overhead. Down on the golden sand below, a couple of swimmers were hurling themselves into the water. I clambered down a hazardous slope and peeled out of my clothes, running at the sea as if it was some enemy to be tamed. It was too cold for more delicate motions and my head was roiling with giant lore. How my skin tingled, shocked into a quivering hypersensitivity by the sudden change of temperature. Pulling on my clothes under a hood of dark granite, I was beaming. The last few months hadn't been easy, but now I was on the road, I felt lighter already, lifting with anticipation for the journeys to come. I peered back at the jagged giants' promontory, like some adventurer eyeing the destination in a romance.

THE MAKING OF ALBION

'So, look at it from a certain angle,' said Anna, 'and you can see a giant.' Wander around Cornwall and you're never more than a quoit's* throw from another storyteller. The other end of the county, up on Bodmin Moor. Old mining shafts pricked the sky, mocking the wind-shocked condition of the hawthorns, and sheep scrambled around the base of a tor known as Stowe's Hill. It was up this tor and against the blastings of the wind that I was being led by Anna Chorlton, author of a story collection called *Cornish Folk Tales of Place*. With her hands sunk in the pockets of her blue coat, brown hair stirred by the breeze, Anna scattered fragments of tales as we climbed around the granite clitter: the hurlers legendarily ossified in a nearby stone circle, the stone-cutter who lived in a cave on the hill, the saint who challenged a giant to a stone-hurling contest, which traditionally explained the stack of granite on the hill's summit.

It's a fine view up there, looking out towards Dartmoor, but the eye is wrenched back to the marvel on the hilltop. So ingeniously are the slabs piled, bulging out from an astonishingly narrow base, they're known as the 'Cheesewring', after a traditional cheese press. Geology credits this wonder to weathering and dates its presence back millions of years. Local lore, of course, has another explanation.

Saint Tue, the story goes, was a plucky evangelist who set a challenge to the giants: if he could beat them in a quoit-hurling contest, the saints would be allowed to stay in Cornwall. A giant called Uther took him on, but he failed to account for the power of Saint

---

* In Cornwall, the term 'quoit' is used for dolmens and other mysterious structures comprising upright stones with a flat capstone on top, dating back to the Neolithic period. Many folk stories tell of giants throwing quoits — in this case the capstones — during their games.

Tue's faith. Despite his diminutive size, the saint's quoits were winged forward, an angel ensuring that he carried the contest. Like the story of Bolster and Saint Agnes, told forty miles south-west, it's a parable for the decline of the old ways and the rise of Christianity. In this case, the losing giant has the name of 'Uther', the same name as King Arthur's father in the legends.

Anna lives with her family just a few miles from the Cheesewring, a short walk from another giant's domain, Trethevy Quoit, known locally as 'The Giant's House', where slabs of granite lean over an ancient path of quartz. Sitting in her house under Monopoly boxes and Harry Potter Lego, drinking tea, and eating homemade cookies, I listened to three generations of her family telling tales — her vivacious daughter Elowen, Anna herself, and her mother, Sue, a locally renowned puppeteer and artist. Sue had brought along a copper picture stand, a 'cornishbhai' inspired by traditional Japanese storytelling, into which she slotted her scenes to spin out a tale. That afternoon, she told one about the piskies, the little folk of Cornwall, stealing a farmer's food after he cuts up the turf where they sleep, and another about a real-life woman called Anne Jeffries, who communed with fairies in the mid-seventeenth-century.

'People in Cornwall are storytellers,' said Sue. 'You see it wherever you go, at gatherings, at tea parties. And it's anarchic, they don't stick to the script.'

For Anna, there's an important theme of 'looking after your neighbour': 'You see this in the piskie stories especially. They help people who are frail, who haven't got much. Life in Cornwall is often harsh and terribly poor. So the piskies help the farmer, the elderly woman, the lonely child, they make their lives a little more bearable.'

These themes are interconnected, born out of Cornwall's position at the edge of (or, as some would have it, next to) England, exploited but sparsely rewarded, left to fend for itself despite all the tin and copper and granite carried over the Tamar. Isolated linguistically as well as geographically and politically, Cornwall was a convenient depot in which to store mysterious things, a fitting abode for tales of giants.

For a week or so, I wound my way around the Duchy. Shifting my backpack on my shoulders, I strolled past surf lodges and signs for holiday lets, ranging across moors and heaths, passing wind turbines and the industrial giants of pyramid-shaped sky tips. I watched gannets dive around the grassy shoulder of a cliff once named for a giant called Wrath, and followed the flight of curlews from the earthwork at Gorran Haven, where I spent the night in a spider-haunted watch-guard's hut from the Napoleonic wars. It's said that a giant was rolled into the sea from the Haven's earthwork, by a cunning physician summoned to cure his stomach-ache. 'We'll need to bleed you,' the physician suggested, pointing to a hole in the cliff. But the hole burrowed all the way to the ocean, so the giant kept on bleeding and the physician rolled his corpse onto the rocks below. The story echoes the one about Bolster and Saint Agnes, a typically Cornish tale, an 'ecotype' to use the technical term, in which the gloomy, perforated cliffs play a key role in the plot.

Cornwall's rocky isolation not only inspired plenty of giant lore among the local population, it also prompted tales by outsiders. And this isn't a recent phenomenon — we're talking eight centuries at least. Indeed, there's a tale about a Cornish giant at the very core of Britain's mythic identity.

On my way into the county, I had stopped to change trains at Plymouth. There, under a seventeenth-century citadel and the green slopes of Plymouth Hoe, I clambered among spears of grey limestone above the lapping sea — a spot known as 'the Giant's Leap'. The story located here was so important to British mythology that for several centuries, a giant and his rival were carved into the turf under the citadel, recorded as late as the reign of Queen Elizabeth I. The tradition was reinstated in 2021 by the artist Charles Newington. 'The site was just begging to have these giant figures in it,' he told me when I spoke to him. After the local council had come on board and the necessary licences were secured, Newington laid out the forms of a giant and a hero — Gogmagog and the warrior Corineus — on the grass-covered glacis under the citadel, traced out with football-pitch paint. 'We had a team from 29 Commando to help us, billeted in the citadel,' he explained, 'and Plymouth Argyle Football Club provided the gunk.' A community undertaking: the local press hailed the operation and so much interest was garnered that Newington was hoping to install a longer-term version, using paving slabs and metal spikes. For Plymouth, it was an iconic episode, up there with the division-three trophy from 1996. After all, for hundreds of years, the battle between Gogmagog and Corineus was believed to explain how the ancient Britons came to dominate the islands that took their name.

'The island was then called Albion, and was inhabited by none but a few giants.' So recorded Geoffrey of Monmouth in his twelfth-century *History of the Kings of Britain*. Long after the fall of Troy, a descendant of Aeneas set out for this 'promised island, and arrived on the coast of Totness'. He was known as Brutus, and he named the island after himself: 'Britain'. The Trojan warriors were more than a match for the many giants that populated Albion, and soon there were few of these monsters remaining.

One day, when the Britons were feasting near Plymouth, they were attacked by a band of these giants. The Britons made mincemeat of them, except for their leader, who was 'of such prodigious strength that at one shake he pulled up an oak as if it had been a hazel wand'. His name was Gogmagog. A suitable opponent, Brutus decided, for his favourite general, Corineus.

It was a perfect match-up. Gogmagog's brawn gave him the upper hand, and he cracked three of Corineus's ribs. But this only incited the Briton, who:

> roused up his whole strength, and snatching him upon his shoulder, ran with him, as fast as the weight would allow him, to the next shore, and there setting upon the top of a high

rock, hurled down the savage monster into the sea; where falling on the sides of craggy rocks, he was torn to pieces and coloured the waves with his blood.

So the last great giant of Albion was destroyed. Brutus gave all the land south of the wrestling-place to Corineus, and he named it after himself. Hence: Cornwall.

To the modern ear, this episode has more holes than a windblasted Cornish clifftop. But, as with many of the monster tales we'll be visiting, what matters is its impact. Fusing Greek mythology with the Bible, Geoffrey of Monmouth's tale offered a foundational myth for a nation still wrestling, seventy years after the Norman Conquest, with its identity. Passed down through various hands, it would influence the likes of Thomas Malory, William Shakespeare, and John Milton — the latter retelling the story of Gogmagog in his *History of Britain*. Along with the turf effigies at Plymouth Hoe, the giant and his rival were fashioned into statues to guard London Bridge. Although they were swallowed up by the Great Fire of 1666, they remained iconic enough to be reconstructed, fourteen-foot guards manning London Bridge until they were destroyed again, in 1940, by the Luftwaffe. Remade once more, they were installed at the Guildhall, where they still glower down on passers-by, awaiting their annual outing in the Lord Mayor's procession.

As for Plymouth, the pitch paintings on the Hoe had already faded by the time of my visit. The only version I saw was a mounted print of cudgel-wielders in Wetherspoons, where the pub sign declared the ancient name: 'The Gog and Magog'. Corineus forgotten, the fallen giant supreme. But it was on the other side of the Tamar that giants would soar to life.

From Uther hurling the granite slabs on Bodmin Moor to Bellerion of Land's End, scooping sailors off the passing ships, Cornwall has scarcely a carn or cliff without its own giant yarn. I experienced this abundance when I joined Mike O'Connor and his friends at their regular storytelling meet-up in Liskeard. Mike, a mercurial storyteller (as well as a fiddler and composer of real power), told a tale about the historical Jan Tregeagle (originally a seventeenth-century magistrate), transformed over the centuries into a giant 'who gets bigger as the story goes west'. A harpist called Barbara Griggs narrated a delightfully fruity version of the tale of Bolster, in which he's transformed into a cactus. A fellow called Geoff delivered the story behind the Giant's Hedge — 'Jack the Giant with nothing to do / Built a hedge from Lerryn to Looe' — a rhyme passed down to explain a 4,000-year-old earthwork. What an evening that was — stories whirling around me, digested with tea and home-made cake, topped off at Barbara's cottage near Launceston, where she played on her harp while her husband Bob kept my glass topped up with wine. Monsters, I thought to myself that night: what a calling card!

Seven centuries earlier, the poet John Havillan declared:

There giants whilome dwelt, whose clothes were skins of beasts ...
These pesterd most the western tract; more fear made thee agast,
O Cornwall, utmost door thou art to let in Zephyrus blast.

In their own story-spinning way, Mike and his circle showed there's still truth to this notion: monsters exist wherever people are telling stories about them. And by that logic, no giant exists more vividly, nor stands taller, than the one menacing the heaths around St Agnes on Cornwall's northern coastline. It was time to meet the giant known as Bolster.

THE GIANT AWAKES

'It started out just us and our families, thirty years ago — and now look! We've never had so many people!'

Brian Hart had been charging up and down St Agnes Beacon,

and he had the ruddy-faced, gimlet-eyed intensity of somebody who's been getting things done all day. Six hundred and thirty feet below, the Atlantic was swatting a craggy cliff line, which slid into an undulating heathland swollen by hill forts and disrupted by earthworks. Gorse billowed between lumps of granite that broke out of the bunch-grass like fists out of the ground. Across a vista of receding hills, mining shafts spoked the horizon between the burned-orange mounds of spoil heaps. Tinning and giant tales: St Agnes is top of the heap for both. The pride in its tin is expressed in a centuries-old local saying: 'Sten Sen Agnes yw an gwella sten yn Kernow' ('St Agnes's tin is the best tin in Cornwall'). And as for giants, well, Cornwall may have plenty of competition in that regard, but these days Bolster is hard to top.

Although he was conspicuously absent that evening. Wooden pallets formed a pyramid, set alight to honour the old tradition of signal-lighting on the beacon. His name emerged from the excited lips of children and the adults playing along with them: 'Bolster hasn't woken up yet, he's still sleeping!' The children chased each other around fluttering banners and a trig point, while their parents rested on the slope, greeting each other over the hissing of ring pulls. Brian counted around 300 people. They were still coming well after dark — a red-and-black trail winding out of the walls of granite in the village below.

Among the stalwarts of the Bolster Festival was Soozie Tinn, who was running the barbecue — moon-faced, red-cheeked, a warm and welcoming presence. She'd written a ballad about Bolster and Saint Agnes, which she and Brian would be narrating the next day.

'Look.' Swivelling away from the burger grill, she pointed over the heath, towards the hills on the horizon. 'Over there is Carn Brea, about six miles away. It's said that Bolster could stand with one foot there and another here on the beacon. That's how big he was!'

To be fair, it's a strange tale: a supersized sex pest bested by a missionary. Historically, Saint Agnes was a Roman martyr of the early fourth century. She may never have stepped foot in Britain, but like in the folk tale, she did spurn a powerful suitor (a Roman nobleman, rather than a giant). As a result, she was condemned as a Christian, sentenced to be dragged naked through the streets of Rome. Some vestige of this tale mingled with the Cornish landscape — the ancient earthwork known for centuries as 'the Bolster'. A church was dedicated to Saint Agnes in the pre-Norman period, and on the same site another church was consecrated in 1484. Through the alchemy of storytelling, the saint and the giant were mashed together in the local folk culture, braided into a tale pitting the village against the surrounding heathland.

In *Wolf Hall*, Hilary Mantel imagined rumours of Bolster spreading among the citizens of Tudor London, fearful of an approaching army of Cornish rebels. Whatever the story's currency in the 1500s, it was certainly well established by the early 1700s. A local landowner and member of parliament, Thomas Tonkin, included it in his account of 'The Parish of St Agnes', describing a ditch (or 'vallum') probably dug in Roman times, said by 'the country people':

> to have been the work of a famous Wrath or Giant called Bolster, who lived at a place of the same name, through which this vallum passeth, perhaps an abbreviation of bolla ter, land intrenched, or cast up, for bolla signifies an intrenching or casting up.

Tonkin narrated the story — with Saint Agnes, in his version, forced to carry the stones to the top of the hill until the giant 'attempting her chastity, she pretended to yield to him, provided he would fill a hole (which she showed him) with his blood'. Although the story would be retold and expanded by William Bottrell and other folklorists of the nineteenth century, introducing Bolster's wife into proceedings, the dynamic of a monster in the wild heaths, harassing the villagers, is there from the start. It remains key to depictions today, as I learned when I came face to face with the giant the following morning, after a night camping on a farm a few miles out of town.

'No valerian this year!'

So said Jo, one of the volunteers who'd brought flowers to the St Agnes Sports Club. Glowing in the morning sunlight were bluebells and ox-eye daisies, celandines, alexanders, and sweet-smelling phlox. Jo and her fellow volunteers were the kind you find in church halls and community centres up and down the land. In this case, however, they weren't here to do the pews at church or decorate a wedding venue. They were here to give a giant a makeover.

'He's about to awaken!'

A couple of burly men carried his body out of a corrugated shed and laid it on a set of trestles beside the football pitch. The granite-like slab of a head was set against the fence, and volunteers started binding ferns to his brow. Technically, Bolster might have been constructed from fibreglass, with a harness of steel and wire so the operator would be able to raise him up. But now, coiffured in ferns and flowers, it was easy to believe the giant had grown from the heathland we'd climbed the night before.

'Don't worry,' one of the children reassured his younger brother. 'He can't do anything. At least,' he added, with a mischievous curl of his lips, 'not till they get the head on!'

The little boy wouldn't be the first to be awed by Bolster. His father, Rich, told me some of his neighbours were so freaked out by the giant they'd done a runner:

'Their kids are terrified of Bolster — so they've gone camping at Sennen!'

The children were all over the story — how much damage could the giant do, they speculated, how fast would you have to run to escape him? As for the flower ladies, they had their own views about this strange old yarn.

'Well, isn't it obvious?' said Jo. 'Saint Agnes is a feminist! I expect poor Mrs Bolster's first stop would be the chiropractor, then the domestic-abuse line!'

For another volunteer, Bolster was a relic of paganism, rooted out by Christian evangelism. 'That's why the church people don't like us celebrating him,' she said with a wry smile.

As for Soozie, who'd sifted old folk-tale collections looking for the core of the tale, Bolster represented, above all, the landscape: 'In the story, he returns to the fields, the gorse and the heather, all these features that are specific to Cornwall, the things that Cornish people have grown up with.'

I could have listened to them all morning. The discussion was a reminder that figures of ancient folklore can still inspire plenty of chatter, far away from academic ivory towers. This was the sort of conversation I was travelling for: eavesdropping all over the world's monsterlands.

DEATH TO BOLSTER!

Q: How many people does it take to slay a giant?

A: A village.

(Or, folklorically speaking, one plucky and slightly devious saint.)

Brian, Tom, Mike — pageant regulars — were tapping out rollies in the car park behind the village library. Stubbing out their butts, they wriggled inside harnesses, under bulbous costumes and oversized foam heads, mounted on tubes attached to bicycle helmets. There was the pompous knight Sir Constantine, boundering along on a pantomime horse, and the tax-raising mayor Samuel Sprocket, onto whom the villagers could project their irritations with officialdom. But the lion's share of sympathy was reserved for Bolster's wife. Her snaggle-toothed, pear-shaped head was straddled with brown braids, and papier-mâché rock was strapped over her hunched back. (And underneath it all? A cheery, bearded fellow called Tom.)

'It is I, old Bolster's wife,' the giantess declared, every time the parade came to a halt. 'I live in fear and panic, / For bearing boulders all my life, I carry up Bryanack!'

'Shame!' came the response from porches and pavements; from the Hotel St Agnes, the Miners and Mechanics' Institute, the Peterville Inn; from the old granite homes of miners and the stone cottages built for eighteenth-century sea captains. Children ran over to drop their coins in the collection tins. We moved as a river — around fifty drummers in black and red, beating sticks against cans, oil drums, and biscuit tins. I'd been in touch with Brian in the weeks leading up to the festival, so now I was assigned a role: as a steward. There I was, in a hi-vis jacket, rattling a collection tin, an honorary member of the community for one magical day.

Did it matter that rain sprayed down on us? Hardly! The procession was rough and rugged; people peeled off to chat to somebody they hadn't seen in a while; children let go of their drum tins to be carried. Mishaps, pointed out one of my fellow stewards, were par for the course: 'Remember that year the Bolster's arm fell down — whacked a poor woman in the back.' 'She seemed all right about it,' somebody else replied. 'How about the time the Bolster's head came off!' 'Had to lift it up on rods to keep the pageant going,' said another. 'It was like Captain Pugwash!'

With cries of 'shame on Bolster!' and 'get the giant!', we slid down to the last pub before the sea — the Driftwood Spars, named for its huge roof beams, salvaged from shipwrecks when it was built in the 1650s. 'Half a pint for everybody in the pageant!' announced the barman. They'd have to work hard at the taps: we were an army of more than sixty. Costumes were unhooked, drums laid down, and a merry scrimmage roared inside the pub.

'It's strange,' said Soozie, sitting under a joist of shipwrecked oak. 'The story of Bolster, it's about people overcoming oppression of some kind. But a lot of us have an attachment to Bolster, despite him being the villain of the piece. We're very fond of him, we're protective of him.'

He was so beloved, she pointed out, that when one of the festival regulars died, they laid Bolster on a pickup truck and drove him to Truro Cathedral for the funeral.

Among the chatter, a few phrases in Cornish were bandied around, a reminder of the local identity in which this story plays a part; a reminder of how stories intersect with a community's sense of itself. Glasses clattered on the bar, rollies were sparked on the porch. In between talk of the giant and the pratfalls he stirred, there were more-intimate snippets of conversation — grumbles about second-home owners and the municipality misdemeanours satirised in the figure of Mayor Sprocket; talk of bereavements and operations, heartache and job losses; whispers of the deeper community resting under the giant lore. We clambered into a minibus to Chapel Porth, and Derek, the lead drummer, started a rendition of an old Cornish folk-song, 'Lamorna'.

'Now,' came a garrulous voice beside me, 'let's do the naughty version!'

In the windscreen of the bus, the sea was a stormy splurge, bookended on either side by misty green hills. Surfers speckled the water, occasionally popping upright like counters in some frantic board game. The spiky-crested granite hill rising above them mocked their motions, and the sea's as well, towering over the 'intrenchment' described by Tonkin, William Borlase, and other antiquarians over the centuries. Pitted down the grassy slope were burrowing holes like some perilous golf course. How far the holes plunged was impossible to guess. Or put it another way: they were exactly the kind of holes that inspired the tale of Bolster's ill-fated bloodletting.

Looking out towards the sea were the doorless towers of mining shafts, with their narrow adits for ventilation, alongside the crumbly remains of a pump room and a miners' bothy. Pallid light turned these relics into perfect retreats for brooding. I stood among them, enjoying a few moments to myself, a break from the crowd. The sea undulated in the openings and my nose itched to the alkaline smell of guano. For all that industry had hammered this heath, not just for centuries but millennia, nature still ruled, and reclaimed.

By the time I climbed back down, the giant was on his way. Four men, steady as pallbearers, lifted him down the track and set him on the brow of the hill, just out of sight of the audience.

'Let's hope the wind doesn't pick up,' said one of them, 'or it'll knock us into the sea.'

> There once was a giant who was fierce and mean,
> The biggest giant you've ever seen,
> His deeds throughout the land brought fame,
> Big Bad Bolster was his name ...

Soozie and Brian chanted the storyline, while drummers flowed down the slope, barrels and snares matching their beat. Bolster's wife moaned down the path, Sir Constantine bobbed on his horse, the mayor twirled about, muttering of taxes. The story was building towards its climax, the pieces coming together. It would all boil down to Saint Agnes — Soozie's granddaughter, in an ankle-length white dress and veil, a picture of Christian purity against the more colourful pagan chaos of the giant.

> One day a girl who was fair and sweet
> Came unbeknownst beneath his feet.
> Her song she sang in dulcet tones,
> Which reached right down to Bolster's bones.

But where was the giant? A problem with the PA, a lull in the communications. Murmurs rippled through the crowd, patience wearing thin. Jo, one of the flower-ladies from earlier, trotted over the crest. As soon as she came back, the drummers started rattling their dirge.

'There he is,' called out a boy with a wooden sword. 'It's Bolster!'

Across the hill on both sides of the ditch, there was a collective intake of breath.

The boulder-shaped head bobbed over the flower-clad body,

arms quivering on the rods. The drums thundered the giant's roar, clamouring at the approach of each antagonist. Sir Constantine's head was knocked to the ground, the mayor was sent spinning down the path. Now it was Agnes's turn, a last resort. She announced her challenge — the giant must prove his love by filling a hole with blood.

Down it flowed — reels of red ribbon unfurled by the red-clad 'blood-runners'. The drummers beat out the giant's groan and he collapsed onto his back. To the sad notes played by Robin the bagpiper, the pallbearers bore the giant down the path, behind the audience to the car park below. Soozie had warned me, 'you'll hear the people's sighs,' and that was true enough. Big and bad Bolster might be, but it was the giant we'd all come for. Victory might have gone to the new world, but for one day at least, the old world had roared.

As I slipped away, after exchanging a few quick farewells, walking along the hedgerows, I felt the poignancy of those sighs. Giants like Bolster remind us that something came before us. We are all, as the saying goes, 'standing on the shoulders of giants'. Whether it's earlier generations living harder lives, or the denizens of the wild places that were eliminated for human societies to flourish, this is the uneasy aftertaste in so many giant tales: in order for us to have our sway, something had to give. It's there in many other monster tales, but it has a particular force in tales of giants, because when we look at them, we can see ourselves.

There goes the fallen giant, I thought, stepping into a blackberry bush to make way for a pickup. For a surreal moment, I was standing by the roadside, watching Bolster sliding past.

'Give you a lift?'

'Ooh thanks, you've saved me a hike!'

I jumped into a 4x4, driven by Guy, one of the drummers.

'Uphill too, much easier to walk down.' He nodded at the windscreen: 'Looks like we'll be following Bolster all the way.'

The back of the giant's head filled the windscreen, and my heart swelled with fondness at the sight of it. The granite-faced monster had cracked open a community for me, and he was a fair representative of the Cornish giants: a mason of the rocks, but also a fool, a terrible husband, a leaker of his own blood, easily outwitted by human wiles, living above the people but never far away. A typical Cornish giant, but in a broader sense, he represented giants the world over: supernatural earth-masons, incarnating the landscape, dissolving back into the ground to make way for human civilisation. Like the Fomorians of Ireland or the Si-Te-Cah of Nevada, he has to be sacrificed so a new society can flourish.

More fearsome beings were still to come, but Bolster had shown the way: how monsters echo their landscapes and join communities together. They don't have to be pulled out of the earth: they can charge down the mountains, rustle through the woods, or hover in the sky. As we'll find with the most romanticised of monsters. Horns curl from its head, wings burst from its shoulders and fire pours out of its mouth. Has the human imagination ever devised anything more magnificent? Time to cross the Channel and set out in search of the dragon.

CHAPTER TWO

City of the Dragon

THE SECOND TALE
Out of the woods it emerges, with horns on its head and spikes on its tail. The prophecy has come to pass: the dragon is returning, after centuries of slumber.

Maria, Lady of the Fortress, gathers all around her. The knights are away, seeking glory. Or, to be more precise: hacking their way through villages on the other side of the Bavarian forest, spraying Bohemia with the blood of anybody who doesn't share their creed.

Even her beloved Udo has gone. He stole into the fortress to bid his farewell, before riding into the forest, Maria's scarf flying from the back of his helmet. Now he is surely dead, trampled under the war wagons of the Hussites, one among thousands of bodies decomposing in the mud of the forest.

War brings people together — hundreds, in this case, seeking refuge from the war wagons. They pour inside the fortress, filling up the courtyards, squabbling in the bailey. The enemy across the woods is formidable enough, but it isn't only human foes they're fleeing, for something far mightier is on its way: the dragon. Maria has heard of only one way to appease its wrath: the sacrifice of a pure-hearted maiden. Leaving the fortress behind, wading through the silence of the streets, she plucks at her robes to keep off the dirt.

She can smell the dragon: the odour of the forest, fungal and mulchy, wildness and rot. She can feel the heat of it, burning like a hundred hearths. Already, in its impatience, the dragon has set fire to a wooden chapel on the outskirts of town. The flames are lapping at the sky, black smoke billowing around them. Through this fiery veil, she can see the ancient golden eyes waiting for her. She steadies herself for the sacrifice and takes her last steps forward.

'Fair maiden, let me succour thee!'

Why, he has the timing of the devil himself! There is Udo, riding towards her: Maria's Udo, back from the wars, with her scarf still hanging from his helmet, although now it's smeared with blood and dirt.

His horse skids across the fire-blackened earth and kicks its shanks at the air. Not a moment to lose. He hands the bridle to Maria and thrusts his spear into the dragon's throat, pumping out blood like water from a spring. Pine trees crackle against the flames, crashing into the mulch. Another thrust, and the dragon goes the same way. A sound like a thunderclap as its body strikes the ground. Udo makes sure of the feat with his sword, prising its head away from those great scaled shoulders.

At last, Maria reaches out, feels his bloodstained beard on her skin and searches for his lips, while the dragon's smoking carcass empties its blood into the blackened forest and fields below.

A WALK IN THE WOODS

Midsummer morning sun: red gold, a dragon's eye blazing at my back. Beech leaves crackled underfoot; pinecones skittered off my heels. I'd crossed the border the night before, clambering around log piles, past rickety smallholdings and the odd stray cottage, tramping under wooden hunters' hides raised on stilts. The Bohemian Forest was the only boundary marker, dividing German- and Czech-speaking communities, as it did in the Middle Ages. A couple of miles into Bavaria, I climbed the ladder of a hide and rolled out my sleeping bag on the boards. From there, it was a short downhill hike to the Drachensee — 'Dragon Lake'.

Light trickled between the trunks, green chlorophyll pulsing with morning's promise. I stopped to breakfast on iced tea and a kipferl bread roll, sitting on a lump of rock beside two beech trees so close together a spider had spun its web between them, like a camper's hammock.

Nettles prickled my arms where the undergrowth was thick, warning me back from the cliffs, and I swivelled around an obstacle course of fallen logs and vines, as if I was putting on a dance for the spirits of the forest. Between the trees, the lake was visible in vertical strips the same green as the firs. A couple was walking a dog between bushels of basket willow and red blobs of burnet. Behind them, the *Dragon Bridge* arched over the water, a rust-coloured artist's installation made from weathering steel, in homage to local legends.

The Drachensee is a flood-retention basin, absorbing the excess waters from the River Chamb, which used to pour into the nearby villages, drowning livestock and wrecking foundations. The name is apt: dragons have long been associated with flooding (to which Bavaria has always been vulnerable, saturated by snow-melt from the Alps, its riverbanks frequently bursting). A mile south-west, up on a rise, is a town so entangled with the monsters it's known as the 'Drachenstadt' — the 'City of the Dragon'.

Stand on the bridge: you have the forest to your east, while to the west are cultivated fields, striped green with wheat and gold with corn. 'Bad things come from the East,' they say in Furth im Wald, and round here bad things have a particular shape: a reptilian quadruped with bat-like wings and spikes on its head, fire spewing out of its jaws. Another thing they say: 'Furth will live as long as the dragon dies.' At a roundabout where the Chamb trickles down towards the lake, a metal dragon languishes under a fatal lance. Opposite a pizzeria, the dragon appears on the doorway of a guesthouse, red-caped Saint George brandishing his spear at its throat. On the façade of the town hall, the dragon and its bane bulge in bas-relief. The saint deals the dragon another mortal blow beside the nearby Portofino Cafe, over the gushing water of a fountain.

Between these scenes of slaughter, there are less imperilled dragons — in a glass case outside the Raiffeisen Bank, hanging over a store for agricultural machinery, carved from wood in the window of a pharmacy. Dragons are the seal of membership, marshalled by nearly every business in town, a sign of integration in the Drachenstadt. They're so widespread, it's easier to identify the stores that don't have a dragon: Takko Fashion, the Commerzbank, big businesses oblivious to the community glue. Kill the dragon to save the town? Or maybe it goes the other way: without the dragon, what would become of Furth?

A DRAGON-SLAYER FOR THE WORLD
Where giants magnify human form, dragons intensify the beasts of the wild — reptiles, bats, birds of prey — through the microscope of the imagination. More remote from us than giants, they pose an even tougher physical challenge. Guile might do for a giant, but to thwart a dragon you need prowess: an arrow in the neck, a well-struck sword. What links them is that both reach back across millennia.

Four thousand years ago, the Babylonian creation myth known as the *Enuma Elish* pitted the hero Marduk against Tiamat, 'the glistening one', a primordial goddess who brings forth the first dragons and fills their veins with poison. Not much later, the *Rig Veda* told how Indra, king of the devas, slew the many-headed Vritra, 'the dragon lying on the mountain', and set the waters of the world free. Fast forward a couple of millennia and John of Patmos was envisioning a seven-headed dragon knocking the stars out of the sky with its tail before the Archangel Michael hurled it down from the heavens. By the dawn of the last millennium, dragons were everywhere — embroidered on the robes of Chinese emperors, carved on the prows of Viking ships, venerated in Mesoamerica, writhing on military standards at the Battle of Hastings.

Whether these creatures were of the same stock is a matter of debate. The Chinese loong, Germanic wyrm, and Roman draco have long been boxed into a single category, but there are many differences between how they have been depicted. What they share is a serpent-like core, representing a universal fear of serpents but also a fascination for the magnificent ways in which such creatures can be portrayed. This combination of terror and splendour is at the heart of what makes dragons tick.

In East Asia and Mesoamerica, dragons were traditionally associated with blessings; they were divine bestowers of wisdom and good fortune. The dragons of Indo-European tradition were very different. Although sometimes represented as protectors (such as the Slavic Smok, preserving crops from its demonic adversary), they are most commonly forces of malevolence. Inheriting the ancient Middle Eastern myths of 'chaos monsters' and evoking the ferocious splendour of Norse dragon tales, mediaeval Germanic storytellers imagined them as river-drinking, flightless 'wyverns', most famously in the form of Fafnir, who falls to the hero Siegfried in the woods outside Worms, and in whose blood the hero bathes, rendering his body almost immortal. But Siegfried was a pagan hero associated with a pagan court. The popularity of his story reflected the enduring power of pre-Christian folklore. If Christianity was to compete with Siegfried and other dragon-slayers whose legendary deeds were being narrated across Europe, it needed a hero to match them.

Saint George wasn't the obvious choice for a dragon's bane. The Archangel Michael had long been associated with dragon-slaying thanks to his aerial victory in Revelation. But George proved the greater pull, a relatable hero for a war-waging age.

Historically, George was a high-ranking officer under the Roman emperor Diocletian (a notorious persecutor of Christians). When he converted to Christianity, he became an enemy of the state. According to a fifth-century Greek text, he was subjected to seven years of suffering. He was poisoned by a sorcerer and cut into ten pieces. His bones were thrown down a well then brought back to life. He was made to drink molten lead, suspended over a fire, and sawn in two.

The supernatural elements of the tale suited him to popular fantasy, along with his growing cult, supercharged by Emperor Constantine's visit to his shrine only a few years after his martyrdom in AD 303. The Bagratid kings of Georgia incorporated the dragon-slaying into their royal arms, but it isn't until the tenth century that we can locate the story we know: in the surviving paintings of dragon and warrior-saint adorning the rock churches of Cappadocia.

Europe was yet to swallow this tale, but the days of Siegfried, Beowulf, the Danish hero Fridleif, and other pre-Christian dragon-slayers were numbered. When visions of Saint George boosted the warriors of the First Crusade, cheerleading them in the Siege of Antioch in 1098 and again in the assault on Jerusalem the following year, it was only a matter of time before the saint would be recast in popular European storytelling.

Cited in a twelfth-century *Passion of Saint George*, the story was given a fuller narration in *The Golden Legend* (AD 1260) by the Genoese archbishop Jacobus de Voragine. George is riding across North Africa, according to this version, when he learns of a dragon dwelling 'in a deep lake as large as an ocean'. The beast prowls the city walls of Silene, poisoning all who come near with its breath. Two sheep are offered every day, but when the livestock runs out, humans have to fill the gap. Lots are drawn and the king's daughter, Princess Alcine, is chosen as the next victim. She is taken to the lake to be offered to the dragon — on the very day the saint passes by.

'In the name of God I will succour thee!' he promises the terrified Alcine. George knocks down the dragon and tells the princess to throw her girdle around its neck. 'This she did, and the dragon, getting himself erect, followed her like a dog on a leash.' So George makes an offer to the people of Silene: come to be baptised and he'll slay the dragon for them. They agree and the dragon's carcass is carried out of the city on a cart driven by four oxen.

It's a story rife with subtext. Not only does the dragon represent the dark forces of ungodliness, but in defeating the beast, Saint George acts out his evangelical purpose, converting the entire population.

The association with Crusade is reinforced in Jacobus's account, which includes Saint George's apparition to the Crusaders and his harrowing martyrdom — beaten with staves, branded with irons, and disembowelled. George hadn't just consigned the dragon to oblivion — he'd dealt a mortal blow to pagan heroes like Siegfried. Where the latter had something of the monster inside him (Siegfried's skin is described as 'horny' after his bath in the dead dragon's blood), George was the monster's antithesis. Depicted in shiny armour, with lance and shield, he was a poster boy for the Church Militant: humanity vanquishing the forces of wildness and everything that Christianity abhorred.

Just as Siegfried's dragon battle had been carved all over Europe in the early mediaeval period, in the high mediaeval it was all about the hero of Silene.* During the same period, nations were lining up to select him as their patron saint: from England to Ethiopia, with Aragon, Portugal, and Moldova in between. George had become the superstar of Christian monster-slaying — although his patronages weren't always the most glamorous. Appropriately, for a saint associated with the rough and bawdy life of the military, he became

---

* From west to east, this obsession can be found in the continent's castles: from Saint George's Castle in Lisbon (chief defence against the Moors, dedicated to the saint in the fourteenth century) to the Castle of Hradec in Bohemia (where, in the same century, the saint's victory over a bat-winged dragon was painted in a fresco cycle inspiring Crusaders to glory).

heavenly protector of sufferers of syphilis and skin disease. For much of this period of ascendancy, his story existed in a world where dragons were plausible inhabitants of earth's extremes, 'the largest of all serpents and of all living creatures on earth', as Isidore of Seville decreed in his seventh-century *Etymologies*. They figured on prestigious maps such as Fra Mauro's 1450 *mappa mundi* and the 1510 Hunt–Lenox Globe. *Hic sunt dracones: Here be dragons.* But they proved conspicuously elusive during the Voyages of Discovery. By the eighteenth century, when Carl Linnaeus published his taxonomies of scientifically attested animal life, it was hard for anybody with geographical know-how to argue there were dragons lurking in the back of beyond.* So they were banished from the world of reality to the realm of the imagination (or, in Linnaeus's classification, the 'paradoxa', along with phoenixes and unicorns).

George's tale remained popular, revived especially by nineteenth-century Romantics. But until the boom of fantasy fiction in the twentieth century, dragon-slaying would never match its mediaeval potency — the same allure that JRR Tolkien and his imitators channelled in reviving them.

Still, there were corners of Saint George's old empire where folk re-enactments had been commonplace, little nooks where the dragon-slayer's triumph was still manifest. I had seen a giant walking in Cornwall. Now it was time to see a dragon breathing fire in Bavaria.

PROCESSION OF TIMES PAST

I'd left my luggage at a campsite near the Drachensee, pitching my tent under an oak tree, next to a sunbathing family with a baby and a flappy-eared dachshund. Now I was sitting on a recess of the mediaeval

---

*   Although reports slowly emerged of a certain flightless and fireless 'dragon' on the island of Komodo in what is now Indonesia, not confirmed to the outside world until the twentieth century.

Pfarrkirche, the parish church. Under a cupola-topped clock tower and a pale pink façade, Saint George was up to his usual antics — stuffing an ironwork dragon's throat with several inches of lance. But I had my back to the scene. Any moment now, the dragon and its mediaeval world were expected to materialise all around us, on the streets of Furth im Wald.

'You have to be patient,' said Erika, who lived forty miles away in Schwandorf. She was sitting on the recess beside me, using her phone to fan herself against the heat. 'They have to make sure everybody's in order, they never start the parade on time.'

'This is Bavaria,' whispered her partner, with a disapproving eye-roll. (He grew up in Baden-Württemberg, he explained, where 'everything' is much more efficient.)

At last, a hoot around the block, like the signal from a departing ship. A dozen trumpeters marched towards us, chequered flags dangling from their trumpets, feathers trickling out of their caps like steam. They were momentarily held up by a pram, its wheels jabbing at the kerb until a bystander lifted it onto the pavement. On they stomped, and what followed came like a river, flooding the street with music and motion and colour.

Knights rode past on horseback, gilt spurs screwed into the heels of their boots, or standing on wagons pulled by draught horses; ladies in hennins on the steps below, lifting the hems of fur-trimmed gowns from the wheels. Boars and eagles flashed on banners raised over the handsome heads of white-maned palominos, and more animals appeared in the wagons of hunting folk in pointed felt hats: a tusked boar, hung by its trotters; a fox and a duck on a mattress of pine clippings. Sunlight glistened on the tips of spears and pitchforks, on the visors of helmets, the golden braids on the ladies' gowns, the drops of beer splashing from the peasant folk's steins — so many textures, it felt as if I was leaning inside the frame of a painting by Bruegel.

So far we had only seen a cross-section of Furth society. Now it was time for the villains. A pantomimic hiss passed through the crowd. A cry of 'Hussites!' Clanking towards us was a high-sided wagon, its wheels nearly loud enough to drown the jeers of the crowd, and the jeers hurled back by the occupants of the wagon. Their theatrical scowls were framed by loose cowls and hoods, their bodies twisting inside dark tunics. Some walked behind the wagons, carrying longswords or trailing rusty spears across the ground. Here, in caricature, was the Bohemian army that wrestled with the knights of Germany in the fifteenth century, whose wagons and war-chants have been passed down in the folklore of Furth. Some of them swung between the crowd, picking on familiar members to taunt or offer a try of their sword.

Familiar — because this is a community parade. It isn't a novelty: it's a tradition, acted out for the people whose ancestors have been acting out the same story for centuries. I met a man whose grandmother was once the parade's leading lady, another who pushed one of the wagons a couple of years before. To call them an audience isn't quite right: they were participants, some years dressing up, some years helping to ferry the procession along. It was their interactions, as much as the paraders' costumes, that gave the procession its mad, marvellous vitality.

Officially there were 1,100 costumed figures, a flowing torrent of mediaeval sensations: quilted hoods and kirtles, bag hats and bodices, bare-chested forest folk with wreaths on their heads and bones or bushy tails hanging from their belts. It was a catwalk of mediaeval fashion, a tapestry of foot-length gowns, padded doublets, and woollen cote-hardies with tin buttons up the front. But for all the glamour of the paraders, there was hardly an eye that wasn't pulled away from them towards the spectacle behind.

Nothing had prepared me for its size — between the breadth of an elephant and the length of a lorry. Wings vibrated over its horned head. Its tail swung behind, its mouth lagged open, steam billowing between teeth the size of stalactites. The street was barely wide enough to contain it, and sections of the crowd flattened as it passed. Fifteen metres long, four and a half metres high, as green as the Bohemian forest. Impossible to turn away — every single one of the crowd was in thrall. I wished it would move more slowly. It swung too fast, so I shuffled down a passageway behind the Netto supermarket, angling for another view.

The dragon had five operators. One of them was Stefan, a landscape gardener originally from Switzerland, whom I met later in the afternoon. 'I started off, many years ago, in the parade,' he told me, 'then I got different jobs on the technical side.' The big shift came ten years before, when he received a call from 'the boss'. A new dragon had been designed, and Stefan was selected as one of its operators.

Twenty different companies, including the German Aerospace Centre, Audi AG, and the special-effects company Magicon, collaborated to make the new dragon, at a budget of more than €2 million. 'Tradinno', they called the project, tradition and innovation, a mingling of heritage with state-of-the-art technology. With its high fuel usage, complex motherboards, the specially patented mathematical formulae that enable it to move, 'so many signals going all over the place', to quote Stefan, it is a challenge to keep the dragon moving.

'Oh, there are so many stories!' His face crinkled at the memories. 'Once the clutch broke, so a local steelworker made a new one for us. We worked through the night to fit it, so we could get the dragon walking in time for the next day's show. That's what mattered, the show went on. When you're involved with the dragon, you really get to know the other guys you're working with, you become friends. Sure, there's a lot of stress. I'm not saying it's easy, but it does bring us together.'

Now I was following the dragon up the hill, past the railway station, down the high street — a dragon-led tour of Furth im Wald. People were standing up from the tables of the cafés. The waitresses froze, trays of iced coffee and cherry cake balanced on their arms. The object of all our gazes might be a jumble of electronic circuits and hydraulic controls, wrapped in clay limbs and nylon wings; its six-metre-long flames conjured out of flammable powder, its mountainous roar transmitted by loudspeakers embedded in its chest — but when it glided down the street, imagination overpowered reality. Today in Furth, we could say: *Here be dragon.*

A STORY ACROSS THE AGES

The Drachenstich (the 'stabbing of the dragon') is Germany's longest-running folk drama — although for how long is impossible to say. For many centuries, the Furthers had a Corpus Christi procession, in which the battle between Saint George and the dragon became a popular element. Documents attest to it: a protocol from 1590, a church account from 1646, a receipt from 1676 stipulating 'payment of two guilders' for the knight who struck the dragon. Growing out of pictorial representation, the Drachenstich developed into a pageant, a performance with actors and props, of which by far the most significant was the dragon.

Imagine you're a peasant from one of the villages near Furth. You haul your wagon into town to sell a few spring cabbages and join the procession cheering Saint George. Out in the fields nearby, the Thirty Years' War is wreaking its poison across the Upper Palatinate. Terrible stories are bleeding back into Furth. But here for one day, you can relish your favourite saint's victory over the forces of darkness. You might laugh when the gravediggers operating the linen-sack dragon lunge a little too vigorously at the sacrificial virgin on the porch of the town hall, or when they squeak at the mistimed spear-thrust of the drunk burgher playing the knight. But when the cow's bladder bursts and the street is sprayed with 'dragon's blood', you can't help believing. Like many others, you dip your handkerchief in the precious ichor, to be buried in your field as a talisman for harvest.

The popularity of the Drachenstich is testified by its survival. But survival is never guaranteed, and official documents show a tempestuous tale, in which it could very easily have been lost forever. It wasn't a battle between hero and dragon, but rather between townsfolk and church.

For the townsfolk, the Drachenstich was not only the most exciting day of the year. It was also the most lucrative. Isolated on what they called 'the most unfortunate Bohemian border', they struggled for meaningful trade 'except for the day that many hundreds of people come to the Drachenstich'.

For the clergy, it was something very different. As far as they were concerned, the Drachenstich was a riot of impiety, compromising the dignity of Christian devotion. By 1754, the gauntlet was down: the Bishop of Regensburg condemned the Drachenstich for distracting from the true meaning of Corpus Christi. Unfortunately for the bishop, the people of Furth paid scant attention, so in 1788 the ban was repeated, by an even higher authority: the Elector of Bavaria. But it's one thing to issue an edict from your far-away courtly eminence, it's quite another to put it into action. So popular was the dragon that when a fire engulfed the town in 1863, devotees dragged its head out of the castle, determined to salvage their beloved totem.

'For a long time there has been thought about dealing with this scandal,' wrote Johann Georg Hierstetter, the pastor at the centre of a decisive incident in 1878. By his own admission, Hierstetter had determined 'to get rid of this nonsense', forbidding the knight and dragon from taking part in the Corpus Christi procession. But the knight didn't steer clear of the procession, so Hierstetter swung back inside the church with the Blessed Sacrament — holy monstrance throwing shade at unholy monster. The result was uproar: 'the whole crowd poured in front of the parsonage', wrote Hierstetter. He was accosted in his chamber by the knight's companions, who threatened to hang Hierstetter and his associates and to burn down the parsonage.

Throughout that tumultuous afternoon, Furth was a cauldron of tension. Men and women piled up around the parsonage — 3,000 of them, by Hiersetter's estimation. The clergy tried to block out their noise by singing the gospels, and the police advised them to stay inside in case of violence. In the meantime, the Drachenstich was played out on the streets. The townsfolk paid back the parson's insult, carrying the dragon up to the doors of the parsonage, where it 'turned around and showed its rear side', a blatant insult to the indignant Hierstetter. As beer casks emptied in the taverns, dirty songs were chanted, fights broke out, and the windows of the parsonage were smashed. 'The howling and yelling lasted until around two o'clock in the morning,' recalled Hierstetter. How could this tension continue?

Hierstetter reported the events of 1878 to the bishop's office and the Magistrate of Cham District, and an inquiry followed, at which the clergy was exonerated. As a form of reparation, Hierstetter was awarded honorary citizenship of Furth im Wald.

On the side of the clergy, reputations had been salvaged. As for the townspeople, they had made it clear they would never relinquish their beloved Drachenstich. There was no going back now. So, from 1887, it became an independent event separate from Corpus Christi, to take place on the second Sunday of August. As it has continued ever since.

Not that it's been without its trials. The conflict with the church might have passed, but Germany was about to enter its most turbulent century. With the establishment of a theatre association from 1880, and a festival committee formed six years later, the Drachenstich evolved away from mediaeval carnival into an organised pageant. Late nineteenth-century innovations included a court jester and a troop of magical dwarves, echoing the era's Romantic sensibilities. In the wake of World War I, the play text grumbled about disarmament, and after the 1929 financial crash, there were complaints about the 'foreign stuff' that 'has to be on your table'. While the dragon was updated — a discarded prop from the Royal Bavarian Court Opera, previously used for Wagner's opera of *Siegfried* — the play-text aligned with the increasingly unconcealed prejudices of the age. During the Nazi zenith, the knight's crusade to the Holy Land was switched in favour of a land grab on Hungary. Christian references were exchanged for the pan-Germanic mythology favoured by the regime. The dragon would be punished for these dark associations: in 1945, American GIs hung it from the back of a jeep and dragged it through the streets, before setting it on fire. But with the war over, a new dragon emerged, designed by a local blacksmith, and with it a new play-text, written by the acclaimed novelist Josef Martin Bauer.

Cold War had replaced the previous conflicts, stretching the Iron Curtain between NATO and the Soviet Bloc; and Furth was on the frontline once again. The perennial burden of border folk was inscribed by Bauer in his script: 'Nobody further inland will stop the dragon if it doesn't happen here.'

Revitalised as a manifestation of ever-present danger, a lively symbol for the nuclear age, the dragon became a politician's photo-op: two presidents of the Federal Republic would attend the Drachenstich, along with all Bavarian *Ministerpräsidents*. But with the collapse of the Iron Curtain in 1989, a new iteration of the story was called for. I would learn more about this version when I met the playwright, Alexander Etzel-Ragusa. His script rooted the story in a particular historical moment: the battle of 1431, when a 100,000-strong imperial army set out against the Bohemians at Domažlice, just twelve miles from Furth im Wald.

It was a Bavarian Charge of the Light Brigade, showing who suffers when communications falter at the top. Elector Frederick neglected to notify his fellow princes on his strategy, spreading confusion through the ranks. Panicked by the ever-noisier chanting of the Hussites' war-songs, the imperial army scattered. Thousands were picked off in the woodland passes. 'Oh what a disgraceful refuge of such active nations,' decreed a contemporary poet: 'Not having seen the enemy, he fled and left behind so many dear ones / To his hard and cruel enemies.'

It is this tempestuous historical moment that flavours Etzel-Ragusa's adaptation, reminding the audience of the wars from which this border region suffered over so many centuries — the bloodstained reality that gave birth to the Drachenstich in the first place.

NIGHT OF THE DRAGON

For a couple of days, I circled the festival, like a serpent winding its coils before the big squeeze. I dived into the museums, tracked down the dragon statues, drank hoppy 'Dragon's Blood' beer under the drapes of a tent village, and snacked on veal sausages dunked in soup. Between the many stalls for mediaeval fare, a falconer pulled off a hood and I gazed into the inscrutable yellow eyes of a real-life raptor.

On the third day, I was inside the arena, mingling with the players. A Hussite with a patch of blood on his brow was sitting on a bench, chatting with a knight in a shiny round cervelliere. A make-up lady touched up the streaks of brown dirt on the bare back of a forest-dweller. Towering over them all was the dragon, so high on its haunches I could walk under its neck and I barely had to stoop. Well, not quite ... As I straightened up, my head collided with a hand-carved chin-spike.

'Careful,' said Sandro, one of the players. 'You don't want to be killed by the dragon!'

My hair was dripping blood — a pinkish fluid ran through my fingers. I did wonder for a moment. But it was too watery to be mine: it was dragon's blood I'd drawn, the liquid dribbling down the creature's neck after the last show.

'It would be a strange way to go.'

'Killed by the world's largest walking robot!'

Silver-haired, with a neat goatee, his arms slashed with decorative stripes and his feet strapped in knee-high leather boots, Sandro cut a swanky figure. He was the villain of the piece — the 'Warden of the Fortress', a local politician exploiting the menace of the dragon. He'd played one of the 'good knights' in the past, but it was much more fun being a baddie.

'We have been involved in the Drachenstich for so many generations — my parents had speaking roles, so did my grandparents. Now my children have a role. So it continues.'

But for Sandro, to be part of this tradition is to recognise its evolution. 'It used to be about the danger from the East. Now it's about terrorism, refugees, about peace. The play adapts and that is how traditions survive.' Sandro remembered fraught times at the festival — mechanical failings with the dragon, forcing the actors to improvise; a year so stormy the audience had to be sheltered in a church and an underground garage. 'And then we all came back out and carried on with the play.'

This atmosphere of solidarity was echoed in the storyline: Lady Maria gathers the refugees from the war with the Hussites, and the people of Furth stick together against their two enemies — the army from over the border, the monster from the wood. Around me, men in shiny helmets were greeting others clotted with stage gore; half-naked forest-dwellers were ribbing each other as they lined up behind the tower: the community of the story overlapping with the camaraderie of show business. Not long until the next show: blood-smeared Hussites, shiny Crusaders, Saracens in pointy helmets, all gathered for their make-up checks. Gowns and tabards were stroked down with brushes. With my camera slung over my T-shirt, I felt conspicuous — a blot of modernity in this mediaeval sea. Still, at least I was standing next to Alexander, the playwright-director, who was in jeans and a baseball cap. We could have been Bill and Ted, stepping out of their time-travelling phone box, straight into a mediaeval crowd.

'This play,' said Alexander, 'it needed to be updated, to move on from the Cold War.' He led me under a parapeted tower into his office nearby, to sit under Lever Arch files and printouts of the play-text. 'The dragon was seen as a symbol of the East, but we needed to ask what is this conflict with the East, to recognise that the fight between good and evil is within every person, and it's also within the dragon.'

As much as the political shift was a change in how the dragon was perceived. 'In our story,' explained Alexander, 'the dragon is not simply a monster. It watches over the people, guards them, keeps away dangerous animals like wolves, and gives them fire. But when it sees what they do with this new technology, the dragon is enraged.'

So for Alexander the dragon represented man's complicated relationship with nature. 'It's echoing some of the issues we are dealing with today, climate change and our ecological crisis. The dragon stands for creation itself, for nature, and how man is treating nature. This is what we see with climate change, when nature strikes back. Christian culture called dragons evil and nothing else, but in other cultures, in China for example, there were different conceptions. Of course,' he added, with a wry smile, 'dragons can represent anything you want them to.'

Alexander was an unassuming presence against the mass of costumed figures. But it takes some willpower to mobilise a cast of this size and tow a mediaeval story into the present day. Sitting in the arena, I felt that power in the crisp flow of the drama, the cinematic switching of scenes. The cheering, chattering atmosphere felt less pre-show than pre-match, as if we were egging on the local team against a longstanding rival. The crowd wasn't confined to the benches — people were leaning out of the windows of the overlooking houses, arms hooked around shutters, legs dangling from sills.

Under the grey walls of a storybook castle, Sandro started off the action. Hands clasped between his flared sleeves, he paced a raised platform, addressing the audience in Machiavellian monologue, letting us in on the Warden's scheme: to exploit the war with the Hussites and the threat of the dragon. A series of vignettes followed, from a Stone Age tribe gifted with fire to Sultan Saladin preaching religious tolerance in Jerusalem. 'People desire your fire for ... destruction,' the loudspeakers boomed. The dragon's wrath was stirred, the tumult was mounting. However deadly the monster, the story was reminding us, there will always be humans who see in them an opportunity.

High-sided wagons rolled into the arena. Clouds of dust swirled around them, evoking the chaos of war, as the refugees gathered in the castle, seeking sanctuary. Tensions mounting, tempers flaring: Sandro's Warden wrangled with Lady Maria; knights and prelates added their voices to the debate. A crescendo building towards a crisis: only a ritual sacrifice, the purging of a monster, could bring the people together.

These events work best under the cover of darkness. We watched the climactic scenes under the glare of floodlights and the glitter of stars. The gates swung open. Claws stamped the ground. The dragon bellied forward like a giant lizard still digesting its last meal. Villagers inched towards the beast with their pikes, knights swatted with their spears, but everybody backed away to the reassuring percussion of approaching hooves. It was time for the hero.

Down the high street he came, galloping into the arena, spear straight as a lightning rod. Flames burst from the dragon's nostrils, but the spear met its target. Udo dismounted — it was a bravura sporting performance, a mixture of dressage and javelin-throwing, with a dash of fencing on the side. Under the thrashing of his sword, a wedge of scaled belly tumbled to the ground. A last roar clawed at the air and the dragon's eyelids dropped in defeat. The voices of the villagers overwhelmed its growl, the soldiers' cheering joined them — a community of triumph resounding over the slain beast. It could have been the dragon of Revelation, or Beowulf's firedrake. But this was the dragon of Furth, and Udo was the victor, running down the platform to clasp Maria in his arms. 'The community that was once so terribly stricken', as the French philosopher René Girard put it in his groundbreaking study *Violence and the Sacred*, 'suddenly finds itself free of antagonism, completely delivered.'

*

Coats were buttoned, bags rustled. People stepped back for each other, murmuring polite farewells. Others clasped each other's hands and stepped onto the high street, shoulder to shoulder. 'Furth will live as long as the dragon dies.' For a few moments, we remained in the shadow of the story.

I looked around for Erika and her partner. I couldn't see them in the crowd, but another audience member, from Deggendorf, told me this was his seventh visit:

'It just gets better and better.'

Later, bedding down in my tent near the Drachensee, I thought over what I'd seen. For all the re-tooling, this was the old story of Saint George and the dragon, of a dashing knight rescuing the noblewoman who is to be sacrificed for her community.

'We call him Udo,' Stefan had said, 'but it's based on the legend, it's based on Saint George.' By weaving in the Hussite Wars and the landscape of Furth, the play had been localised. A universal myth had been grafted to local soil, enabling it to flourish here in Bavaria. And with its themes of religious cooperation, the effects of war, the plight of refugees fleeing from terror, and some consideration of female empowerment, Alexander's play offered a twenty-first-century spin. Like the dragon itself, the tale was 'Tradinno' — tradition plus innovation, ancient and modern combined.

Dragons reign supreme, spreading their wings over the fantasy genre, in books and TV adaptations and movies. Seeing the dragon's procession through the streets of Furth, seeing the awe in which it was beheld, I was stirred back to my own long-standing fascination for dragons, back to the thrill I remember as a child turning the pages of *The Hobbit* and encountering Smaug. A dragon is such a magnificent beast. It incorporates features we fear but also admire in nature — flight and fire, the sharpness of talons, the menace of horns, the shiny reptilian alienness of scales (and many other combinations, depending on where your dragon emanates from). Among all the thousands of monsters imagined over the centuries, it remains unequalled. Where giants are clumsy, poignant in their resemblance to humans, dragons remain thrillingly unfathomable, mysteries of the supernatural that represent, if they represent anything at all, recognition that there are things beyond our knowledge and our power.

But monsters come in so many forms, with their different meanings and associations. In the months after my journey to Bavaria,

I travelled in search of others. I followed a trail between the USA and Mexico, trekked across Europe from the Balkans to Britain, and roamed among the mountains and temples of Japan. It was in the latter that I sought out some of the most ancient monsters of all, demonic figures whose earliest depictions — horned and bristly, wielding clubs and ferocious snarls — are set among the fiery torments of hell.

CHAPTER THREE

The Ogre on the Purple Mountain

THE THIRD TALE

There is no city as refined as Kyoto. Gold and silver gleam over the scarlet colonnades of its shrines and temples, where worshippers clasp rosaries made from lotus seeds and meditate among moonflowers. Outrunners tow palm-leaf carriages down streets scented with burning firewood, and through the leaves can be glimpsed noblewomen with dangling sleeves of coloured silk, their faces whitened with nightingale dung, their hair clasped with combs and kanzashi sticks.

But for all Kyoto's refinement, its population is quivering with fear. People are disappearing — guardsmen, court musicians, the daughters of ministers. The emperor's master of yin-yang, Abe no Seimei, consults his tools of prophecy:

'A terrible oni is at work. They call him Shutendoji. He has fifteen

eyes and five terrible horns and a taste for human flesh. He lives in the Iron Palace on the top of Mount Oe.'

The bravest of heroes is sent to tackle this monster — Minamoto no Yorimitsu, known as Raiko. With a band of warrior companions, Raiko treks up the steep slopes of Mount Oe, after paying respects at a mountain shrine.

'*You must disguise yourself,*' warns a *yamabushi*, a mountain priest. There are four of these ascetics. They accompany Raiko's group, giving them the ragged clothes they need for disguise.

Up they climb with the priests, passing the bleached bones and entrails of the ogres' human victims, drawing closer to the great walls of the Iron Palace. Behind the gate stands a fierce-looking guard, a horned figure in a tiger-skin pelt.

'*We are poor priests of the mountains in need of shelter,*' they tell him.

The gate groans, admitting them into the cavernous compound. As they step across the iron-floored hallway, more of the oni gather. In their centre, sitting on silk cushions and surrounded by drinking cups, is Shutendoji, huge and red-faced. Though large, he doesn't appear as horrifying as his reputation suggested. He invites the visitors to dine, to eat the flesh-meat he's torn off his victims' bones, to drink his foul-smelling liquids, to hear of how he caused a flood that sent hundreds of peasants to the land of the dead.

'*Please, have some of our saké — it's the least we can offer.*'

One of the priests opens a jar and the ogre king pours it down his throat. Now he's stumbling, lunging for another powdered bone to line his stomach. Too late: he crashes to the ground in a drunken stupor. His minions scuttle forward, pulling him into his chamber, where his snores can be heard from behind a heavy iron door.

Perhaps this is no demons' lair, after all. Beautiful women appear in the guest quarters, enticing Raiko and his companions with artful ways. Musicians pluck the strings of *biwas* and beat on drums. But the warriors see through the shapeshifting, discerning the horned oni as well as their human captives — a minister's daughter, a priest's page.

'We must slay Shutendoji!' Raiko declares.

Behind the great iron door, the beast is sleeping off the effects of the poisoned saké. The priests chant mystical incantations, causing the door to melt. There he is, fifty feet long, his head bristling with five horns, his arms yellow and blue, his legs black and white, his true ogreish appearance clear to see. The priests grab his limbs so Raiko can cut off his head. But no sooner is the mighty head severed than it swoops into the air, eyes rolling, teeth snapping, a last vengeful lunge before Raiko knocks it down with his sword.

Now that Shutendoji is dead, the warriors make quick work of his minions. Through the palace they charge, swords slashing until the iron floor is slick with demon blood and the only sounds are the exhalations of relief from the liberated captives.

Raiko and his men lift up the oni king's massive head. The priests wish them well. They are more than priests, for now they reveal their true selves — they are the deities the warriors prayed to at the beginning of their mission. They fade back into the world of the spirits, leaving the heroes to return to the court with the liberated captives, announcing the end of Kyoto's nightmare.

TO THE SHRINE OF A BEHEADED OGRE

Monster-questing is often a journey on the peripheries — marginalised places like Cornwall, border regions like eastern Bavaria. Now I was soaking up one of the grandest cities of all. For it's said that Shutendoji, the ogreish villain defeated by the hero Raiko in the mediaeval tale, was slain on a mountain near Kyoto, and his head was brought back to the edge of Japan's imperial capital.

The city of 'Purple Hills and Crystal Streams', some call it: straddling a pair of rivers, the Kamo and Katsura, criss-crossed by bridges, framed on three sides by mountains. Kyoto contains 2,000 shrines and temples, stretching around vast courtyards and compounds. Darkwood torii gates guard them, with the horned heads of oni (the idiosyncratic ogres of Japanese mythology) snarling from their ridgelines. Tourists, worshippers, and temple maidens in scarlet kimonos all receive the oni's glowers; even Buddhist monks and Shinto priests in orange robes or black washi-paper hats.

The robes of the Shinto priests are based on the imperial uniform of the Heian period (794–1185), the flowering of Japanese culture. This was the era of *The Tale of Genji* by Lady Murasaki and the charming *Pillow Book*, as well as the monster tale about Raiko's victory over the great oni Shutendoji. Almost every building from that time has burned — swallowed in the conflagrations from religious disputes or wars over imperial succession. So the splendour that glistens around Kyoto, in the dark wood pagodas of the Toji Temple or the vermilion colonnades of the Heian Shrine, is an artificial vision, a re-creation of past glories, like the luminous painted faces of the geishas gliding between the shuttered wooden houses of the Gion Quarter.

Illusions are Kyoto's métier. Flanked by misty, forested mountains, the imperial capital developed in contrast to the wildness around it, at the same time as it cultivated nature's beauty into its exquisite gardens and architectural patterns. Magic and ritual provided antidotes to the threats in the mountains, and now I was on the lookout for that magical world. My search would take me far from the tourist magnets, burrowing among places that were, on the surface, less lovable.

A short walk from the imperial palace, past wine shops flanked by red paper lanterns, mini-markets, and mechanics' workshops, I reached a shrine dedicated to a tenth-century mystic. Beyond a simple torii gate, water spilled through a bamboo pole into the jaws of a metal dragon. A five-point star decorated the ground — a pentacle, associated with the five-fold elemental system of Chinese philosophy (air, water, fire, earth, and metal) and an embroidered banner showed the yin-yang master Abe no Seimei stoking a visionary fire, revealing the giant head of Shutendoji.

The most iconic of mediaeval Japan's court magicians, Abe is a household name who features in many tales. Painted scenes from the shaman's life spanned the courtyard over the red berries and lance-shaped leaves of heavenly bamboo. Here was Abe, watching his supernatural mother, who takes the form of a white fox. There he knelt over a yin-yang board near an eerily placed skull. Here was Raiko's erstwhile fighting partner, Watanabe no Tsuina, disarming a shapeshifting oni who appeared in the guise of a beautiful woman approaching him on a nearby bridge. Not much inkling of a path — where my map suggested a track, all I could see was a white ripple, the route signposted by animal spoor.

Some shrines pulsate with spiritual magic. This is one of them, with its twelve-square board carved on the ground, its sacred tree, its statue of a white fox and a serene-looking bronze Abe, ready for visitors to rub his knees. A small, out-of-the-way shrine in a working district — but this was no site of abandonment. A steady flow of petitioners was filling the courtyard — a woman with a traffic warden's gear around her waist, a worker in a hi-vis jacket, a smartly dressed elderly couple, clapping their hands together (a traditional Shinto gesture that goes back at least as far as the third-century AD) and tugging on a pull-rope.

Now it was time to climb up the mountains, en route to Shutendoji's kubizuka (a term for burial mounds containing severed heads). A path known as the Philosopher's Way towed me alongside a canal, between camellia and laurel bushes. A similarly meditative atmosphere flowed through the Sekiya Zenin Shrine, past glowering thick-browed oni and an upside-down twisted zoomorph, to a priest reciting a mantra under carved elephants, golden lions, and a rooftop monkey (a ritual pun for warding off demons, since the word for a monkey, 'senu', can also mean 'go away').

The priest's reassuring chant echoed off dark wooden beams and mirrorwork; I could still hear the repeated 'om' as I climbed to a moss-clad shrine hidden in a fretwork of trees, until it was smothered by the clinking of chimes and the thud of falling snow. The higher you go, the more the monsters and monuments overlap; the worldly gives way to the wild.

Over snow-filled rivers banked by bending willows, past thrift stores and stained apartment blocks, I crushed my boots in the ice of Nishikyo Ward to the west of Kyoto. Snow powdered my shoulders from the pine trees as I made my way towards the metal gleam of a bridge. No chance of a path to follow — where my map suggested a track, all I could see was a snow-filled pathway, the only route forward marked by animal spoor. Green patches of moss glowed through cracks in the snow. Above a wood-cutter's shed, a snow-clad mound rose like an iced pudding, lifting up a stone torii gate under bending bamboo trunks and towering pines.

Here, on the top of the mound, it's said, lies the head of Shutendoji: a simple wooden installation surrounding the interment, with a pull-rope and a couple of bells. Its association with adventure is signified by the offerings: a miniature plastic hero left beside the rope; a bottle of frozen saké wedged into the snow. Customarily, visitors make an offering of saké or another alcoholic drink. I did my best with a can of Sapporo beer: amber drops trickling over the demon's snowy covering.

Silence, except for the occasional snowfall. I stood there, shivering a little, dizzy from something that was definitely not the Sapporo. Here I was at the snow-clad shrine of a decapitated ogre king from a mediaeval fantasy tale! To stand under the cowl of the trees, the pale residue of light oozing between pine trunks and stalks of bamboo, darkness threading out beyond, was to feel the very meaning of monsters, their legion of possibilities. On wooden panels beside the pull-rope were writings about Shutendoji. But there was no stream of visitors like at Abe no Seimei's shrine in the city below. Only the desperate would bring their prayers to the sepulchre of a monster. Or so I assumed.

Further down the hill, past log sheds and a few wooden bungalows, a well-wrapped-up woman greeted me, clasping her hands when I explained I had come for Shutendoji. 'The great oni,' I suggested, but she had another term: 'Daimyojin', the 'shining deity'. She pointed to her head, her smile flattening to a look of gravity and possibly gratitude. In an addendum to the tale, it's said that Shutendoji's spirit regretted the vicious deeds of his life and used his powers to heal those with problems in the head or neck. And so people still come here, every once in a while, to pray for his help.

A WORLD OF DEMONS

The oni are 'undomesticated expressions of nature', in the words of the folklorist of Japan Michael Dylan Foster, 'denizens of a wild territory beyond human agency'. In many of the traditional stories, they dwell on the outskirts of civilisation, intruding only for quarry — to steal away captives or treasure, to wreak their revenge or recover lost limbs. In one tale, an oni carries Raiko's companion Watanabe into the sky by his topknot, before the hero slashes off his arm with his sword. Later, Watanabe receives a visit from his aunt — who turns out to be the oni in disguise, slyly retrieving the severed arm. In another tale, a young woman marries a wealthy suitor. Her parents hear screams from the bridal chamber and put them down to wedding-night antics. Only in the morning do they discover she's been eaten: her husband was a shapeshifting oni. There's a point to these disguises: intruders from the wild the oni might be, but they are able to ape the civilisation they despise and hold a mirror to human failings. In one of the grisliest of all oni tales, narrated in the eighteenth century, a Buddhist monk grieving for his catamite consumes the corpse's flesh and turns into an oni before being redeemed by a sacred verse.

To understand the oni better, I sought out a husband-and-wife team living in Tokyo, who have established themselves as experts on Japan's many-layered spectrum of monsters. Hiroko Yoda was raised, like many Japanese children, with stories of the oni. Among these was the folk tale of 'Peach Boy', in which a boy born from a giant peach sets out with a talking dog, monkey, and pheasant to quell a band of oni.

'One of my favourite books as a child,' she told me, 'was about the crying red oni who wants a friend, but humans are so fearful of him. I thought: "I'm more than happy to be friends with you!"'

But as Hiroko grew up, launching a career as a writer, editor, translator, and photographer, crafting dialogue for comic books and computer games, researching books on Japanese folklore, she developed a different view of the oni.

'It's a powerful being,' she said, 'that gives you a feeling of awe.'

She was sitting in her study in Tokyo, next to her husband Matt Alt, her collaborator on numerous writing projects. I first came across this remarkable duo when I read *Yokai Attack!*, a book as dramatic as its title, packed with full-colour images and thrilling fact files and featuring a dizzying range of monsters, from the terrifying (the giant skeletons known as O-dokuro, the ghostly Yurei) to the weird and kitsch, such as the Bura-bura (a creepy-eyed lacquered-paper lantern) or the Tofu Kozo (a little boy in a straw hat who drains your life with jiggly blocks of tasty tofu).*

Ensconced behind a pile of books, several of which they had written themselves, Hiroko and Matt talked about the phrases in common currency, such as *kokoro wa oni ni suru* — 'making your heart an oni', applied for 'tough love'. Digging into the roots of the oni, Hiroko mused about the kami, the deities of Shinto tradition, expressed through animism and the personification of natural phenomena. Like many ancient monsters, the oni peel off from the fearsome divine. But in the storytelling around them, there's another root, with a particular significance in the tale of Shutendoji.

'Some stories of oni in the mountains,' Hiroko explained, 'might be traced back to people who had to run away from the capital of Kyoto. That part is not just folklore. Some outsiders were portrayed as

---

* Yokai are, as Matt and Hiroko put it, 'the faces behind inexplicable phenomena, the personalities behind the strange hands that fate often deals us'. They span the spectrum of the supernatural, from man-eating monsters to household tools come to life to kindly spirits or mysterious weather patterns.

monsters, back then. That's something that happened in reality.'

Fantasy creatures with roots in human history — here's an oft-heard tale. *Other* people, *almost* like us. Scholars have suggested the origins of Shutendoji's band can be found in the copper miners of the Heian period or ironsmiths (hence the name of Shutendoji's palace), or the tribes suppressed by the Yamato people, who established their dominance in the early centuries of the first millennium and inaugurated Japan's royal dynasty.* A scholarly treatise, *The Birth of Shutendoji*, by Masaaki Takahashi, describes the oni leader as an abandoned orphan wandering the mountains, a child drunk on liquor and magical power who represents a challenge to the royal status quo (and must therefore be quashed). For Professor Noriko Reider, author of *Japanese Demon Lore*, Shutendoji has a strong flavour of 'otherness', people disenfranchised by the state or a local deity displaced by the religious elites, 'someone or something outside the powerhouse of hegemonic authority'. Here's a definition that could be applied to almost any monster — a reminder that storytelling, for all its appeal, can be a cloak over more sinister processes of persecution and othering.

We find parallels in ogre-like monsters and their depictions around the world. Homer's Cyclops, for example, has been interpreted as a representation of non-Hellenic pastoralists denigrated by city-building Greeks; while the ogres depicted in Europe's early fairy tales have much in common with the forest-dwellers (some of whom, like the ogres, were forced to live in caves, and many of whom were deformed and malnourished by their poverty) who appalled and

---

* One of the terms the Yamato gave to their enemies was 'Tsuchi-gumo', or 'earth spiders', which evolved over time into a story about the slaying of a giant earth spider by Raiko and his companion Watanabe. The human origins of Shutendoji have long been suggested: so the seventeenth-century Japanese philosopher Kaibara Ekken wrote that 'Shuten Doji was originally a robber who donned the appearance of a demon to scare people so that he could steal their wealth and abduct women'.

fascinated the literary elites of their time. Not only is history written by the winners, but monsters are made by them. Just as the author of the mediaeval *Song of Roland* turned the Christians' enemies into giants and supernatural freaks, so the storytellers of Heian Japan made oni out of the emperor's enemies.

For Hiroko and Matt, this point played into their role in a very modern update of the Shutendoji story — the World of Demons video game. Although Raiko remained the hero, they were conscious of the ambiguity around his nemesis. 'Using Shutendoji as the antagonist made sense,' said Hiroko, 'because he is big and powerful, but he also has a human nature — he likes to drink, he welcomes the warriors. When you see how they defeat him, it's difficult to see Shutendoji as absolute evil. It's the heroes who are the dishonest ones.'

Here is the crumbling of our conventional morality around monsters. Bad monster, good hero: this binary dynamic isn't borne out in the stories that have endured. From the cunning Odysseus, blinding the Cyclops in whose cave he'd trespassed, to the agony of Grendel, tricked by Beowulf before having his arm ripped off by a hero as ferocious as himself, monsters are defeated not only by prowess and courage but also by deviousness. Dragons may be battled with heroic valour, but giants and ogres tend to be humanity's dupes. In besting them, the heroes often show their less honourable qualities, and in the process they illustrate how we have vanquished the wildness (and the so-called 'wild people') around us.

THE DEMONS' MOUNTAIN

Winter's thaw, a few days out from spring (according to the old calendar, when it starts on 4 February). But the train out of Kyoto groaned to a standstill. Ploughs and blowers were being marshalled against the snow, which hung so thick in the forests it was hard to distinguish from the clouds. It smothered the cars and covered the roofs, burying the overlapping shingle. Only the ceramic sea monsters

THE OGRE ON THE PURPLE MOUNTAIN

known as 'Shachihoko' broke free of it, their carp bodies and tigers' heads twisting off the ridgelines.

In the heroic tale, Raiko and his accomplices clamber up the mountains to take on the great oni. Now I was travel-dreaming in their wake, turning my back on the bright temples of Kyoto, changing at Fukuchiyama and stepping down at the foot of Mount Oe, where great sheets of snow soared above me, fading away into darkness.

The path was snow-clogged, so I kept to the road until a mud track carried me under snow-camouflaged pines and maples. The slopes sent the river water tumbling under icy bridges and stalactites daggered from the eaves of mountain cottages, hundreds of them, like a frost giant's armoury.

Above a corrugated-iron bus shelter, a green-haired oni sat cross-legged over a bowl of saké, inside the frame of a billboard. Nearby was a sign outside a school: 'In case of flood, earthquake or other natural disaster please gather here.' A boozy monster and an information sign for natural disasters may seem an unlikely pair, but together they underscore how monsters answered the puzzles posed by nature. In a country that sits on the fault-lines of every possible disaster — volcanoes, earthquakes, tsunamis, typhoons — it stands to reason there would be a high rate of monster stories. For a society to survive in the midst of so many natural threats, it needed to be diligent and precise; and in order to absorb such disasters, it needed to be imaginative.

As Hiroko pointed out: 'In the old days, people thought there was a spirit in everything: the sun, wind, rocks, the sea — and that concept is rooted in animism.' With mountains accounting for 80 per cent of Japan's landmass, 'people were divided and different traditions developed', which helps to explain the variety of supernatural beings in Japanese folklore. But the oni, associated especially with thunderstorms and natural disasters, remained consistent, because they are rooted in an ancient conception. The word 'oni', which appears in Buddhist scriptures from as far back as the seventh century, originally denoted invisible spirits causing diseases or infirmities, but they became associated with images of demons ferrying the sinners in Buddhist hell-scrolls — armed with horns and clubs, dressed in tiger-skin loincloths. Depicted in the hell-scrolls, in temple iconography, later in picture-scrolls and woodblocks, they are one of the most uniformly imagined of monsters. In themselves, they represent wild abandon, but the regularity of the depictions underlines the codified culture that made them.

Their habitat is varied — abandoned storehouses, the upper tiers of city gates, isolated chapels, bridges, and other 'twilight' places, but also the wild places such as forests and mountains. Mount Oe became a popular habitat, since its location to the north-west of Kyoto tallies with the direction of demons imported from Chinese cosmology (a direction associated with the ox — which explains the oni's curved horns). Their closest Western counterparts are ogres — with which they share their tusked, brawny, bipedal form, their wild attire and clubs. But their connection with the Buddhist vision of hell, their horns, and their ability to disappear, fly, and shapeshift add layers to the oni's mythology, warning us against drawing too straight a parallel across cultures.

The road snaked between the shiny wet cliffs of a gorge, under a suspension bridge, between organ pipes of bamboo and glossy sprays of fern. The trunks rattled, branches shuddered, and a clump of snow slammed against my shoulder. As I turned, I felt the creep of melting snow slithering down my back.

Euchhh ... It was tempting to blame those blue-and-red figures, with their tiger-skin shorts, starting to appear by the side of the path. But they were only statues, after all, commemorating Mount Oe's prominence in the folklore of oni, less a hindrance than waymarkers. The biggest of them — five metres high, a giant oni head smothered in snow — was snarling beside a compound of brick and glass. Under horns the size of aeroplane wings, his brows were ribbed like missiles ready to drop. His eyes glared over a broad nose and fangs like slabs of carved stone. Here was Shutendoji's severed head, or a sculptor's take on it, with so much snow between his teeth they looked as if they had been smeared with some kind of celestial toothpaste.

Inside the building were more oni than any oni-hunter could hope for. Sculptures from temples — the 'onigawara' erected on roof ridges to ward off other evils — ran in a hemisphere, facing masks and models, murals, and advertising plates. The older ones were broken, hieratic, evil suggested in a few broad strokes from a carver's knife. As they lurched through the centuries, the oni grew more complex. Their eyebrows thickened, their tusks lengthened, and they developed beards — ribbed, fanned, waved. An 1195 oni had a single horn and teeth like piano keys. One from 1543 had a coiled, scaly body like a dragon's. The oni of 1895 had a dandyish moustache like Kaiser Wilhelm. The message of the museum was that the oni is consistent but also versatile, susceptible to changing fashions, yet always recognisably itself.

I was near the crest of the mountain, where a monument to Shutendoji and his oni companions had been erected. Uphill from the museum, the snow sucked down my boots. As I climbed higher, it swallowed more of me, until I was sinking to my knees. I levered myself out and tiptoed as lightly as possible along the ridge of the track, wishing I could miniaturise myself to the scale of the birds and burrowing creatures whose delicate tread-marks scored the snow. Where the sun beamed down, the snow was bright and warm, but as I moved under the mountain's shadow, the surface grew darker, grey-blue and cold. No sign of the oni monument across the vista. *Do I turn back now, or carry on to the next corner?*

Movement upslope: something huge, sliding forward. Could that be a pair of horns protruding from its head? *I must be suffering some kind of snow-driven brain fog!* With a movement like the shifting of a partition door in one of Kyoto's traditional houses, the figure rolled out of the shadow and into the light. So much for horns: they were walking poles, sticking out of somebody's pack. Half a dozen hikers were coming towards me, in salopettes and skiing coats, conspicuously better prepared for a mountain hike than me.

'The oni? They are very high! Go up, behind the trees, there you will find them.'

I followed the hikers' advice. Maple and pine trees shuddered snow on my head, but their rimy branches offered handholds to the crest. Stone and bronze shimmered behind the last row of trunks, guiding me towards a plinth supporting three black oni stained with green splotches of verdigris. The statues were the work of Tohl Narita, who designed the latex-suited alien superhero Ultraman (an iconic figure in Japanese pop culture), and they had something of that series's dynamism. They weren't just hieratic figures representing an idea but characters in a scene: knees braced, arms flexed, ready for battle. The oni nearest me had his club embedded in the plinth, ringed in snow. High-horned and fanged, in a shapeless cloak, he pointed across the sky, towards Kyoto. A reference to the story, underlining the oni's ever-present threat to civilisation.

I imagined Raiko and his companions slashing with their swords. Channelling my inner child, I swung around in the snow, throwing my fists around, chopping the air with karate kicks. When I'd done enough shadow-boxing, I looked across the milky sea of clouded peaks, a vast greenness streaked white and red with snow and maple. Giant cedars writhed over the gorge, where moss flashed like iridescent gems secreted in the snow. The hiking party was a series of specks in the distance, as small as the burrowing animals whose tracks I'd followed. Outcasts the oni might have been, foreign labourers, or menacing cloud formations. But whoever has the heights has power, and others look up to them with awe.

ONIMAGERY

Look around for the monsters and you'll find them — that was becoming one of the lessons of my monster-quest. Only a few days in Japan and I'd seen horned oni advertising giant sushi rolls in the supermarkets; raccoon-dog creatures known as 'tanuki' outside saké bars; webbed, river-dwelling kappa stationed in front of restaurants; and kaiju movie monsters in pachinko-parlour arcade games.

In Osaka, I took a subway to a leafy suburb where the oldest known version of the Shutendoji story is stored. In the elegantly laid-out Itsuo Museum, among picture scrolls of geishas with kanzashi sticks in their hairdos and lovers framed by chrysanthemums, was the fourteenth-century Oeyama Picture Scroll. In the image on display (the rest of the story concealed inside the myriad windings of the scroll on either side), a black-helmeted Raiko roamed with brown-cloaked hermits, seeking directions to the ogres' palace from an old woman under a spiny tree. To see the story so close to the time of its conception was to eavesdrop on the early tellings. It was to witness a time when the oni (suggested by a pair of red horns in the corner of the picture) were manifestations of authentic terror, long before anybody imagined them as marketing tools for sushi.

Yuki Fushimi, curator of the wonderful Miyoshi Mononoke Museum of Miyozi (popularly known as 'the Yokai Museum'), traces this transition to a particular moment in time.

'The monsters are expressing people's fears and desires,' she said, guiding me between an 1881 shadow picture with black demons prancing against a red background and an 1895 painting based on a kabuki performance of the Shutendoji tale.

Above our heads, on a luridly decorated kite, a hungover Shutendoji puffed out his cheeks under Raiko's raised sword. For Yuki, the older images, especially the oni, reflected the power of natural phenomena:

'When people could not understand things such as storms, they explained them as oni.'

But over time, fear of nature gave way to market forces. From the seventeenth-century Edo period, 'they published many books about the yokai,' Yuki explained. 'People could see the variety, and they were very popular, so people made more and more, and they imagined more yokai.'

'So success breeds monsters? Commercial demand?'

'Yes, before that period, these images were not available to ordinary people — the emaki [picture scrolls] were only available to the high-class people. But since the Edo period, all people could enjoy these images, and they wanted more.'

From something to be feared to something to be treasured: collected and put inside a frame. This is a significant moment in history — a marker of the emerging modern world, when the things we feared became sources of revenue. Monsters had been disseminated in earlier centuries in European, Indian, Chinese, and Middle Eastern romances, encyclopaedias, pseudo-travelogues, and illuminated manuscripts, but not to such a wide spectrum of the population. Matt Alt and Hiroko Yoda in Tokyo had also noted this process: 'Japan,' said Matt, 'is where commerce and folklore intersected, earlier and more thoroughly than anywhere else.' It's a process that I saw in vivid polychrome in an artist's studio in the town of Otsu, a short train ride from Kyoto.

Oni everywhere: lurching under dark beams and a poled ceiling, baring sharp teeth and curved horns. They were painted on wooden boards and bowls, on saké jars and teapots, on driftwood and seed-paper. Here was an oni plucking the strings of a biwa over a saké bowl, another sitting in an onsen hot bath. Here was a wide-mouthed, terror-stricken oni, shinning up a pole in fear of a mouse. The images were as lively as the artwork in manga cartoons. They were comical scenes, poking fun at the oni as well as the public figures they were aping. But they represent a tradition that stretches back 400 years.

For Shinsuke Shozen — a zen-like figure in horn-rimmed glasses who showed me around the studio — this is more than just a life's work. It's a heritage connecting him with five generations of ancestors.

'We have been making these paintings since the seventeenth century,' he explained.

Here, in the same studio, his father painted, and his father before him, with the same traditional paints and techniques that Shinsuke uses today.

'We must keep up with the tradition, but it is complicated. It isn't any good just remaking the old ones, you have to come up with new designs.'

There are other images beside the oni — geishas and samurai, a tiger leaning over a branch, frolicking white rabbits. But the oni dominate. The reason for their popularity, Shinsuke believes, is that they combine the fear of monsters with human frailty: the most popular image shows an oni dressed as a Buddhist priest, with a gong and a subscription list, poking fun at the corruption of the clergy.

'The oni,' Shinsuke suggested, 'are close to human beings with all our blemishes.'

This is one way to define them. Not so much the awesome godlike figures of older myth, more like distorted mirrors to ourselves. The oni of Otsu remind us that we all have the potential to become ogres. Which brings us to the festival of Setsubun — a time of year when the oni are at their most visible, and all over Japan, shrines and temples take action to dispel them.

EXORCISING THE ONI

According to a mediaeval legend, a solitary monk was living on Mount Kurama, to the north of Kyoto, when an oni interrupted his prayers. No matter what sacred verses he recited, he couldn't rid himself of the monster. There was no sword, no bow; all he had was a few roasted beans. So he hurled them at the oni. It let out a scream, scratching at its blinded eyes, and disappeared back into the world of the spirits.

This is one of the stories told to explain the origins of one of Japan's enduring national rituals. During the Muromachi period (1392–1573), the legend of the bean-blinded oni established itself in a courtly ritual, when aristocrats in Kyoto hurled beans out of their houses, targeting invisible spirits. Over the centuries, the ritual has accumulated a matrix of traditions. *Oni wa soto, fuku wa uchi*, people cry: 'out with the oni, in with good fortune'. Marking the onset of spring, and coinciding with the new year in the old lunar calendar, Setsubun represents a moment of seasonal transition, an appropriate time to dispose of the old and ring in the new.

In the run-up to the festival, the oni were massing. You could hardly pass a supermarket, or even a mini-market, without coming across a horned, red-faced snarl. Kyoto didn't have the monopoly; they were visible in Tokyo, Osaka, Hiroshima, usually appearing over a roll of fish-filled nori-maki. In Cornwall, I'd seen a village gather around a giant. In Bavaria, a city had paraded around a dragon. Here in Japan, an entire nation was forming around ogres.

Nowhere does Setsubun more grandly than Kyoto's Heian Shrine. The vermilion pillars, curled green roofs as scaly as dragon hide, and glittering light of the shrine make an ideal setting for a monster purge. That morning, priests and acolytes gathered inside a cordon. Kneeling on tatami mats, they recited sacred Shinto verses, lashed the air with sticks, and nocked their peach-wood bows to pin the corners of the shrine with the psychic protection of arrows. A shaman, in a four-eyed mask, proceeded around the courtyard, escorted by a group of young acolytes in blue tunics. Behind the compound gates, monstrous manes were visible, and to the beat of a gong came the oni — brown-faced, red, purple, orange, wielding clubs and axes and sporting pantomime breastplates. They stomped across the courtyard, passing inches from the pulsing skin of the crowd, and took up position between the pillars in front of the shrine. It was a comical upturning of convention — instead of priests wreathed in incense and prayer, the temple was delivered to ogreish misrule. The oni leader waved a golden sceptre, shaking his fist at us all.

His reign lasted, by my reckoning, all of eight minutes. From behind the pillars came temple dignitaries, armed with the ultimate weapon — kryptonite for the oni — the artillery known as soya beans!

Oni wa soto! — 'Out with the oni!'

Clawed arms flailing, the monsters staggered across the courtyard, a slow-motion retreat until they had all been swept out through the gates. The temple was back under the priests' control and we all turned for their blessing: the ritual of mame-maki (a pun on the homophony of the Japanese characters for 'bean' and 'destroying evil').

Throughout my time in Japan, I had been charmed by the codes of politeness, the courtesy with which people acknowledge each other — hands clasped in thanks when you hold a door open, traditional phrases bandied over the shopping till. This refinement, distantly related to the intricate codes that governed life in Heian Kyoto, collapsed around the bean-giving. Like Brits under the influence of booze, the people of Kyoto transformed: jostling, tugging, elbowing each other out of the way, people grabbed at the sacred packets. Setsubun was a spotlight on Japan's ambiguities — the submission to shrine authority in a secular society; socially sanctioned anarchy bursting out of an intricate repertoire of rituals.

All over Kyoto, variations on oni eviction were taking place. Under the monkey-crowded, jungly hills of Arishiyama, to the west of the city, I climbed past saké barrels and statues of holy figures to join the crowd awaiting a kagura dance in the main courtyard of the Matsunoo Taisha Shrine. This was another ancient art form, performed by men in magnificent gowns, one with a bow, another in the high-browed mask of an emperor, weaving steps around each other to the music of clappers, a flute, and a drum. Incense billowed behind them and onto the stage crept a pair of oni — horns spearing black manes, in gowns as splendid as their adversaries', golden tassles hanging from their sleeves, tapering green leaves and red flames swirling between golden patterns appliquéd to black velvet. This quartet danced in antagonistic, ritual steps, mincing around each other, the archer raising his bow, the emperor his sword, the oni shaking their arms. Their nimble feet traced webs around each other, mingling hunter and the hunted, while the drums continued to pound, the clappers to rattle, the flute to pipe. At last, they were separated: one oni was shot with an arrow, the other stabbed with a sword. Lurching in slow motion, the monsters doubled up on the walkway projecting over the crowd — for a few moments, there hung the threat of a monstrous crowd-surf — before tumbling backwards to retreat behind a curtain.

'It is a sacred privilege to perform the kagura.'

So said the emperor. His mask removed, he revealed himself as a young, bespectacled actor, calling out to his fellow performers on the path behind the stage. 'To fight the oni, this is very ancient.' It took several years' training, he explained, to master the dance, with bi-weekly sessions, following techniques passed down through dozens of generations. 'It is for the kami, the spirits. When we dance the kagura, we are asking them for blessings.'

So dense were the crowds at Setsubun, such acres of humanity, at times I felt as if I was peering at the rituals through a crack in a wall. I sensed something deeper going on, a continuity unbroken over many centuries, not an isolated once-a-year occurrence but an echo of rituals and beliefs enacted across the seasons. If only somebody could show me what it meant — show me how it felt. I looked around and asked, and at the Yoshida Shrine in the north-east of Kyoto, I met a student seeking solace in community, who helped to make it a little less blurry.

Slightly built, in a black hoodie, Ryouta had an air of soft tension, as if it was unsettling, but also a little bit liberating, to be approached by this long-limbed, bearded foreigner. He came from a small town in the neighbouring Hyogo prefecture but had moved to Kyoto after winning a place at the School of Informatics.

'This is the first time I spent Setsubun away from my family,' he told me.

We had passed through the fairground crush at the foot of the shrine, ranging past Hello Kitty toffee apples, candyfloss, and fried fritters shaped like sacred sardines, and we found connection as solitary strangers in the thickening crowd.

'Every year we celebrated Setsubun at home,' Ryouta explained, as we climbed the long flight of steps together, up to the main courtyard.

'The same thing, every year, so it feels strange to me to be here.'

He bit the top of his lip as he drew me a picture of home life: his father in the civil service, his mother who worked at a school, his sister completing her high-school diploma.

'I'm usually the one who wears the mask.'

'You become the oni?'

'Yes!' His lips curled back, a bashful, boyish laugh. 'I like it. Especially if I can scare my sister!'

'And everyone else throws beans at you?'

'Yes. Then we gather up the beans at the end and however old you are, you have to eat that number. Plus one extra for the coming year.'

We had reached the courtyard, where the crowd was thickening around us, humming with anticipation. Under a roofed area in front of the main shrine, priests in coloured gowns and black lacquered hats sat down on stools, reciting ritual incantations. They were performing a tsuina ceremony, a purification of evil spirits.* Darkness swallowed up the compound, and fire glared from brands held by boys in their own black hats. At their head was a magnificent, freakish figure. A single horn speared the red mask, which was lit by four eyes, tangled in a golden mane and beard. In his gloved hand was a triple-pronged spear. A monster? Or a shaman?

'Is he an oni?' I asked Ryouta.

'He is the good oni. Not an oni exactly — but he is from the spirit world.'

They call him the 'hososhi'. This was the name for an official minister and priest, charged with officiating at funerals and leading rituals of exorcism. His four eyes represent the four cardinal directions, from which it is his duty to perceive and thwart demonic activities. As a court seer, the hososhi evokes the likes of Abe no Seimei, who sent

---

* These rituals go back to the Heian period, and according to the scholar Komatsu Kazuhiko (in *An Introduction to Yokai Culture*), oni masks were worn in tsuina performances of that time.

Raiko to Shutendoji's Iron Palace — a sorcerer inhabiting the world of monsters and men.

This one led his cohort around the courtyard to the humming of the recited verses, while the sound of growling rolled down the mountain path. Fire starred the corners of the courtyard, and across the blaze lurched three oni — blue, red, yellow, a trio of monsters in loincloths. Arms spidered the air, legs slashed forward with jerky, stabbing motions. However much the howling had prepared us, still, they erupted in our midst with the shock of a monster in a fairytale. The shaman was their mirror, with his mane, his red face and horn, but also their opposite, a picture of zen-like serenity. Proceeding around the shrine, he lifted his spear and prodded at the oni in steady, ritual jabs. They staggered backwards, twisting on their heels, scowling at the crowd. Their faces were livid in the candlelight, which gave a beatific light, conferring magic on the ritual; and under this glare, the monsters were dispelled.

'What do the colours represent?' I asked Ryouta.

Red was miserliness (also associated with passion and greed), blue was anger. Yellow was the hardest to define, associated with 'worldly attachment' and 'restlessness'. We wandered between the stalls, snacking on sardine fritters, warmed by the fires, musing on the semiotics of oni colours. Ryouta turned, catching my eye.

'It was the right decision to come here.'

In the bobbing of his head, I could sense how much he'd wavered. I felt a squeeze of affection for him, recognising my own uncertainty around communal gatherings.

'Otherwise, I would just be in my room at the campus. And I would think about my family too much.'

'Yes, I know what that feels like.'

Here at the shrine, he was part of the community; and in a small way, I was too. I wasn't holding a collection bucket like in Cornwall, or mingling backstage like in Bavaria, but something I'd learned over the course of these community gatherings was that you don't have to be front of stage to be part of it. As long as you're anticipating the monster — as long as you have the giant or the dragon or the ogre in your sights — you're one with the crowd.

There was one more ritual to witness that night. Into a cage of lashed bamboo, people were casting omamori — amulets containing written prayers sealed inside pouches of brocade, hung in the home as good luck charms and burned at the end of the year.

'It is bad luck to keep them for more than a year,' explained one of the volunteers helping to manage the offerings. 'We get rid of the old and we welcome the new.'

'And the oni are part of it?'

'Of course! We are getting rid of all the bad things.'

Flames were thrown into the cage and the crowd thickened, fixated by fire like communal gatherings the world over. I stood beside Ryouta, gazing at the red and golden tongues swimming inside the cage, the bamboo trunks turning black, twisted and charred. I thought of the dragon in Furth im Wald, the dazzling pyrotechnics conjured from its nostrils, and the fire on the hilltop in Cornwall. But I thought, more, of bonfire nights with my family back home, my youngest on my shoulders, our eyes on the fire, warm embers dancing in the dark. Like Ryouta and his family, like so many generations of Japanese families: shared rituals, passed down through the generations, connecting us to the people who came before, but more importantly, connecting us to each other.

Life can be so lonely, and we need rituals to bring us together, to cast out the demons that keep us apart. Because the forests and the rivers and the mountains aren't the only places where the monsters dwell. We've always known that. It's inscribed in some of our earliest art and our oldest stories. It's there in the shapeshifting of the oni, and in the figure of the horned shaman who dispels them. If only the monsters were *out there*, only ever out there, fended away from the battlements that supposedly keep us safe ...

Wouldn't that make everything so much easier?

PART TWO

When They Become Us

'Beware that when fighting monsters you yourself do not become a monster. For when you gaze long into the abyss, the abyss gazes also into you.'

Friedrich Nietzsche, *Beyond Good and Evil*, 1886

CHAPTER FOUR

Shapeshifters at Sea

THE FOURTH TALE
Who can match Odivere for prowess — his force of arms, his skill on the hunt? His bride is blessed indeed — however fair she may be. But they've scarcely been married long when Odivere straps on his helmet and spurs, kisses her farewell, and sails across the sea.

Word comes back of blood spilled in the Holy Land, piles of pagan corpses, ferocious sea battles and lavish banquets where the mighty Odivere celebrates his triumphs with his fellow Crusaders. But reports won't keep you warm at night. For Odivere's lady, pining in the castle, life is a pale litany of routine. Sitting by the window of her chamber, she looks down on the stewards and chambermaids as they go about their duties, the grooms leading the horses, the servants mopping the flagstones. At last, a knight comes knocking on the gate. He brings tidings of her husband, so she bids him dine with her.

He also brings a ring — which she recognises. For he was her first love, before Odivere won her for his wife, and now that affection is rekindled. He mesmerises her with tales of life at sea, and tells her stories of Odivere as well, how he's been dallying with the ladies of Micklegarth (which some call Constantinople). He has brown hair and large brown eyes, and his brown coat reaches his ankles. There is a sparkle in his eyes and in his words, the taste of other places, far beyond anything even her husband knows. She can no longer resist. She brings her visitor into her chamber. Long after he has gone, she sits by her window, looking out to sea, a hand stroking the swell of her belly.

Her lover's name is San Imravoe, and he is a leader among the selkie folk, with his court on the mysterious isle of Sule Skerry. When he returns, the lady is holding a baby in her arms. He will visit again, he informs her, to take the child away and raise him as a selkie. For the boy has the same power as his father, the ability to transform into a seal. Though the lady weeps at the prospect of giving him up, she knows he will never fare well in human company, not when tongues can wag so freely.

When Odivere returns from Crusade at last, the castle glows with celebration. Bulls are slain for the feast, red wine poured into horns, tales told around the table. But Odivere is never one for rest. He soon tires of feasting and sets out to hunt.

'Look at this one, I swear I recognise the chain on its head.'

He's caught a seal pup on his latest expedition. The lady only has to see the golden talisman she wound around the little boy's neck. She throws herself onto the body of her slain son, her tears mingling with the salt water seeping from his sleek brown body.

'So you've lived a life with the seal folk, I see!'

Odivere doesn't take long to work it out. Oh, the ladies may have beguiled him in Micklegarth, but that's no excuse for his wife in his castle, no excuse at all! He has her stripped of her finery and locked in the highest tower, to wait until the day she'll be led to the stake. But howling noises are heard along the shore. The waves are broken by fluked tails and

Odivere cannot resist — he sets out to hunt the whales. How many harpoons do his men hurl? And how many whales do they catch? Not one! When the lord returns to his castle, fuming at his misadventure on the waves, perplexed by the seals diverting his ship and evading his spears, he stands before the tower where he imprisoned his wife. The iron door has been thrown to the ground, and of the lady there is no sign.

'Where is she?' he exclaims, the salt water drying on his beard. 'Will nobody tell me where she has gone?'

He would have burned her. But there is no fire to light now; only a different sort of fire, scalding his heart. How often Odivere wanders the shore, how many lonely nights he stands on a clifftop, gazing out to sea. And among all those seals' eyes looking back at him, he can never find an answer to the question tormenting him: where oh where oh where has she gone?

THE SELKIES' DANCE

An hour before dusk, the sea around Orkney was a cold grey soup. Out of the vat popped a little lump of meat, mottled and shiny. Inky spots around large brown eyes; whiskers spraying either side of a nose as black as a dog's. The seal turned, one way, then another, posing in profile before facing the lone human sitting on a rock on the shore.

I was delving among stories of shapeshifters. Humans transforming into ferocious beasts; strange creatures taking on human form: the search would carry me to the mountains of North Africa and the swamps of the Deep South. But first, I was trudging around the island of Sanday, whose cusped and rangy outline was likened by the novelist Eric Linklater to a fossilised bat. I had left my hired bike beside a farmhouse and clambered over shoreline scree. Slipping into a couple of unexpected rock pools, I followed the squiggly curve of a bay towards a tidal islet.

Sanday has a special association with folklore. It was here

that some of the earliest stories of selkies — magical seal folk who transform themselves into human form by shedding their skins — were written down and preserved. One of the darkest tales is told about this particular patch, the gloomily named Holm of Ire.

When a shepherd killed a seal cub, the story goes, he put himself in the way of the selkies' wrath. The next day, he left his flock on the Holm, but when he looked for them in the morning, none could be found. Here was the silent revenge of the seal folk: for the most part benign, but, like the animals that inspire their stories, occasionally they bite.

All evening I watched the seal, and for some of that time the seal watched me. A companion emerged, another head popping out of the water. The two of them danced around each other, one disappearing under the surface, then the other. They floated around each other, rising and ducking. When one had been absent too long, the other periscoped its neck, letting out a moan so plaintive that when I closed my eyes, I imagined a little boy weeping. I stayed fast to my rock, reluctant to leave the seal. As if in some way I was a substitute, until the other one returned.

Low tide was seal-watching time. Another evening, I crossed a field of machair and clambered around barnacled rocks, picking my way between whelks and limpets. An amphitheatre of slab-like ledges formed, a gathering place for seals. I kept my distance, wary of disturbing them. With my chin on a nub of rock, I could see their claws joined by webbing, dappled on the other side with fur. Half a dozen seals, maybe more on the deeper ledges. Lying on their sides, sprawled out, as if they'd just finished a banquet and were having a nap. Flippers drummed the rock, and the air pulsed with some wonderfully satisfied-sounding belches.

I thought of the tale, recorded on this very island, by a nineteenth-century farmer-scholar called Walter Traill Dennison, about the 'Goodman of Wastness', who spurns every woman he meets until one moonlit night he spies a circle of dancers with long brown hair, slick and shiny from the sea. He watches them, mesmerised, and notices the seal skins spread across the rocks. Before they can plunge back into the water, he steals one of the pelts, forcing its owner to follow him back to his croft. For seven years she lives with the Goodman, bearing seven children and brewing the strongest ale on the island. But when he sets off on a fishing trip, one of her children tells her where the skin is hidden. She bids the child farewell and flings herself into the sea. However much she loves her children, she cannot resist her own true nature.

Stories of this kind have been spun all over the world. In Bulgaria, tales are told of samodivis, fairy-like beings dancing in the woods. In Nigeria, the heroine is an 'elephant woman'. In some places they are swan-maidens, in others mermaids, disempowered by the theft of a magic comb. In Orkney and the Hebrides, and a few places on the Scottish mainland, they are selkies. Hundreds of tales about these shapeshifting creatures have been collected— about men like San Imravoe, who takes his lover back to his mysterious home on Sule Skerry; or women like the melancholy wife of the Goodman of Wastness. 'Orkney' means the 'islands of seals', from the Norse for seal, 'orkn', and the suffix 'eyjar' for islands.* So it makes sense that seals feature in some of the archipelago's most iconic tales. But as I travelled between the islands, I wondered how deeply they influence Orcadian culture today.

*

'Twenty-four, that's the record.'

Ruddy-faced, with a shock of white hair and a ready smile, Geoff was in charge of the community bus. Every day, he drove around

---

*   This is a Norse interpretation of an earlier name, which possibly goes back to the Gaelic term for a wild pig. When Norse settlers arrived from the eighth century onwards, they took the name 'Orc' to refer to the common seal, 'orkn' in Old Norse.

Sanday, ferrying passengers to their drop-offs. 'That's the most we've seen on the beach at Burness.' His garden was near the beach, and after a storm, he'd found a seal pup there: 'We wrapped it in a bedsheet and carried it down to the beach.' It still had time to snarl at his cat, before returning to its natural element.

Geoff's was one of several seal stories I heard over that week in Orkney. Some were sweet, or uplifting, some were strange. There was the woman who'd swum with seals, and remembered the tickle of their snouts against the bottoms of her feet. There was the macabre story of half a seal found on a beach, the other half ripped away by a ship's propeller. For marine biologist Mònica Arso Civil, the biological reality of seals is far more intriguing than any tale that can be told about them.

'Each seal has a unique pattern on its pelage,' she explained, 'and it remains the same when they moult. So we can recognise the same seals over a long period of time.'

Telemetry tags and photographic data enable close recognition (so that Mònica can identify around 200 seals at the site she's been monitoring). As a result, she is able to notice the variety in seal behaviour and characters. On one skerry, she observed a mother seal with numerous pups suckling from her; while other mothers pushed away those they hadn't pupped themselves. Once, Mònica saw a bull seal hurtling into attack, neck stretched out: 'He was barking and he went off like a torpedo, he wanted to show it was his territory.'

For the people who lived at close quarters with seals, over the centuries, this range of behaviour inspired stories. Around peat fires they would be passed, over bere bannock and home-brewed ale, tales to while away the cold winter evenings, chewed around on fishing boats and the long hours of waiting at the harbours. They helped to make sense of the unexplained — drowned sheep, lost fishing tackle, strange sounds in the night. But Mònica, as a scientist, was wary of anything that veered towards anthropomorphism:

'When I look at seals, I don't think how we're like them. I think what a tough life they have: giving birth every year, moulting their pelage, feeding their young, diving for fish. And the things they can do — holding their breath, the way they communicate underwater. There's still so much about them we don't understand.'

But for storytellers, our parallels with seals are too striking to resist. Perhaps the most haunting seal story I heard that week in Orkney was from a storyteller called Tom Muir. He was recalling an incident near his family's farm on Orkney's main island:

'One night I was at Valdigar, smoking, as I did in those days, when I heard a sobbing sound. Now this was a place where people used to go for a little bit of privacy, if you take my meaning. You'd often hear them, whether you liked it or not. Some falling out, perhaps, and the more I listened, the sadder she sounded. Poor girl, I thought. I wondered if something had gone wrong, maybe she needed help. Then I heard a groan, and it was like no sound any human had ever made. And that was when I realised: it was a seal.'

Reflecting on this years later, Tom could well imagine why seals inspired anthropomorphic tales. 'They're very human in their curiosity, their love of music, their playfulness. I've stood on the beach and whistled, many times, and they'll come closer. And I've seen seals playing chicken with the cliffs — young seal boy racers going on the tide to the cliffs, then flipping around.'

On Sunday, I camped at the Bay of Brough, near the pebbledash farmhouse where the folklorist Walter Traill Dennison wrote down many beloved selkie tales in the nineteenth century. As the colour was bleeding out of the bruised purple sky, I peered into the bay, feet popping on bubbles of rockweed. There in the water were two seals. Their snouts faced each other's, rubbing up like lovers greeting each other under the moonlight.

Many of the tales tell of lonely men, enticed by the dances of the selkies, irresistibly drawn to the beautiful women who emerge from the wet and shiny pelts. In others, a lonely woman weeps seven tears into the sea and a handsome male selkie emerges to comfort her. The stories confound the distinctions we draw between human and beast. To call a selkie a 'monster' seems wrong, morally as well as taxonomically. But they are part of the spectrum of shapeshifters, a range that grows snarlier and bloodier as we move along. Not all the old stories, the selkie reminds us, treated the 'other' as savage beings for heroes to slay. Throughout storytelling history, men and women have imagined the possibility of falling in love with the weird. Through the varied tales of the selkie — gently pining for her stolen life from a farmer's croft, or savagely drowning a flock of sheep in wrath — we see the swirling mists of ambiguity in which all our shapeshifters lurk.

THE MANY CLOAKS OF TRANSFORMATION

A twisting tunnel in the foothills of the Northern Pyrenees. Running 400 metres deep, the limestone cave complex drills past hundreds of other figures until it reaches the chamber known as 'the Sanctuary'. Here, 280 animal figures, including mammoths, ibex, and bison, speckle the walls underneath a bipedal being that has been given the name of 'Sorcerer' or 'the Horned God'. Short-tined antlers burst from a head with rounded, owl-like eyes; a penis pokes under a bushy, tufted tail like a wolf's. His feet and toes, as the archaeologist Henri Breuil suggested soon after the image's discovery by gaslight in 1914, 'are rather carefully made and show a movement similar to steps in a "Cakewalk" dance'.

Painted and engraved high above the cave floor, around 13,000 years ago, the Sorcerer continues to rouse inconclusive speculation: a deity, or a shaman, channelling the powers of the animals thereabouts? Why wouldn't humans envy those animals — their heightened sense of smell, their strength, their predatory skills? And why wouldn't humans imagine what it might be like to become such a beast — to have the reactions of a deer, the strength of a bison, the hunting prowess of a wolf? Or, if you lived near the sea, the speed and grace of a seal?

This fantasy is expressed in many ancient tales — the 'wild' Enkidu in *Gilgamesh*, for example, who has more in common with beasts than with men; the 'horned' skin of Siegfried, after he bathed in dragon's blood. To be like an animal is one thing. But other stories take the idea further, metamorphosing humans into animals — the hunter Acteon, transformed into a stag for spying on the bathing goddess Artemis. For transgressing taboos, for poor kingship, for failing to submit to divine authority, miscreants are reduced to the status of beasts. But the line between the beast-like hero and the beastly misdoer is a narrow one. Being beast-like, ancient stories suggest, can be a blessing as well as a curse. It can help you beat the monsters, or it can turn you into one.

Selkie stories are as old as the sagas that were told with gory relish across the mediaeval Norse-speaking world.* Since they were transmitted mostly in oral form, they can be hard to date, but the story with which this chapter began, the so-called 'Play o' de Lathie Odivere', has been traced to mediaeval times (the scholar Simon W. Hall has called it the 'first truly indigenous fragment of Orkney literature') and the storytelling assumes its audience's familiarity with the nature of selkies. One of the features that distinguishes selkie stories from some other tales of shapeshifters is the priority of the animal form. The default is the seal rather than the human. A selkie may hang around in the human world for many years — as a melancholy bride, or a lonely lady's fancy man, perhaps — but as soon as the chance arises, they return to the sea. The call of the wild trumps the comforts of the hearth.

AN ISLAND OF STORIES

It was the tales set down by Walter Traill Dennison that had lured me to Sanday. I'd come on a ferry from Kirkwall, sliding out from Orkney's

---

* In the thirteenth-century *Laxdæla Saga*, a large seal swims near a grounded ship, 'and everyone aboard was struck by its eyes, which were like those of a human'; soon after a failed attempt to spear the seal, the ship capsizes and all but one of the sailors is drowned, the seal acting as an omen of disaster.

main town, after a rainy night crouching under a bike shelter next to the mediaeval cathedral. A relief to lie down on the ferry, leaving behind the solid seawall and the long line of hotels and pubs, the labyrinth of cobbled streets with their gable-ended shops. Sliding over Kirkwall Bay, you taste the salt on your tongue, ground so they say by a pair of magical millstones under a whirling stretch of sea known as 'the Swelkie'. There's a thrill to edging out there, ever remoter, where Picts and Vikings and Gaelic-speaking settlers mixed their stories along with their blood. Gannets plunge like shooting stars, terns wheel over the ferry's antennae, and a cross-shaped shadow on the surface of the water signals a cormorant hovering overhead.

You don't need jungles or mountain precipices for a place to feel wild. Orkney's jagged coastlines, the rock stacks and 'dark rounded hills' (to borrow a phrase from the much-loved Orcadian writer George Mackay Brown) have inspired a smorgasbord of monsters that's a match for Japan. Well, on a per capita ratio, at any rate: hogboons and trows creeping out of ancient burial mounds known as 'howes'; sea-trowies with their monkey-like faces and seaweed hair; the winter spirit Teran and his enemy the Mither o' the Sea, a giant known as the 'Cubbie Roo'; ghosts in the kirkyards; witches casting spells on isolated shores; horned devils, mermaids, and mysterious finfolk. Orkney has two powerful forces in particular — time and the sea — conspiring to prompt speculations about its ancient wonder-works and to pull in surprises, like a sea serpent spotted by three sailors in Shapinsay Sound in 1910, or a mermaid detected by a fishing crew near Deerness in 1913, which 'rose out of the water to the height of three feet', according to a report in *The Orcadian*, 'and looked like a lady with a shawl round her shoulders'. The same forces have carved out drama around the islands' cliffs during their several millennia of human habitation, in clefts and blowholes and rock arches traditionally attributed to the actions of magical creatures.

I hired a bicycle from one of the island's two shops, and for a couple of days, I rolled around Sanday. Dropping the bike by a sign,

I stepped along the marram grass towards a chambered cairn — Quoyness. Sitting in the grass like a giant's hat, the cairn is flanked by a corridor of stone leading to a central vault with chambers on all sides and a pit in the central one. It was built 5,000 years ago, and when it was discovered in the nineteenth century, there were bones arranged ceremonially, suggesting some long-forgotten ritual for the dead. How strange it felt to sit there, comforting and queasy at once, hugging my knees, wondering if I was in some megalithic torture chamber, or a dream pod designed for access to the other world. Like so much of Orkney, the Quoyness Cairn is a tantalising glimpse of an ancient way of life that has conceded little evidence of the daily reality behind the rituals. Which is why the surviving folklore is so precious.

Cycling north, I followed the curve of a bay where curlews were poking in the mud like a team of detectorists on a treasure hunt. A whimbrel called to a partner and a flock of geese honked overhead. Down a tarmacked road, a roofless church rose over a graveyard. Tombstones lurked under lichen drapery and the nave was sprung with nettles. I followed the steps up the cracked-open northern flank, looking for six long divots at the top, traditionally known as 'the devil's claw-marks'. Which ensured that islanders gave the church a wide berth at night.

Inhabited for millennia, Sanday became a centre for Orcadian storytelling, its tales put in order at last by the nineteenth-century scholar-farmer Walter Traill Dennison. It was Dennison who preserved 'The Play o' de Lathie Odivere', about the Crusader's wife and her selkie lover; as well as 'The Goodman of Wastness', in which the selkie returns to the sea after finding her long-hidden sealskin.

Down from my tent, the bay curled past flat, moody fields of machair. The lack of trees has been a boon for archaeology, forcing the early settlers of Orkney to build in stone, leaving behind their craggy refuges to be puzzled over by later discoverers. It has nurtured a landscape in which the past is ever present (at least, ever on the verge of jamming a farmer's plough). It hasn't been burned to ashes but remains, rough-hewn and tangible, ready any moment to trip up the present. And wherever the past is alive, magic and supernatural creatures are never far away.

I picnicked that day in a ruined croft near the road, munching on bannocks filled with creamy Westray cheese. I had to keep my legs clear of the nettles, balancing on the round crest of a barley-drying kiln. It was the kind of building where the selkies in the stories were forced to live — low-slung, built to withstand the blastings of the wind. Another barn was part of the farm complex at West Brough, the smells of the animals trailing out of the stalls. Behind this compound was a pebbledash house, with a stepped roof under the chimney. There, Dennison collected the tales he'd heard, as well as other antiquities gleaned from the fields around — a Viking axe in a wooden handle, the remnants of old ploughs, a Queen Anne teapot, and the first china cup and saucer to reach the island.

'The whole of Dennison's life was spent on Sanday,' wrote the Orcadian historian Ernest Marwick. 'This was for posterity a fortunate occurrence, for the island was particularly rich in its recollections of folk tradition.' The stories he collected were in danger of draining away, lost to the tidal pull of modernity. It fell to Dennison, as the storyteller Lynn Barbour put it to me, 'to shine a lantern on it'.

Many of Dennison's stories hum with otherworldly magic. But what makes them so charming is the Orcadian earth in which they're rooted. The heroes are ordinary people, like a misfit called Brockie, who blows his nose on a gentlewoman's pew in church and is punished with an iron collar, fastened to the church wall (before leading a riot and kicking an official into the sea); or Vallyon, a drunkard who manages to beat the devil by throwing a keg of gin at his horn with a psalm stuffed inside it. Against the rough-hewn characterisations, supernatural glamour sparkles: ghosts swaying on pillars of fire over a graveyard; San Imravoe's army of seals herding the whales away from the bloodthirsty Odivere.

'It is now well-nigh fifty years since I first heard parts of this ballad,' Dennison wrote in a preface to the latter tale, in 1894, 'and for fifty years I have been gathering up fragmentary scraps of it from many old people in different parts of Orkney.' As a relic of Orkney's literature, it is significant, but it also stands out as the oldest known selkie tale (and some of the 'fragmentary scraps', as Dennison called them, inspired ballads sung on many of Orkney's islands, noted down by other lore-collectors in the nineteenth century*). Its antiquity is manifest in its language, which incorporates many of the words used in old Norn, the Norse tongue spoken on the islands into the eighteenth century (words such as 'peerie' for little and 'skeeted' for hit).

This underlines how the idea of selkies, of strangers coming in from the sea, spoke to Orcadians, enough to keep passing the story along, long after the words had fallen out of fashion. The selkie is a classic outsider, stranded against their will, in many of the traditional tellings, yearning to return home. Many of the stories are about how these outsiders are taken in and sheltered, sometimes exploited, sometimes treated with kindness. They reflect the daily life of a place which 'had always been open', to quote the scholar Jonathan Westaway, 'to the possibility of something washing up on its shore, a place where it is possible to imagine that anything could happen'.

STORYTELLERS OF STROMNESS

As I set off across Orkney's main island, I was hoping to learn more about this world of magical possibilities. I had two particular people in mind, who I hoped could teach me more about the archipelago's storytelling heritage — and the selkie tales in particular.

Among the cairns and barrows and standing stones that spread

---

*   One such fragment was transcribed in 1859 by a minister on the island of North Ronaldsay. Its lyrics evoke the heartache of a mother who has to give up her selkie child, mirroring the narrative of 'The Play o' de Lathie Odivere': 'But how shall I my young son ken / An' how shall I my young son know? 'mong a' the Selkies i' Sule Skerry / He will be midmost among them a'.'

between the lochs of Harray and Stenness, twenty-seven megaliths (some as high as fifteen feet) tickle the sky, earning their place in local folklore as dancing giants transformed to stone by the rising sun. Other passengers were debating whether to disembark for the giants or hold on to Skara Brae, the neolithic settlement uncovered on the island's western tip. Halfway between these landmarks, I climbed down at a crossroad. A sprawling pebbledash house guarded the moor ahead, looking over an abandoned croft and a garden bobbing with buoys and rocks and fishing nets. The mute figure of a Huldufólk — a ragged doll representing a supernatural being — sat inside the doorway like a sentry. Music poured out of the room behind her. A door swung open, fragments of fishing nets hanging from the pane, and there stood the storyteller Lynn Barbour.

'So you've come to visit, have you? You should've phoned!'

In her black overshirt, a silver trinket shining on her chest, grey hair swooping around her cheeks, she had something of the shaman about her. An air of impatience as she rattled around the house, showing me her library of folklore and the planked hall where she performs her tales, perfumed by incense sticks. Dolls spanned the breadth of the hall, among potted plants and ferns, and frescoed over the mantelpiece were sailing folk and magical Orcadian creatures.

The layer of frost soon thawed. Lynn pointed out books for me to read and recalled the stories she tells. Soon she was perched on a stool, dishing out reminiscences and tales while her dogs scrambled around her knees. She hails from West Scotland, but Orkney drew her in. She came first in her mid-twenties to set up a dance academy, reviving traditional island dances from the nineteenth century, and returned a few years later. Now she has her folklore and storytelling centre, where she narrates tales about selkies and other creatures of Orcadian folklore, along with classes in dance and tai chi. For Lynn, it's all connected: every dance has a story in it. 'The Play o' de Lathie Odivere,' she pointed out, 'was originally sung to music,' and many other stories began their lives as ballads. Dance introduced Lynn to people across the isles, and over the years she's heard most of Orkney's stories, picking up its phrases and proverbs. She's even taught the descendants of selkies, as far as local tradition is concerned:

'One of my dance students, she had webbed feet. There's a few like that around here, and if their feet are webbed, they say it means there was a selkie in the bloodline.'

Associations of this kind have been made for centuries — at least as far back as Odivere's lady and her selkie child. 'The selkies are Orkney folks' cousins,' to quote a traditional verse. The Orcadian writer Ernest Marwick knew a woman from the isle of Stronsay 'who sprang from union with a seal man', describing 'thick horn skin' on her hands and feet, 'a greenish-white tegument fully a sixteenth of an inch thick which was cracked in places and had a strong fishy odour'. If somebody doesn't fit in, if they have a melancholy look, if they're too quiet, too grave, or too spirited perhaps, tales of transformation help to explain the anomaly. For Lynn, the stories about selkies have something to say about mental health, troubles that, in the days before psychological treatment and cognitive therapy, were understood through allegory:

'You remember the melancholy look on the selkie's face when she's gazing out to sea? In the story of the Goodman of Wastness, but it happens in a few of the tales. A woman suddenly moved out of home, finding herself pregnant, looking after her babies in a house that will never feel like her own. It may be that the tale speaks to something about women and what they go through in childbirth. It may be it speaks about postnatal depression.'

The selkie's shapeshifting can be an analogy for the bodily changes and psychological challenges of puberty, for sexual fluidity, gender dysphoria, manic depression, migration trauma, and many other states of change. Lynn talked about the role that selkie stories have played in workshops on cognitive therapy, and I thought of times I had dipped into other magical stories — folk and fairy tales, weird stories, episodes in sagas and epics — how they'd helped me find my own equilibrium, helped me when I was tipping close to the edge.

I thought of some of the stories I'd read: a mean-spirited fisherman who lives with the selkies for a year and comes back gentler and kinder; a notorious seal-hunter taken to the selkies' underwater cavern, given the shock of his life and a sack of gold, who spends the rest of his days protecting the seals he used to hunt. These are not heroic tales. They're stranger, more fluid. Many are framed around recognition of the cruelty that humanity inflicts on animals, as well as on each other. The lessons they teach us aren't new. Odivere belongs to a line of bloodthirsty hunters cut down to size in traditional tales.[*] The selkie stories remind us that storytelling has always come in different forms, with different angles of meaning; even more so in the past, when people gave themselves more time to hear them.

I had hoped to catch one of Lynn's storytelling evenings, but with autumn stealing away the daylight, her season was drawing to a close. Still, I was only a few miles from another storyteller, and if I could trust what I'd heard about him, I would surely hear a tale or two from his mouth.

In order to reach him, I needed to walk down to Stromness. It was a six-mile stroll, past low-built farmhouses and stone barns. The drooping sun was turning the sky amber, like it had been washed with mead, except for the dark flash of a great skua in flight. Sheep grazed on the sloping pastures, while the oat fields were patrolled by lines of stooks. The Loch of Stenness acted like a compass, with the Brodgar giants on its far side. I followed the shoreline, the giants shrinking to dwarves, the road tipping me towards the grey sunless sea.

Stromness is the sort of harbour town you'd expect to find bulging with tourist tat, but it remains defiantly dour, its thin lanes tight with secrets. It's a practical place for long-term residents rather than a lure for holidaymakers, with its community fridge and the shuttered façade

---

[*] A few examples: Agamemnon, provoking the wrath of Artemis by killing her sacred deer (for which he ultimately has to sacrifice his own daughter); the stepmother in the Chinese tale of Yeh-Shen, who kills and cooks a holy fish containing the heroine's guardian spirit; Odysseus's crew, destroyed by Zeus for roasting the Cattle of the Sun.

of the Royal Hotel, the grey pebbledash and narrow windows oozing melancholy.

That night, the Met was threatening seventy-miles-per-hour gales, sideways rain, and floods. Which was a little bit unfortunate if you happened to be camping.

'You're not the one in the tent?' asked a doughy-faced campervanner at the Point of Ness.

His wife grasped her hands, as if the funeral was already underway. Above us, the sky had turned the colour of coal ash.

'Well,' I said, 'at least I'll have my pick of the pitches!'

I tucked my tent beside a drystone wall, hoping for protection from one side at least. I could feel the wind from the moment I bedded down — plucking at the sides of the tent, as if hogboons were scampering out of the mounds, perhaps out of the raised greens of the golf course on the other side of the wall. I learned that night why Orcadians coined so many words for rain. Whether it was a driv, a rug, a murr, or a hagger spitting, thrashing, sideswiping, or crashing down from on top, I'm putting the final assault down to a hellyiefer. Drenched, exhausted, but weirdly stimulated by my tussle with the elements, I dragged my gear into the toilet compound. The tent flapped behind me, as if it was undergoing its own supernatural mutation and would rematerialise as a guillemot.

All morning it sloshed down, filling the walkways with puddles, so fiercely southward that from one direction the wind pushed you forward, the other it rushed against you. On the narrow lanes of central Stromness, you had cover, steep walls to see off the squalls, but refuge was still necessary. I found it in the museum, browsing between marlinspikes, stitch mallets, and baleen plates, a wonderful array of maritime gear — the chest of a murdered sea captain from Tankerness, the snowshoes worn by the explorer John Rae in the Arctic — as well as George Mackay Brown's rocking chair, on which the beloved writer used to muse in his pebbledash flat across the way, imagining tales of selkies and trowies and other magical things. Further along the street, up a flight of stone steps, a lion-headed knocker snarled over a pot of ferns. Rainwater was dribbling over its muzzle as Tom Muir flung open the door.

'Let's get you in, this is no weather for staying outside.'

Behind an Amish blanket, hung up to keep out the draught, he led me into his drawing room.

Rain or not, I could have sat there all day. A stagecoach lantern was mounted under a baby carrier from Borneo. Hung over a fan-heated stove was a painting of the eleventh-century Battle of Clontarf, one of the great contests of the mediaeval North, which drew a pagan army out of Orkney all the way to Ireland, falling under spears and axes, portents of boiling blood and iron-taloned ravens. Similarly eclectic were the books lining the walls beside us. They ranged from international folklore and literary classics to Orcadian favourites such as Mackay Brown and the prickly angler Eric Linklater's *Sealskin Trousers*. Tom poured out drams of whisky, opened a tin of shortbread, and tipped books off the shelves to illustrate his points. With his thick woollen jumper and his broad frame, he put me in mind of a bear, scooping honey out of a tree. Send him back a thousand years to Clontarf, and Tom would look just right in a bearskin. He certainly seemed like a child out of time; or, as he put it:

'I was born at the tail-end of something that no longer exists.'

He grew up on a farm called Valdigar, with five other siblings. As a child, he'd help sorting the hay, mucking out the cattle sheds, the rigours of farming life. There were few books, and bedtime tales were rare. 'The family got a TV just before I was born, so that way of life was gone. In fact, it was through the TV that I got interested in stories — through *Jackanory*.'

As a schoolboy struggling with dyslexia, Tom was picked on by fellow students as well as the staff. His nose still bears a scar from a meeting with a teacher's ruler. He left at fourteen, wriggling out of the way of official warnings against truancy. Schooling may not have suited him, in the form it was taught, but he was fascinated by the past. Work on archaeological digs led to a job at the Orkney Museum in Kirkwall, where he was put in charge of an exhibition for the 100th anniversary of Dennison's death in 1994. Tom's natural gift for storytelling was drawing in audiences, and over time he was dispatched around the islands, telling stories to local communities on islands like Sanday, Westray, and North Ronaldsay.

'People didn't always like it. Some of the older folk were against it — they thought it was backward, they'd been raised with this church attitude of seeing stories about magical things as wrong. But young people couldn't get enough of it.'

I'd heard this before: clerical opposition to the Drachenstich in Bavaria, mutterings about tension with the church in St Agnes. So often, traditional monsters hark back to the beliefs that predated Christianity. Even if the stories pay formal homage to Christian teachings, the glamour — in every sense — lies with the ancient beings.

Tom retold the stories in Dennison's collection, and sifted other sources: mediaeval sagas, old newspapers, tales he heard by word of mouth. Many of them hadn't been aired for decades. He told them in performance, and published collections as well, establishing himself as Orkney's most prominent teller of tales in the twenty-first century:

'Now those selkie tales are popular, especially with girls. Whenever I visit a school, the girls always say, "Do you know a selkie story?"'

For Lynn Barbour, the selkie stories expressed something about postnatal depression. For Tom's wife, Rhonda, they echoed escape from an abusive relationship: 'losing your identity,' in Tom's words, 'and getting it back.' Shapeshifters resonate for people who've lived a double life, which may explain the particular appeal the selkie has for female storytellers (Cathie Dunsford's *Song of the Selkies*, Laurie Brooks's *Selkie Girl*, and Kirsty Logan's *The Gloaming* are just a few twenty-first-century examples). Tales of identity and agency sublimated by masculine control are echoed in many of the selkie narratives. The stories keep coming, because the idea still chimes with life's realities.

But the selkie is also a creature of Orkney. Not exclusively, of course, but it does have a special connection with these islands. Tom believes this is because 'the selkie stories originate here, that's my gut feeling. We have so many selkie stories, and they don't get mixed up with other stories. In Ireland, they mix up selkies and mermaids, but here there's no confusion between a selkie, a mermaid, and a finfolk. We know exactly what they are.' They reflect the 'mixture of different cultures in Orkney. We have stories you find in the Nordic world, the Scottish world, and stories that don't belong in either. Because Orkney lay on a cultural crossroads.'

When travel by sea was faster and more efficient than by land, the Swedish scholar Bo Almqvist argued that 'the Orkney earldom was a formidable naval power, backed as it also was by the forces of the whole of western Scandinavia. It would not be inaccurate to say that Orkney played a role in the North Sea similar to that played by Venice and other mighty Italian republics in the Mediterranean.'

This interconnectedness is visible in surprising details — Romanesque features in St Magnus Cathedral in Kirkwall, for example, journeys to Constantinople recounted in literary works like 'The Play o' de Ladhie Odivere' and the *Orkneyinga Saga*. Like Cornwall and the border towns of Bavaria, Orkney is pigeonholed as peripheral. But that hasn't always been the case. Its position at the heart of trade routes brought people to the archipelago and made it a fulcrum for storytelling; just as its later marginalisation enabled these stories to survive. So many monsterlands are places that mattered, before the wider world left them behind.

The rattle of rain had been the ambient noise to our chatter, like a radio playing in the room next door. But now it had fallen silent. Looking through the window, behind the Bornean baby carrier and the stagecoach lantern, I saw flat puddles among the cobbles.

'It's calm now.'

Tom marked the change in weather by pouring another dram and launching into a story about the Mither o' the Sea, who stills the storms and fills the waters with life, battling for supremacy with the spirit of winter. The story was still bouncing around my head as I slid down the cascading steps towards the harbour. I looked out at the grey water around me, waiting, and waiting, and waiting.

No luck this time. No dappled head breached the surface, no whiskery snout turned in profile. It was hardly the weather for waterdancing. So I turned from the grey vat of the sea and made my way to the bus station.

The forecast was bleak, the ferry several hours delayed, but it ploughed its way across the stormy firth. The tilting corridors were rancid with vomit, noisy with the moaning of seasick passengers, with the jostling elbows of people who looked upon each other as potential carriers of plague. Travel was only just resurging in the wake of the global pandemic, and there was a suspicion in many eyes that I didn't remember from before. Any one of us might be the shapeshifter, the demon, the plague-carrier. Safer to shun them all and keep to yourself.

That's the menace of these tales. When creatures from the other side can make themselves look just like us — who can you trust? These stories force us to ask difficult questions not only of the wild, mysterious places from which the creatures emerge, but also of ourselves. In a world in which shapeshifting is possible, anybody could be a selkie, or a werewolf, a skin-walker, a púca, a fox spirit, or even — heavens preserve us! — a jinn.

Two and a half thousand miles separated me from a different kind of shapeshifter. They might, like the selkie, emerge out of the sea; but they might appear out of heat haze and desert mirages, or even turn up in your drains. They've inspired some of the richest supernatural storytelling, and they remain alive in a culture that never stops whispering about them. For the jinn may be the most invisible of 'monsters', but when it comes to their presence in ordinary life, they're as visible as it gets.

CHAPTER FIVE

The Realm of the Unseen

THE FIFTH TALE

Along the Atlantic Coast, soldiers are standing on ramparts of stone. Sweat pours under their domed helmets, like juice squeezed out of oranges. They perch between the bastions, fanned by the Portuguese flag, looking down on the dust-caked Africans below.

Deals have been struck, God has been invoked, gold and silver have exchanged hands. But there has been raiding along with the trading, too many captives led in chains, too many camels and cattle stolen from the plains. Now the people of the Maghrib are uniting, hearing the call of the Sufi leaders, gathering around the sultan at his court beside a mystic's tomb. Smoke burns in braziers, sulfur fizzes in the flames. Some say they saw the jinn among the clouds of smoke, some say they saw them floating out of the fire.

That night, a soldier at the fort is bragging of his deeds — the bodies he's slashed apart, the blood that has puddled around his feet; blood his squire is still wiping off his leather boots. He looks up at the fat moon with its African tilt and laughs at the deeds he's relating. But there is nobody listening now. Across the rampart, sweeping up the muddy path behind an iron-bossed gate ... impossible ... but too beautiful to ignore, in her long gown, black hair as long as a horse's tail behind the musical sway of her hips, the scent of musk from her glowing skin, the promise of those blood-red lips.

'Who sent you? Ah, no matter, it's been too long a while.'

Shaking away any misgivings, the soldier draws an arm around her waist and guides her into the shadows. But what he sees in the darkness is no mortal woman. Huge teeth hanging out of a demon's head and down below those alluring limbs have turned into the furred legs of a camel. Before he falls, his mind has already snapped.

When they find his charred body, a bell is ringing from a bastion on the other side of the fort. Two men have fallen, three, four, dead before any can give an account. And in the gaps left behind by the guards, men with mysterious words scribbled down their sleeves flit between the shadows.

'What is attacking us? What is it? Tell us!'

The Portuguese commander roams the ramparts, his voice bristling with panic. Sufi dervishes are taking over the fort, driven forward by mysterious powers. Down in the dungeon, the commander grabs hold of a prisoner, demanding he explain what is happening. But instead of shivering with fear, the prisoner's face blazes defiance:

'You have awakened her! The blood is on your hands!'

Wrenching his chains, he smacks his head against the hard stone floor. Blood flows from his brow, spilling down his neck, but a smile shines through the wreckage of his face. He smacks his head again, as the commander looks on in horror.

'The daughter of the King of the Jinn is here in our world. We call her Aicha Kandicha, and she is your destruction.'

All over the land, word is spreading. The enemy may have cannons between its parapets, arquebuses and muskets; it may have gold and silver flowing out of its mines like water out of fountains. But the Maghrib has something more — it has the jinn.

CITY OF THE INVISIBLES

Once there was, and once there wasn't, as they say in the old Arab tales. And once, long ago, I was a student in Morocco. I stumbled around the narrow alleys of the medina (the old walled town) of Fez, breakfasting on delicious pastries and glasses of mint tea, turning up to classes in Modern Standard Arabic, wrestling with the intricacies of a language I could never quite master, and apprenticing in a tannery where I plunged into pits of lime to soak the hides and carried them onto the rooftops to dry. I loved those months in Fez, hanging out with the shebab, the local lads who invited me onto their rooftops, sipping tea, puffing on hash pipes, watching the pigeons in the coops and the flights of swallows overhead. I had studied and worked as a teacher in Palestine, but it was in Morocco that I came across stories about the jinn.

Now I was returning, and memories of those stories came flooding back: amulets containing prayers for safety from the spirits, copper Hands of Fatima hung on doors as defence against the jinn, herbs and incense sold to ward away or (in some cases) attract them. I remembered a friend telling me how he had once been possessed by a jinn, and another pointing out a troublesome pigeon in the coop on his parents' roof, a sure case of jinn interference. Over time, I heard of particular spirits, with their own names and caprices. There was Baba Hammou, jinn of the abattoir, and Shamharush, so-called 'King of the Jinn', whose white-washed tomb gleamed from a ridge as I trekked up Mount Toubkal in the Atlas.

Most sinister of all was Aicha Kandicha. First she appears as a beautiful woman, beguiling men (especially, but not exclusively) and leading them into deserted places. There, like the optical flip on a

Rubin's vase, she reveals a different side to herself. Huge teeth jut from her mouth, fur bristles down her legs, which end in a pair of cloven hooves like a camel's, or in some tellings a goat's, or another hoofed creature's. If her victim cannot protect himself with the power of his faith, he is doomed.

'People have a real fear of Aicha Kandicha,' said the literary scholar Fatima Zahra Salih, who I visited on my return to Morocco. Sitting in her elegant front room in Rabat, surrounded by gold-tooled books and brochures from a storytelling festival she had curated, Fatima mused on the presence of the jinn in Moroccan culture:

'There are certain things you are expected to do, or not do, especially after the Asr prayer in the evening — such as not taking a shower, because hot water disturbs the jinn in the drains.'

But alongside the apprehension about jinn in real life, Fatima recalled their vivid presence in storytelling:

'When I was growing up, we had a nurse who told wonderful stories. Of course, many involved the jinn.'

Among these was a charming tale about a girl who pledges her love to a lantern that leaves her presents every night; another told of a young man who marries a jinn, and when she disappears from his life, he seeks her across the heavens on a magical eagle. These are the sort of 'genie tales' familiar all over the world. But as Fatima put it, 'there is a fluency between reality and the imagination'. In her own family, there was a story about her grandfather encountering a jinn while he was working on a railroad in the desert.

'And what was strange to all of us was that my grandfather was a very serious man,' said Fatima, 'he was not somebody who invented stories.'

In Meknes and Fez, I often heard about strange goings-on: a collapsed house blamed on a vindictive jinn; a party during which a mysterious voice warned everybody to leave — which they did, straightaway. In Casablanca, the British writer Tahir Shah showed me his garden where, according to a much-reported story, a jinn treasure was said to be buried (his gardener swore he'd met twenty-four jinn in a room overlooking the garden who claimed prior rights over the property — and lest they be disrespected, they had left a decapitated cat, broken windows, and numerous other signs of their power).

But where do you go to look for jinn — or at least, to hear the stories about them? They tend to arise in unexpected places, and so it was for me. I spent many hours roaming around Meknes, and followed many trails. Travel can be like burrowing around a maze — try enough paths and hopefully one of them will guide you to your target. Wandering outside the medina's mud-brick ramparts, I found myself climbing between whitewashed walls, to a door as bright as the fruits in the nearby market: lemon yellow, pomegranate red, grapefruit pink. Hexagons swirled around dotted stars, framed in wave-like swirls and trails of white like lacing on cloth. It was the most beautiful shrine entrance I'd seen in the city, drawing me in like a secret garden. A pair of entwined trees loomed overhead, with oranges and bananas hanging among the leaves, and underneath them stood the shrine's guardian.

Salam-u aleykum.

W-aleikum as-salaam.

Peace to one another. Abdel-Wahed was thin but sinewy, an intellectual craftsman with gimlet eyes shining above pronounced cheeks and a tightly clipped moustache. A face burning with thoughts, lined with experience.

The perfume of recently burned herbs followed us inside the mausoleum, where Abdel-Wahed showed me the green cloth-covered shrine of a sixteenth-century weli (saint), the carpeted prayer room where he had painted the names of God across the walls, the graves of patrons. He had studied Islamic art and carpentry, in between working in the army and academia, and spent most of his days at the shrine.

'Look here — you see this panel.' He showed me a board near the tomb, embossed with black Kufic Arabic against a gold background. 'There is an invisible army that protects this city.'

'An army of jinn?'

'These are the good jinn. Do you understand? There are satanic jinn, but there are also jinn among the faithful.'

They had come to him, he said, in dreams and reflections, inspiring him with images, offering advice.

'They are not always easy to tell,' he conceded, kneeling over a gas burner, brewing tea, 'it is a matter of faith.' But when it came to the 'satanic jinn', he was adamant: those encounters were incontestable.

'Once, some years ago, I was staying on a farm, it was not so far from Meknes. Late in the evening, I heard a noise. It sounded like a howling, the sound a wolf might make. But there are no wolves in that area. And I felt a prickling in my head, I knew I was in the presence of something with a more-than-human power.'

Wolves, he explained, were common forms for jinn to take, along with black sheep, scorpions, and black cattle. But he had ways to repel them: herbs to burn, salt to sprinkle, a ritual phrase: *audhu b'illah min ash-shaitan ar-rajim* ('I seek refuge in God from the outcast Satan').

'This is how you know it is a satanic jinn,' he said, 'because they are afraid of the word of God.'

During that week in Meknes, I met Abdel-Wahed nearly every day. We'd sit on his couch, drinking vervain tea, or crouch around his gas burner, eating kefta (meatballs). His generosity was of the unfettered kind I had encountered so often in Arab and Muslim societies. We talked about many subjects, including tricky political ones, but my favourite conversations were the ones about the jinn. We worked over some of the tales from the *1001 Nights*, the mediaeval Syrian poet al-Maari's *Epistle of Forgiveness*, and the jinn mentioned in the Quran.

'Well, of course I know a few of the hikayat [tales],' Abdel-Wahed said. 'As it happens, I made a book about them.'

They were stories heard in the streets, in teahouses and at communal gatherings. Appropriately, he'd called his book *Invisibles of the Everyday*. It included the jinn of the bathhouse, a jinn that appears to a man digging in the hills near Meknes, and many stories about the jinn associated with the nearby Mount Zerhoun, especially the notorious Aicha Kandicha.

'Praise God, there are a lot of stories about this jinniya,' he said, and narrated one about a man who falls in love with Aicha, dazzled by her supernatural beauty, but forgets about her and settles down with an ordinary human. Cue a major bout of jinn jealousy: 'So she appears to the man late at night, no longer beautiful — now she has hooves on her legs, her teeth are very big and ...' He sliced a hand across the air to indicate the fatal strike.

There were other stories, in which Aicha appeared to a miller, a pair of lumberjacks, a madman 'who was living a normal life until he met Aicha. But she told him to wear only ragged clothes and never cut his hair, and he wandered around as her favourite.'

Did I want to know more about Aicha Kandicha and the other jinn of Mount Zerhoun? In that case, I should come to the moussem — the religious festival taking place over the coming days.

'Hmmm ... funny you should mention that.'

'You were planning to attend? Then let us travel together, God willing.'

It was the abundance of named jinn that had drawn me back to Morocco. Not just generalised spirits but individual characters, each with their own qualities and quirks. Among them, none is more 'monstrous' than Aicha Kandicha. Which makes it all the stranger that she is at the heart of the festival in which people gather to ask the jinn for help.

THE PEOPLE OF FIRE

'I seek refuge in God from the outcast Satan.' So went the phrase Abdel-Wahed had taught me, a reference to the jinn's back-story in the Quran. They were created before humans, out of 'fire free of smoke'. Granted dominion over the worlds, they ravaged it with their mischief-making until God grew weary of their misdeeds and dispersed them.

One of their number, called Iblis, was brought to heaven to be raised among the angels. But when God ordered the angels to bow down to Adam, Iblis refused: 'I am better than he. Thou didst make me from fire, and him from clay.' So he was hurled out of heaven, and Iblis pledged to hinder humanity wherever he could.

Not all jinn are of the devil's party — but doctrinally speaking, if they're causing trouble to humans, that is their provenance. We can understand them better if we delve into the roots of the word. 'Jinn' derives from the letters jim and nun (j and n). As the scholar Amira El-Zein points out in *Islam, Arabs, and the Intelligent World of the Jinn*, 'each time the two letters jim and nun occur together, like in jinn, they convey the meaning of invisible, unseen, or hidden.' This is key to how they are perceived: something mysterious that cannot always be seen with the naked eye. Every so often, someone will be granted a sighting, and their life will hinge on the encounter. But among the many descriptions — gaseous figures, translucent, brightly lit, or barely distinguishable from humans — none has monopolised the consensus. For the great mediaeval polymath Ibn Arabi, the jinn were beyond human vision: 'we see them in the eye of the heart rather than with the physical senses, and take it on faith they are with us.' But for many other Islamic writers, they can be perceived, if indistinctly. The thirteenth-century cosmographer al-Qazwini, for example, saw them as 'aerial animals, with transparent bodies, which can assume various forms'.

This last detail is at the heart of jinn identity, and was key to the descriptions I heard during my visit to Morocco: their ability to change. If a being has no fixed form, how do you define it? There's only one way, surely: by looking at the stories.

In the West, jinn or 'genies' are associated with the wonderful tales of Scheherazade — the wrathful jinn outwitted by a plucky fisherman and trapped in a cask; the magnificent jinn who fills Aladdin's house with treasure and conjures him a palace next to the sultan's. Powerful beings, formidable but ultimately benevolent. But a truer sense of their complexity is suggested when we learn how capricious they can be.

Among their many appearances in classical Arabic literature, one of the most illuminating is the mischievous jinn called Abu Hadrash, who features in *The Epistle of Forgiveness*. In this extraordinary eleventh-century text, which follows a literary pedant's often comical journey around the heavens (anticipating Dante's *Divine Comedy* by nearly three centuries), we meet Abu Hadrash in the paradise of the jinn. He describes his many adventures: stirring the minds of drinkers, cheating notaries, turning middle-aged women mad while they cook for their children. He's a down-and-dirty villain, using his powers to sow discord. In one of his adventures, he tells us that he targeted a young woman, transforming himself into a rat. Her family set their cats against him, so he turned into a viper and then a blustering wind, so confusing the girl's protectors that he was able to strike her with a fit. With such a comprehensive CV of misdeeds, it's a little surprising to find him rewarded with a berth in 'paradise', but Abu Hadrash has seen the errors of his ways: 'my repentance was exemplary,' he tells us, 'after I'd lived a life notorious for disobedience.'

What is unusual is his self-articulation. In the poet al-Maari's fantasia, we are taken inside the mind of a jinn. They have their own secret tongue, as well as knowledge of human languages; they can compose and recite poetry, are skilled in philosophy and the art of disputation. Add to that their ability to shapeshift: 'Anyone of us could be a speckled snake if he so wished, or a sparrow if he wanted, or a pigeon.' The selkie can only shift from seal to human, but the jinn can morph into anything they like: animal, object, element ... But what makes them especially unsettling is their ability to present themselves uncannily like humans.

Of all the shapeshifters that appear in Moroccan storytelling, Aicha Kandicha is the trickiest. Even her name keeps shifting: Contessa Aicha, Lalla Aicha, Aicha Soudaniyya, Aicha Dhughiyya, Lalla Aicha Hasnawiyya, Aicha Gnawiyya, Aicha Hamdoushiya, and other names besides. She has been traced by some to the Canaanite goddess of love, Astarte, who was also associated with war: 'we have reason to suppose,' wrote the scholar Edward Westermarck, 'that Aicha Kandicha is the old goddess of love degraded to a Moorish jinniyah of a most disreputable character.' The god-to-monster downgrade so common throughout world mythology.

Similarly vindictive she-monsters can be found seething across the world's cultures, reflecting male fear of female power, while evoking the old fertility goddesses, such as the donkey-eared Babylonian monster-goddess Lamashtu and the terrifying Umm Duwais of the Arabian Gulf, who like Aicha lures errant men into deserted places, where she reveals skeletal features and claw-like hands. The Moroccan stories locate Aicha Kandicha in a variety of places — on the banks of the river Sebu; in the deserted places around Tangier; in the Doukkala region, where she was associated with stories about the insurgency against the Portuguese outposts of the sixteenth century. This version inspired a Moroccan British actress and writer called Safia Lamrani to pen a play about her, depicting Aicha both as spectre of death and defender of the nation. Safia was drawing not only on a national folklore, but on family stories, for in Morocco nobody is more than a couple of degrees of separation from an encounter with the fearsome jinn:

'My grandfather saw Aicha,' said Safia when we talked in the UK. 'Well, that's what he told everyone. He was walking near a graveyard in Tangier when he heard her calling him. She was wearing a white dress, but when he drew closer, she was a skeleton, completely terrifying.'

Stories like this are rarely told openly. They are hashuma, Safia pointed out, taboo; but over the years, she'd heard about the jinn appearing in every form you could imagine — emerging out of mirrors, pouring out of upside-down shoes. 'If you recite the Quran then you'll be free. That's how my grandfather escaped. They're created by Allah, so you can seek protection from them, there's a way out.'

So Abdel-Wahed suggested, with his sacred phrase and his smouldering herbs. This is the reassurance around the jinn: if you have faith, if you belong to the community of believers, there is the possibility of being saved. And to reverse that process, if you have faith, you may be able to call upon them. It's a path fraught with danger, and not to be undertaken lightly. But if troubles are piling at your door, what is there to lose? So it has always been, and so — I had heard — it continues in a small town on Mount Zerhoun.

MOUNTAIN OF MYSTICS

Olive trees run in undulating rows, under the soaring cliffs of the Zerhoun massif. The sun grills the valleys around Meknes, but occasional greenery bursts out in smoky-green plumes of fig and caper, carob and palm, defying the brown austerity above. As severe as the cliffs are the barriers with police vans. Gendarmes in peaked hats pat down passengers and shine their torches into the cars. Behind them, the road cuts into the mountain, depositing the latest batch of sweating pilgrims in a holy town named after the seventeenth-century mystic Sidi Ali.

'He is to be classed (may God have mercy upon him) among the sheikhs of the mystical tradition in which the ecstatic trance is powerful', wrote the nineteenth-century Moroccan historian Muhammad bin Ja'far al-Kattani. Establishing himself only a few miles from the burial place of Morocco's first Muslim preacher (Moulay Idriss, who came here in the eighth century), Sidi Ali drew a large following, who 'spread throughout many lands'. Miracles were attributed to him — among them, a rockfall crashing on the troops of a hostile sultan and the transportation of holy-oil jars by a gang of jinn. As with holy figures in other parts of Morocco, the stories about Sidi Ali inspired an annual celebration — a moussem — and over time, a village of clay-block houses grew around the weli's tomb compound, which ranks as one of the largest in Morocco.

But the moussem remains contentious, both for its rituals and the people it attracts — hence the police checks on the road. Away from orthodox centres, Sidi Ali has become an enclave where people not accepted in mainstream society can find a spiritual home. Sitting in a teahouse at the edge of town, Abdel-Wahed and I had barely sipped our first glass of mint tea before an old-timer in a chequered shirt, with a brush moustache and a pair of narrow eyes, sidled over to poke us with questions.

What was I doing here?

By whose authority had I come?

Did I intend to make a report about the things that go on in this place?

I was frog-marched to a police hut, my passport photocopied, my details written in triplicate, an anxious phone call relayed to a superior officer. 'Sidi Ali is a secret,' I had been told in Meknes; and many believe it should remain that way. There is a long history of keeping foreigners away from Zerhoun. Until 2005, it wasn't even possible for non-Muslims to spend the night in nearby Moulay Idriss.*

Doubts had riddled me over attending the moussem, but so many people in Meknes had talked about it, and their words of encouragement drowned out the policeman's severe expression. So, with much arm-waving, and after drinking several glasses of tea, at last we set off, following the muddy lanes through a knot of stalls selling incense-burners and iron castanets, beads and babouches and medallions to ward off the evil eye. The glitter of these gimcracks was offset by the cages and pens between them. You could hear them before you saw them — the whining, bleating, unhappy sound of hundreds of livestock — sheep, goats, roosters, guinea fowl, and a few

---

* The suspicion of the police is connected to the controversial nature of the moussem. As the anthropologist Vincent Crapanzano has written: 'Many Moroccans, especially Berbers and the educated Arabs, look askance at the practices of the Hamadsha [the Sufi brotherhood that follows Sidi Ali and plays the leading role in the festival]; they consider them to be uncouth, unorthodox, disgusting even, and are often embarrassed when reference is made to them by foreigners.' As a result, there have been very few accounts of the practices at Sidi Ali, and the moussem remains little-known outside Morocco.

emaciated cattle. There wasn't space for all the animals, not in these narrow alleys. They were squeezed together, horns and hooves ringing against the iron bars, the stench of their droppings mingling with the more fragrant aromas of lit perfume sticks and freshly polished copper. The only consolation was that many of them wouldn't have to wait long before they'd be put out of their misery.

Down we dropped, past women daubing bare legs and arms with henna, their complicated cosmographies tracing intricate patterns that reached as high as their customers' knees or as deep as their elbows. The lane snaked under canvas shading, past a carpeted den where a band of Gnawa musicians — black-skinned, descendants of slaves — was practising on long brass horns, oboes, castanets, and several kinds of drums. The castanets are particularly distinctive: their shape and sound echo the chains that shackled their ancestors' limbs centuries ago on the long walk across the Sahara. It is from those further reaches of Africa, so the theory goes, that many of Morocco's animist and magical traditions are drawn, and in the legend told about Aicha Kandicha on Mount Zerhoun, it is said that she herself hails from the 'land of the blacks'.[*]

'You see — this is for Lalla Aicha.' One of the players, with a wide smile and cowry shells wound around his cap, pointed to a black cloth hanging over the carpets. Beside it was a red banner, representing the slaughterhouse jinn, Baba Hammou, and there was a green one for Shamharush, King of the Jinn.

'They are all here,' he said. 'When we play, that is when we feel their presence the most.'

---

[*] One of Aicha's names is 'Aicha Gnawiyya', and the name 'Gnawa' is believed to derive from the West African nation of Guinea, birthplace of many of the slaves. 'It has sometimes been suggested that Moroccan [supernatural] possession comes from black Africa', wrote the French anthropologist Raymond Jamous, adding that 'it has been displaced from the centre to the periphery or margin of society'. This bears repeating: what happens in Sidi Ali is far from representative of Islamic society, and as Jamous points out, 'is considered as a deviation from the norm'.

I sat among the players, my ears warmed by the notes of the oboe and the alluring rhythm of the drums. Further along the alley, a dervish in a patchwork gown (which represents a folkloric figure called Bu Ali) was holding a staff strung with ribbons and topped with a bronze orb.

'Shamharush is here,' he told me, tapping the orb.

'The King of the Jinn?'

'Yes, he has a great power.'

'A good power or ...?'

'A very good power. He protects us all.'

A couple of men, hands clasped tight, sidled past; so did a trans woman in a tie-dye dress, face glowing with an expression of ecstasy. Sunlight slid down like a gateway of light, signalling the end of the stalls and the approach to the shrine.

Sidi Ali's mausoleum stretches across a land-bridge, joining the village to the ridge of the adjacent mountain. A hexagonal green-tiled roof gleams over a whitewashed compound, with a doorway spanned by green pillars. Inside is a large courtyard, where people lie down on a carpeted dais, praying or meditating or chattering in small groups. Some were sitting, legs outstretched, gazing ahead, like patients in a hospital waiting to be called.

Abdel-Wahed had stepped inside the mausoleum straightaway. I sat in the courtyard, biding my time. I could hear noises within: a shrieking sound, then a wail. I perched on the dais, steeling myself, trying to recall what I had read and heard about the legends of Mount Zerhoun.

At the core of the legendary cycle is an acolyte of Sidi Ali, called Sidi Ahmed, who is known for his boldness. In one of the stories, he shoots the sultan's vicious son with an arrow; in another, he chews on spiny cactus like a camel. In the most famous tale, he is tasked with a mission by Sidi Ali: to travel to the 'Kingdom of Sudan' and bring back the hal, the mysterious power associated with ecstatic trance. In an instant, he finds himself in this kingdom ('Sudan' being the 'land of the blacks', but in some interpretations, it is a byword for the kingdom of the jinn). He steps past sleeping soldiers and gathers up the hal, in the form of a flute, a drum, and the jinn Aicha Kandicha. The soldiers chase them on the return journey, but through the meditative powers of Sidi Ali, these relentless pursuers are transformed into frogs. This is one of Sidi Ali's last deeds — by the time Sidi Ahmed returns to the mount, his master has died, and the distraught acolyte grieves passionately, slashing his head with an axe (an act of mutilation that inspires emulators to this day). Aicha establishes herself in a small cavern near the burial-place of Sidi Ali, beside the spring of Ayn Kabir, where she assumes the invisible form appropriate to a jinn, and people have been coming to this place ever since.

Under a tiled cupola lay Sidi Ali's tomb, inside a wooden catafalque and a covering of green cloth. A couple of dozen worshippers surrounded it. Some were chanting holy verses, some meditating and reflecting. Over the murmur of recitation, another sound grew dominant: an anguished growl that seemed to emanate from within the tomb itself. I followed the pattern of movement — clockwise, with people who laid candles on the tomb or sprinkled it with orange-blossom water. A woman in black was accompanied by a boy with a balloon; another was bare-shouldered. On the far side, a woman in a striped kaftan was pressing close to the tomb, shuddering, groaning: this was the disturbing noise I had heard. Another woman reached out and clasped her hand, while the growls continued. At last, she collapsed to the floor, letting out deep, exhausted sighs.

'It is not her pain you hear,' said Abdel-Wahed. 'It is the pain of the jinn inside her.'

Here, in this holy place, the burial-place of a weli long associated with miracles, the evil spirits were vulnerable. Here, the afflicted had a better chance of being exorcised.

Over the three days I spent around Sidi Ali, I sat for many hours in the corridor beside the mausoleum, received a greeting from the shrine guardian, and studied the abstract patterns on the dadoes. It was during one of these periods of quiet contemplation that I found my hands clasped inside an elaborate pattern of henna. Beside me was a moon-faced middle-aged woman in a striped djellaba. She wrapped her arms around me, leaned across, and kissed the top of my head.

'I had the jinn inside me for twenty-one years,' she told me.

Her eyes were bright, looking deep into mine. There were tears still drying on her cheeks.

'It will come back,' she said, 'but for now I am safe, God willing.'

Farah had been 'maskuna', inhabited by the jinn. Having tried different remedies, such as shrines, clairvoyants, and the burning of various herbs, she had come to Sidi Ali to pray for help. That morning, she had performed a ritual trance known as 'jidba'. As I looked into her eyes, gleaming with tear-stained kohl, I couldn't help feeling for her, for her fraught struggle, her fears of a relapse. I thought of my own struggles — times I had felt ashamed to vocalise the darkness inside me, times I had been crippled with sadness and grief. Yes, if there was a ritual that might solve it all, if it was endorsed or encouraged by the people around me, then ... why not?*

A few months before, I had taken part in a panel event at the Muslim Literature Festival in Manchester, alongside a Muslim clinical psychologist, Professor Rasjid Skinner. Many of the patients at Ihsaan, Professor Skinner's clinic in Bradford, were concerned about the jinn. 'We look for physical and psychological symptoms first,' he told me, 'but in about 5 per cent of the cases, we suspect there is a paranormal influence.' In those cases, a raqi is called in — somebody trained in the Quran and qualified to deal with the unseen spirits. 'Mainstream psychological services [in the UK] don't give people

---

* There are several stages to this ritual process. The patient must attain the entranced state of hal, and proceed from there into jidba, which according to the anthropologist Vincent Crapanzano is 'comparable to a state of extreme rage' and 'is usually attributed to Aisha Qandisha or another jinn'. Such rituals often end with a verse: 'O Aicha, rise and put yourself in the service of God and his prophet.' In this way, Islamic monotheism is respected at the same time as accommodation is reached with the jinn, for the goal of the ritual is not so much to exorcise the spirits as to reach an understanding with them.

confidence,' Professor Skinner suggested. 'You need to be able to speak to somebody who shares the way you understand the world.' During our panel, we heard about a range of cases: split personalities and schizophrenia, haunted buildings, levitation. 'Our conclusion from the psychotherapeutic view,' said Skinner, 'is don't dismiss it if it helps the patient's recovery.'*

Wandering around Sidi Ali, that day and the next, Abdel-Wahed and I were joined by others — a mercurial flute-maker called Halim, dressed in a patchwork 'Bu Ali' gown, who clasped my hand before holding up his flute and playing lovely, tripping tunes; a lively bakery assistant called Ashraf, who talked passionately about Islamic philosophy, outlining the difference between 'materialistic Sufism' and the 'path of truth'. We roamed between herbalists' stalls, listened to the music of the Gnawa players, and sat together around a plate of couscous, joined by Farah, who was still smiling, still relieved to be freed of the jinn. 'She is drunk on hal,' said Abdel-Wahed, affectionately. I loved the camaraderie, the easy goodwill shared between pilgrims. It was the fellowship in faith that bonded pilgrims in different milieus across the world and across time, a fellowship that more sceptical regions have lost.

---

* There is, however, a less optimistic way of looking at these things. All over Morocco, there are zawiyas, often run by descendants of the Sufi weli who founded them, where people come to be delivered from their troubles. In some cases, the afflicted become dependent on the shrine guardians, vulnerable to abuse. At the notorious shrine of Bouya Omar near Marrakesh, patients were reportedly beaten and starved, chained by the neck, and thrown onto the streets if their families failed to pay the shrine guardians their exorbitant fees. For the Moroccan scholar Mohammed Maarouf, the danger in the zawiya system lies in the power dynamic: 'It disciplines them [the patients] to submit to the centres of distribution of prosperity and power, and thus collaborate with the forces that dominate them.' The same system, Maarouf argues, encourages its followers to attribute all life's calamities to the jinn — marital breakdowns, job failures, accidents in the workplace or at home, sudden deaths — thereby binding the community of believers to the shrine guardians in a system from which they can never gain true independence.

But there was a darker side to this place. We saw it in the shawafa stalls — little dens where magic arts were practised, with strips of lead hanging over red-painted doors, bowls full of herbs and yellow blocks of sulfur laid on the tables. The lead could undo curses, it was said. The sulfur was more active.

'That,' Halim told me, 'is if you want to make trouble for somebody else.'

Lower down, at the deepest point in the town, water trickled from a spring and devotees washed in partitioned chambers.

'Aicha is mistress of the river,' Abdel-Wahed explained. 'People believe she has special power here and that she likes to eat living flesh.'

We were standing under the soot-blackened, cobwebbed walls of a cavern, up a flight of steps from the spring. Candles were laid on mattresses of henna grass. On the walls behind, writing had been scrawled in henna. As I stepped forward to light my own bunch of candles, a woman brushed a live black chicken across a brazier. The shrine guardian took it away, returning with a knife gleaming red. Rolling up her sleeves, the woman held out her arms, and the blood was smeared across her skin.

'Baraka,' was the word I heard, repeated around me. 'Blessings'. The woman closed her eyes, her arms rigid.

'She is calling on Aicha Kandicha,' said Abdel-Wahed.

The jinn as a granter of wishes and blessings — baraka. The root of all those magical tales; as 'mistress of the river', an echo of the old nature spirits that predated Islam. A monster? Or a goddess? Or something in between?

THE HONEY TRAP

Two hundred miles south-west of Mount Zerhoun, the Bastion of the Angel looms over the sixteenth-century fortress of Mazagan, on the edge of the modern city of El Jadida. I stood there, looking out towards the sea. Below the stone crenellations, the Atlantic was flat and glassy, at least until the boys on a narrow pier hurled themselves into it. The water shattered around them, exploding shards of seawater swirling around their heads.

The Mazagan fortress was named after the local Amazigh people, whose single tower was absorbed into an impregnable fortress by the Portuguese. They built it in the form of a four-pointed star, with bastion towers at the corners, linked by parapeted ramparts. Two drawbridges connected the fortress to the mainland, but otherwise it was an isolated outpost. Impregnable too: Portugal continued to hold Mazagan long after they had lost their other presidios along the Atlantic seaboard, retaining it until 1769.

Today, its ramparts are climbing challenges for daredevil teenagers, its walls are regularly thumped by footballs, and the niches between the parapets supply clandestine spots for lovers. The call to prayer floats from a massive yellow-trimmed minaret towering over the old Portuguese clock tower, while rhythmic Sufi chant can be heard from the religious complex below, behind windowsills clotted with cats.

These coastal towns hold the ruins of Portugal's African ambitions — colonial Renaissance grandeur repurposed by descendants of the communities strong-armed into building it. A church has become a theatre; defensive walls provide shade for market stalls. In Safi, ninety miles further south, I stepped under walls of stone and mud, in between the mausoleums of Sufi welis and the parapets built by the Portuguese. At tiled fountains, shirtless boys were washing themselves under the blind arches of a sixteenth-century cathedral, after clambering around the ruins of a sea-fort that hangs over cliffs of crumbling sandstone and clay. Near one of the fountains, I stopped beside a bossed wooden door in a wall of thick stonework.

'Salam-u aleykum!'

A friendly renovator invited me inside. The light vanished for a moment like the parting of a curtain. A wooden plank wobbled under my feet, which tilted down some steps, under an arch moulding, into the choir of the cathedral. Above me, stone vaulting looped in magnificent swags, forming an eight-point-star that hung like a giant spider's web, with medallions in its heart like a spider's cocooned prey — a pair of crossed keys, a bishop's mitre, the armillary sphere of King Manuel I. Here was a shard of history, fixed in time, where all around it the Portuguese remains had been retooled, swallowed up by the ever-growing medina.

It was 'From the Portuguese threat and internal conflicts', wrote Jamil Abun-Nasr in *A History of the Maghrib in the Islamic Period*, that 'there arose in Morocco a call for unity.' Nothing like a shared enemy for knocking regional disputes aside and gluing a nation together. In this case, the glue was the Portuguese, and especially their raids into the interior. Unwittingly, they fostered Moroccan unity, because they insisted on single leaders to negotiate over captives. One of these, a Sufi master called Sidi Barakat, pulled together a collection of tribes in the south, under the leadership of the Saadian ruler Mohammed al-Qaim. The latter's position was consolidated by association with a Sufi preacher called al-Jazuli, whose burial place became a focal point for the Saadian court, before al-Jazuli's corpse was buried, alongside al-Qaim's, in the new capital of Marrakesh.

Safi was al-Jazuli's home for a time. While there, he stirred up followers against the Portuguese and tussled with the merchants who preferred to trade with the Europeans. A memorial to al-Jazuli stands near the sea-fort, a hooped building shaped like a wagon's canopy. It's a tribute to his influence, which extended politically to leaders like al-Qaim and doctrinally to Sufi brotherhoods such as the Issawa and Hamadsha, the tariqas that gather at the moussem on Mount Zerhoun.

What these connections underscore is that Sufism is not a reclusive system, nor an inherently pacifistic one — certainly not in Morocco. Sufis led the struggle for independence, and they also directed the relationship between the people and the jinn. History records the bloody battles that took place, while folklore interleaves them with tales. Few of these are as striking, or as enduring, as the one about the young woman pitting herself against the invaders from the sea.

Sometimes she appears in black, sometimes yellow or white, luring Portuguese soldiers away from their watchtowers. In some of the stories, she is a human, slitting her victims' throats in revenge for her own slain kinsfolk; in some, she is a Portuguese countess who fell in love with a Moroccan chief (and whose title — 'Condessa' — has been Arabised to 'Kandicha'); in others, she is a jinn, presenting a glamorous female form before she unveils the monster within. In the version of the story Abdel-Wahed had written down, she is a silky-haired beauty who appears on the ramparts of the fortress, luring the Portuguese soldiers in the time-honoured way. As they step towards her, expecting to encounter sexual bliss, she transforms into the cloven-footed Aicha Kandicha, enabling the Moroccan fighters (the 'mujahideen', as Abdel-Wahed called them) to break through. These are the stories passed down over the centuries to explain how Morocco freed itself from a great European power — by harnessing an esoteric power from within its own culture. It was a power that I saw, in one of the most startling experiences of my journey, on my last day on Mount Zerhoun.

NIGHT OF BLOOD

That final afternoon of the moussem, I had one more place to visit. Abdel-Wahed wasn't sure that I should. What went on there, he said, was a long way from orthodox Islam: 'People think their wishes will come true, but they are not following the methods of Sidi Ali, nothing they pray for will come to pass.'

Still, the hufra (literally, the 'hole') had a gravitational pull. To come all this way and not have a peek? Curiosity had taken hold of me, tight as any jinn. You could hear the livestock being dragged there, the crying of animals with only the dimmest sense of what was about to happen. Boys pulled the sheep forward, pilgrims strode down the path with roosters under their arms. A woman with her eyes to the sky staggered past me, letting out a strange, shrill laugh. A dervish sat on a rug next to a sheep-pen, beating a snare drum. I'd left Abdel-Wahed talking to Halim in his stall. This was a place I needed to see for myself.

Ahead was darkness and light. Over a scorched-black wall, henna leaves formed mattresses for spluttering candles. Pilgrims were pressing at the niches, setting down their candles, splashing the scorched wall with orange-blossom water. Some of them presented animals to be sacrificed in an adjacent tiled room, holding out their arms to be anointed with blood.

I had a few candles of my own. The first few lit quickly, but I struggled with the last. A woman in a black gown, her face and hands tattooed with henna, helped me. She picked at the wick with practised fingers and pointed out where to install it.

'Is Lalla Aicha here?' I asked.

'Always! If your prayer is ... pure ... then you have her blessing.'

She lifted her eyes, reciting a verse, while hand drums beat behind us, played by a row of dervishes in green acetate gowns.

Sunlight spat through the rips in the canvas shading, dripping off the edges of drums and the beads swinging from dervishes' hats. Members of the Hamadsha, adepts of Sidi Ali, were moving down the path. At their head was a young woman, long brown locks swinging over a face glazed with serenity. She could almost have been a dancer in a nightclub, in perfect sync with the music. She bobbed at the waist and swung her head, so that her long hair leaped in front of her, momentarily gilded by the light through the canvas. Around her were several boys with snare-drums, chanting 'Ya Lalla Aicha!' In one yoked-together group, they slid behind a gate.

I followed them, under a corrugated-iron roof and banners of green, red, and black: the colours of the presiding jinn. People were tipping their heads, nodding to the music, swaying to the beat of the drums, so I did the same. It was only when I saw the blood, scattering in thick drops from a knife, that I realised why the gate had been closed.

The knife was held by a man — I'd not even noticed him, my eyes had been fixed on the dancing woman. He was young, probably no more than twenty, dressed in a blue kaftan with white embroidery around the neck. His eyes were empty whites under a cowl of curly black hair. He swung the knife and sharp metal made contact with skin.

Again he swung, blood dribbling down his face, and again. He struck himself five times before letting out a low, bullish grunt. His arms collapsed to his sides. His dark curls shone with blood: a matted black gel. Staggering, still deep in trance, he followed the dancing woman back through the gate, to the rattling of castanets, beating drums and cries of 'baraka' and 'Lalla Aicha', pouring into a group of men driving a bull, flowing towards the area of sacrifice.

I was so stunned by what I had seen, my heart was beating like one of the Gnawa players' drums. What I had witnessed was hal: the state of trance, the power brought back in the story from the Kingdom of Sudan. The ineffable power composed of the flute, drum, and Aicha Kandicha.* I would have liked to linger, to ask about the ritual, and how it is perceived. But, with eyes sliding away from the Hamadsha, they took in the witnesses. One of the shrine guardians jabbed a finger at me and shouted. Recalling the police officer in the teahouse, I figured it was time to leave. It was Abdel-Wahed and his friends who helped me to make sense of what I had seen.

'With hal,' Abdel-Wahed explained, 'a man can do things that are impossible for an ordinary human — he can eat glass, he can throw himself from a cliff.'

This is the Sufi's secret weapon — a form of intense mental fortitude, a meditative victory over the receptors in our nervous systems. Hal — is this what enabled the Sufi brotherhoods to drive out the Portuguese? I flinched every time I saw the knife striking

---

* To the ethnographer Vincent Crapanzano, hal is the 'ecstatic trance, into which the Hamadsha work themselves', and in respect of Aicha Kandicha, 'the Hamadsha ... are her special devotees. Many hold her responsible for their trance.' This is why, in the tale, Aicha is brought back as part of the hal: she is an indispensable part of it.

the Hamadsha's head. But is there any point in travelling if we limit ourselves to the world we understand? I was an outsider here. I wanted to know what the insiders thought.

'This man was in *ghayb*,' said one of Halim's friends, as we sat around steaming glasses of mint tea in the stall. That is: in connection with the 'unseen' world.

'He does not care what he sees in the mirror — only his love for God matters,' said another.

It was Halim whose interpretation stuck with me: 'Lalla Aicha likes blood,' he said. 'The man who does this, now he has the baraka, and he can do a lot of good with it.' It was known for people to anoint themselves with the blood of adepts after such rituals, in order to receive the blessings.

At its heart, Sufism encourages the annihilation of the self in order to reach closer to God: 'fana', as it is called. The practices of the Hamadsha, however, are slightly different. It is the welis whose baraka enable the adepts to reach hal, and through that state it is the welis' baraka that are released. But it is the jinn (and often Aicha Kandicha) who encourage the adept to slash themselves, they say. In this sense, what I had seen was a man shedding blood through the agency of the jinn. Blood, Abdel-Wahed had told me, is the conduit through which the jinn can reach inside their human subjects, controlling their thoughts and actions; but in the doctrine of the Hamadsha, it is also how people's suffering can be eased. Ambiguous to its core: the essence of the jinn. In ritual and traditional beliefs, as well as in storytelling, these tantalising beings straddle the line between harm and help, between good and evil. They are the perfect form for the mysteries they embody.

There are fiercer shapeshifters, although I know of none as unsettling. But if we cross the Atlantic, riding beyond the Portuguese fortresses, flying over the ocean, if we step foot in the New World, we can find shapeshifters of a different order. Red in tooth and claw, visible and tangible. Time to head for the swampy delta of the Deep

South, to meet one of the scariest of shapeshifters, whose roots in history stir up a remarkable range of influences. Blood enables us to see the jinn, it is said. But in the tales of the rougarou, it is through the shedding of blood that the cursed can be freed.

CHAPTER SIX

Who's Afraid of the Rougarou?

THE SIXTH TALE

Night falls hard on the bayous of Louisiana. Cypress trees stalk out of the water, closing off the sunlight. Fishing boats hurry home against the slurp and bubble of the creatures around the banks. Inside a house on stilts, candlelight is glowing, feet are stamping on the boards — it's a Cajun house, and the evening's dancing is about to begin. But Jean has his back to the brightness. He's fallen out with his sweetheart, Celeste, and he's piling tackle gear onto his pirogue.

Off he punts along the river, keeping a wide berth around the red eyes of the alligators. He peers between the trees, watching out in case of anything more deadly. But his net remains empty, so he ties up on a piling and takes out his hunting knife. He can hear heavy breathing between the rushes. Stealthy does it ... he'll show them all he knows how to hunt.

'Sweet Jesus!'

He falls backwards, crashing into the reeds. One swipe was all it took — over his mud-splattered body swings a clawed hand, covered in fur to the ragged remains of a shirt. Foul breath wafts down on him, a dark snout lunges, and he screws his eyes shut against a vision of saw-like teeth.

So this is how it ends ...

He grips his fist around the knife he's still holding ... the knife ... he swings with a desperate, curving slash, feels the slice across its nose, and a gobbet of blood plops onto his face.

A scream — not a beast's scream. No, it sounds almost human. Jean pulls himself up, blinking against the impossible sight. By the pale moonlight, he can see ... a man, arms around his knees, eyes gleaming with terror.

'Why, ain't that ... ?'

He edges forward, emboldened, scarcely believing what he's seeing, except he knows the stories they tell.

'Ain't that Theophile — the shrimper's son?'

The boy has a jagged shirt and a pair of white shrimping boots, but not much else. And from his mouth comes the same foul smell ...

'Why, Theophile, they been lookin' for you so long ... and this is what it's come to? You're a ... a rougarou?'

'Not any more I ain't — not now you cut me. But you keep those lips sealed, you hear? Else you'll get the curse. You know how it works.'

'I sure do. A year and a day and I can't tell a soul.'

'But I thank you all the same. Never could help myself, could I? Took a black chicken to the crossroad, drank its blood just so's I could see what'd happen.'

'Oh, Theophile ...' he sighs, reaching out in sympathy. The fellow's hand is no longer clawed, but he can't quite bring himself to clasp it.

'Well, you saw what happened to me all right. The rougarou done got me. Now you don't be tellin' tales back home, else you know what's gonna be yours ... that curse is what!'

Days and weeks pass, and Jean can't help brooding on what he knows. Nothing like a secret for keeping you apart from your loved ones, and making them scratch their heads in wonder ...

'Won't you give away what's eating you? Here you are, feeding us all. But I can tell you're holding something back.'

Celeste grips him by the hand, leading him onto the porch. Any Sunday soon they'll tie the knot, but she's looking into his face like she might just be able to find the answer written on his skin.

'I can't, Celeste ... I just can't.'

'I swear it, Jean, whatever it is, I won't whisper to a soul.'

He bites his lips and looks over her shoulder. Inside, the dancers are forming their lines. There's a celebration going on, paper flowers scattered on the floor, among the cracked shells of crabs and bottle corks.

'C'mon, Celeste, let's go back inside.'

But later in the night, when he sees her dancing with ... when he sees the fellow who's turning Celeste around the floor, with his white shrimping boots, his jagged shirt — that's when he snaps.

'You can't dance with Theophile!'

'Why ever not?'

'Because ... because ...' He can't help it now, the truth bursts out before he can stop it: 'Because he's a rougarou! He was, I mean, he's ... he's dangerous, that's all.'

'Oh, Jean, that's just stories, ain't it?'

Feet are pounding the boards behind them, the fiddles are sawing away. They join the dancers, and Jean tries to forget all about his worries. Try and enjoy his time with his sweetheart. But when he's turning Celeste on the floor, she asks him:

'Jean, could you not squeeze me so tight? And you could maybe pare down those nails of yours, they're digging ever so deep.'

When he pulls away, he can feel the fur thickening under his sleeves, the claws pointing outwards. He touches his neck to be sure — there's fleece all the way down from his beard. In the whirl of the dancing, he's too fast for anybody to see what he's become.

A year and a day, Jean: ain't that the rule? And when you break it, you know what happens ...

Off the porch he hurls himself. Drags himself through the swamp, ignoring the cries of Celeste on the porch. His blood is boiling, but what he took for anger, now feels like something else. He leaps into the woods, sinking his jaws into the juicy flesh of a muskrat. Only now does he realise how hungry he's been, how ferociously hungry ... and maybe that's not such a bad thing, for there's a lot of creatures out here, and a helluva lot of killing to be done ...

DOING THE ROUGAROU

Out of New Orleans on a Greyhound: down the I-10, between the corrugated warehouses of supply depots, RV showrooms, and boat yards, the stretch and sprawl of the Deep South. Forest billowed on either side, green-gold morning light seeping between the limbs of cypress trees and tupelo gum, cottony tufts of morning mist clinging to dead oaks half-sunk in the swamps. Rickety bridges clattered under the bus wheels, fly rods flashing from pirogues in the water. Over the bayous, clapboard houses rippled in receding vistas, with their identikit porches and swing-chairs, stars and stripes fluttering on flagpoles in the yards. It was the roofs that drew my attention. Some were missing patches of shingle; others had been ripped clean off, like the Little Pigs' houses after a visit from the Big Bad Wolf. A wolf that went by the name of Hurricane Ida.

I was making for Houma, a city named after a Native American tribe and known for its large Cajun population — descendants of French-speaking immigrants who landed in Louisiana off the back of a nightmare in the eighteenth century; a city curiously associated with one of the South's most enduring folk legends. Houma is precariously situated, deep in the wetlands of south-east Louisiana. Levees built against flooding have been holding back sediment and triggering subsidence, which is exacerbated by salt-water intrusion and the destabilising effects of access canals for oil companies. It's a city that's long been on the edge, but lately Houma has been struggling to keep itself out of the abyss.

In August 2021, Hurricane Ida came to town and gave Houma a pounding. There were reports of flying metal roofs, oak trees snapping like matchsticks, buildings smashed to rubble when the hurricane's eye wall swept the city with gusts of 150 miles per hour. On climbing down from a rare, rackety cross-city bus, fourteen months later, I found myself flanked by broken buildings: sheared roofs, stores sealed with hardboard, shattered transoms. The occasional pavement crumbled into holes in the ground or gave way to the road. A mural showing old-time Houma — Cajuns in palmetto hats hauling shrimp, Choctaw tribespeople in feathered headdresses — looked as fantastical as the red metal wolf on the other side of the bayou, and less telling than the board with stickers bearing residents' modest aspirations for 'regular maintenance', 'free of drug use', 'more reason to come by'.

Unpainted shacks were collapsing into the bayou, slimy trails of garbage leaking between the pilings, bottle-glass shining in the bankside weeds like alligators' teeth. Against all this deprivation, the city's mascot seemed out of place: the red metal wolf in his double-breasted jacket, carrying a cane and hat, a bushy tail curling under his coat-flaps, like he'd swaggered out of a Disney movie. Can a loup-garou or rougarou — a werewolf — do anybody any good when their home's been ripped apart and the rising sea levels are ruining their livelihoods? When Louisiana's losing twenty-five square metres of land per year?

'Children are so anxious,' said Celeste Roger, a mental-health worker who I met later that day. 'They're having nightmares, their appetites are off, their routines are off.'

Another mental-health worker, Jessica Domangue, also a local councillor, had lived for a year in a house with no walls:

'It's too much for the children to take in. Some are living in campers, or they're living with family and they have to share space with others. Their parents are wondering if it's even worth staying here.'

But like a scraggly beast hiding its kindly inner nature, Houma is a city with resources; with a community mixing Cajun, Creole, Native, and African American and other identities into a classic American patchwork. I'd timed my visit for an annual event: because once a year, Houma comes together, for music, laughter, and huge vats of gumbo, gathering around the tale of a werewolf.

South of town, past block after block of hurricane-hit clapboard, a park stretched between the City Library and the Marriott Hotel. Here was the heart of the Rougaroufest — a tent village of canopies and marquee tents, cables snaking between them, generators whirring beside the stages. Volunteers were cooking up crawfish fettuccine, fried catfish, and gumbo. Stall-holders were touting jewellery and dreamcatchers, painted rocks, pepper jelly, and beard products. Beside a Haunted House marquee, there was a 'rougarou board' with a hole for little heads to squeeze through and a 'pin-the-tail on the rougarou'. Across the park, you could purchase a rougarou T-shirt, a bag of chewy chocolate labelled 'rougarou pooh', or pose under a giant rougarou in a lumberjack shirt, growling out of his articulated snout thanks to a voice recorder.

'That's what my mommy used to say: "You be good or the rougarou gone get you,"' said Troy, who was stirring the jambalaya cauldron. I heard the same story from a woman called Jeanie, who was serving gumbo, a woman at the Haunted House, and Jonathan Foret, the mastermind behind the festival.

'I grew up with this tale,' Jonathan told me. 'A big, warm bearded man with a bear-like hug, he was darting around the park on a golf buggy, making sure everything was going to plan. "Don't go into the woods or the rougarou will get you," that kind of thing. But I could sense people were losing connection with the story. Kids growing up down the bayou: "the rougarou, what's that?" And it made us realise we were losing a part of our oral traditions. People are moving away, we're losing so much land to the salt water, people are losing their livelihoods. So this gives people something to come back for, it enables them to share who they are.'

That cultural cohesion, celebrated with helpings of gumbo and tales about the rougarou, was being marshalled by a team of volunteers

— among whom was one highly unlikely member.

Oh yes ...

As with the Bolster Festival in Cornwall, I'd got myself on the duty roster. Alongside Lanor, a stalwart of Houma's Native American community, I was assigned to the Narrative Stage, flanked by a banner and a screen, where storytelling and folklore-inspired interviews took place over the weekend.

So here I am ... holding up a microphone, throwing questions at an alligator farmer, while he passes his baby gator for me to hold, listening to the beats of an African American drummer — all the while our discussions playing on the screens around the park. As darkness engulfs us, I'm sticking on a werewolf mask so I can go with the flow, jostling with thousands along the parade route, watching pumpkin-headed creatures, witches, warlocks, Mandalorians, acrobats, cheerleaders swinging over metal bars mounted on a pickup, a *Ghostbusters* truck with a screen declaring 'I ain't afraid of no rougarou!' The parade spins its saturnalia of horned, furred, candlelit chimeras, all the way to the rougarou queen — Celeste, the mental-health worker I'd spoken to earlier in the day, now in a folksy dress dripping with tree clippings, oyster shells, and thirteen coins (because the rougarou, so the legend goes, can't count beyond twelve). Finally, here comes the rougarou himself — furry arms bursting out of the sleeves of his lumberjack shirt, hurling sweets to the kids clamouring around his float. It's a full-blown candy storm. I'm socked in the jaw by a Tootsie Roll, my ear takes a hit from a packet of Takis. All around me, kids are scrambling for the treats, returning from the track with scoopfuls of Starbursts and Milky Way Minis.

I loved being a small part of it, slipping inside a community. But oh was I tired! My arrival at what I had anticipated to be my hotel was greeted by a scene out of a zombie apocalypse: a jumble of crumbled boards, fallen stanchions, and walls buckled under ragged sheets of plaster. At the next-door store, I was told the hotel hadn't been open for a year: 'Not since Ida.' Megan, a kindly shop assistant, let me use the store phone to call the company I'd booked through. *Nowhere to stay now: all the budget rooms had been snaffled.*

A kind of fatalism overtakes me when things turn south. *So this is how the story goes ...* I dawdled along the bayou and stopped in smoky late-night bars where husky old-timers were doing karaoke to Loretta Lynn. I loitered around gas stations, counting off the passing minutes. I was feeling a little crabby, and hadn't managed to strike up any conversation in the bars. One of those evenings when it feels like there's a barrier a mile wide separating you from every other human being.

The peace of the bayou seemed preferable. Sitting down on a bench, I could feel the moonlight around me like a pelt. I put on my headphones and listened to Lana Del Rey. I'd barely made it past the bell chime on 'Video Games' when blue lights were reflecting back at me from the water.

'Sir, you need to understand we've got laws about vagrancy.'

Under his powder-blue uniform, a cop's hand rested on the holster of a chrome-plated Magnum. He offered a few sympathetic grunts to my tale of a hurricaned hotel, before insisting:

'Sir, we can't have you loitering.'

And so it was that I bumped into Mikey. He was like me — a bum on the streets with nowhere to stay. Unlike me, his situation was long-term. He told me he knew about a rooming house 'where you can sleep for ten bucks'.

'Show me the place, and I'll pay for us both.'

His hard leather shoes were fastened up with straps and he had decking rope around his trousers instead of a belt. He reminded me of a stray dog, with his scruffy hair and sad puppy eyes, and a weather-beaten precision to the creases on his face, like they'd been carved with a knife. He was dragging a shopping trolley down Main Street, with a laundry sack stashed inside:

'Come outta the hospital today. Said I'll be okay now, but Ma's not here to look after me. Used to take real good care of me. Now she got dementia.'

He shook as he said this, the trolley rattling against the cracks in the pavement. Something about Mikey hypnotised me. I knew I shouldn't give him any money, I knew it, especially after I'd gone into a gas station to buy us a couple of fizzy drinks ('Can't go inna that place,' he said, 'they took agin' me last time'). But I buckled when he told me the rooming house was just a block away and, if it was all the same to me, he'd rather be seen to 'pay my way'.

Did he say it was just up the block? Oh no, that's some kind of misunderstanding:

'You just hang there. You gonna look after my bag, see. Won't you relax none? Just need to fix me up some weed. Don't you worry, Mikey ain't no junkie.'

Hmmm, well done, Jubber! When it comes to travelling, you've really got the smarts, haven't you? So what's the plan now? Just wait till the cops show up and ask you what's in the sack?

While I was standing under the flyover, a one-legged man rolled by on a shopping trolley, pushed along by another guy. A car with tinted windows glided past, turtle-pace. Somebody shambled out from a nearby house, leaning into the driver's window. There were shouts across the street, somebody calling out: 'Fuck your eyes, man!' Footsteps behind me, and I swivelled round. Mikey, maybe, back already? But no ... I was looking at a crop of ginger spikes and a pair of glazed, zombie-like eyes.

'Say, fella ...' came an amiable, slurring voice, 'you wanna pitch in for pussy?'

'Um ... thanks but ...'

The relief I saw in Mikey's blue eyes when he made his way across the road at last — well, it was probably matched by mine. He'd sourced a supply, and I could hand back his bag.

'Ain't you gonna sit?'

He suggested 'a spot near the water. We can smoke it there, ain't nobody gonna give us no trouble.'

And just one more thing ... how would I feel about palming another twenty bucks, maybe thirty, he sure knew a good way to use it ...

'Sorry, but I think this is where we split.'

There's a phrase in these parts, for when you've had a troubled, sleepless night: 'I did the rougarou.' From karaoke bars to run-ins with the cops, from my tour with Mikey to the slow hours with my back to an oak tree on the edge of a bayou, stunned every so often by the blue lights flashing on the other side ... I reckon I can say I 'did the rougarou' that night.

Dawn washed out the night like sudsy water on a kitchen floor, and I huffed around a café with a rougarou pasted to its window. A shot of caffeine should be enough. Sure, I might have 'done the rougarou', but I had no real worries about making it through the coming day, because I was wired on anticipation. Because today I would be talking to storytellers about shapeshifters and werewolves. And after a night on the streets of Houma, I felt like I wasn't completely in the dark when it comes to the things that howl in the night.

TIME OF THE WOLF

The werewolf 'has left his stamp on classic antiquity, he has trodden deep in Northern shores, has ridden roughshod over the mediaevals, and has howled among Oriental sepulchres', as Sabine Baring-Gould put it in his typically baroque way in 1880 (as the author of *The Book of Werewolves*, he knew a thing or two on the subject). More than any animal, the wolf strikes the perfect balance between our fears and desires. Lupophobia — the fear of wolves — is an inherited evolutionary anxiety — we fear its sharp teeth and claws, its howling, its ability to pick up a scent and plunge in for a kill. Wolves were a menace to early pastoral societies, and keeping them at bay was a key factor in survival. But as human societies have pulled ever further from wildness, something about the wildness of wolves has increased its appeal, reeling in the repressed id in human nature, stifled by civilisation and yearning for the quick pulse of danger. As Baring-

Gould expressed it, stories of werewolves can be found all over the world. But few have matched the lycanthropic intensity of sixteenth-century France.

To be a peasant child in Gascony, in the early 1600s, was to be at perpetual risk of being gobbled up, or ripped apart, by a loup-garou. From fields and country lanes, children were being snatched. A three-year-old girl was eaten, a baby was seized from a cradle in a cottage, several others were killed, and a thirteen-year-old cattle-herder called Marguerite had scars from a wolf's attack — she had only survived because she fended off the beast with an iron-hinged staff.

As it happened, Marguerite and some of her companions were able to identify the attacker. They had been approached by a very dirty thirteen-year-old boy with matted red hair tumbling down to his shoulders and pointed black fingernails, called Jean Grenier. He had, he claimed, eaten several children already, and a few years later he told one of his visitors that 'he found the flesh of little girls particularly delicious'.

He certainly had a relish for telling his tale. At the High Court in Bordeaux, Grenier was equally candid. Having run away from his violent father, he narrated, he had been inducted by another youth into the cult of the Lord of the Forest. This lord, dressed in black and riding a black charger, had kissed him on the mouth, plied him with wine, and struck him on the thighs. Presented with a wolfskin, Grenier slathered himself in a magical ointment and donned the skin. Instantly, he was transformed, scouring the countryside on all fours. Racing alongside the lord and his fellow youth, he scented prey across the fields, seizing the three-year-old girl and launching himself against Marguerite, among several attacks.

Although the court officials were doubtful about his sanity, they were disturbed by the corroboration between his confessions and the details of recent wolf incidents. Given his young age, the judge decided not to pass the death sentence. So Grenier was sent to the Friary of St Michael the Archangel in Bordeaux, to be locked in a cell and never let out.

When a writer called Pierre de Lancre visited him in 1610, he reported 'very long and bright teeth that were wider than normal, protruding somewhat and rotten and half black from being used to lash out at animals and people ... he walked in such a way that one could be sure that it was a four-legged animal. Then he went as fast as a dog running away, and at the end of the room he turned so quickly that I practically lost sight of him ... He confessed to me also, in a straightforward manner, that he still wanted to eat the flesh of little children ...'

*

We find the association between man and wolf throughout world mythology — from the wolf-suckled progenitors of the Romans or Turks to miscreants enduring divine punishment, such as Lycaon in Ovid's *Metamorphoses*, transformed into a wolf for acts of cannibalism and defying the gods. Shamanic solidarity on the one hand, diabolic vilification on the other: to become a wolf can be a power, but it can also be a penalty.

Over time, as human societies increasingly detached themselves from their natural environments, they saw wolves less as our kin in the animal world, more as evil predators to be annihilated. But the gulf between these perspectives was filled by an enduring ambiguity. In mediaeval European literature, there are several wonderful tales about wolf-men, in which we are encouraged to sympathise with the shapeshifters and scorn their less enchanted antagonists.* But these

---

* See 'Bisclavret' by Marie de France. In this remarkable twelfth-century story, a royal favourite is unable to resist the lure of the forest, where he transforms into a wolf. When his horrified wife hides his clothes — the means of turning back into a human — he is forced to dwell in wolf form. His gentleness and loyalty attract the favour of the king, and he becomes a beast of the court, which gives him a chance for revenge. He bites off his wife's nose and attacks her new lover, leading to the revelation of his wife's betrayal and his restitution to human form. In Marie de France's beguiling narration, it is the werewolf's gentle, courtly qualities (at least

are exceptions. For most of the pre-modern period, wolf-men were figures of terror, and the stories about them still chill the blood today.

'It is during the sixteenth century in France especially,' wrote the occultist Montague Summers, 'the rank foul weeds of werewolf flourished exceedingly.' The case of Jean Grenier was one prominent example. Others included the brother and sister Pierre and Pierrette Gandillon in the Jura region, the latter killed by a mob, the former burned at the stake; and Jacques Roulet, a wandering mendicant in Caude, in the north-west of France, found half-naked with blood and gore on his claw-like hands, who confessed to eating several children and was confined to a madhouse in 1598.

Werewolf stories may have prevailed throughout human history, but the volume of stories from sixteenth- and seventeenth-century France are of particular significance when we consider the rougarou: because it was from areas such as Bordeaux, where Jean Grenier's trial took place, that emigrants set sail for the Americas during the 1600s, ancestors of the people who would become known as the Cajuns. But those grisly French tales weren't simply transplanted on new soil — the 'New World' had old tales of its own. When it came to shapeshifting or demonic possession, the indigenous storytellers of the Americas had some of the richest material around.

TALES BY THE BAYOU

'I was sixteen when I saw the monster. Out on the bayou. Didn't just see it, I'm tellin' you, I smelt the thing.'

Grey Hawk Perkins was sitting next to the Narrative Stage. A shell necklace in the shape of a woodpecker hung over his T-shirt; a drum was on the table beside him. A chief of the Choctaw tribe, he was an invigorating presence; just being around Grey Hawk did the same job

---

in respect of the king; less so towards his wife) that enable him to be restored, making him an unlikely forerunner to the likes of Wolverine and Teen Wolf.

as several shots of caffeine. Puffing on a Cuban cigar, he told me about a journey in his youth, when he'd canoed along Louisiana's bayous because 'they're much faster than the roads'. He and his companions had seen something: 'It was big, hairy, and it smelt like a dumpster truck — that's my main memory of it, the smell! We call it the Chitagoula.'

Grey Hawk was still telling tales when Lanor directed us onto the stage. Some people just can't stop. He warmed up the audience with a 'stomp song', a call-and-response performed on his drum, before launching into a tale.

'So let me tell you about the skin-walker,' he announced. 'It's our rougarou, you could say. But here's the thing about the skin-walker. They can be good, they can be bad. You choose to be a skin-walker, it's not something that's forced on you, but if you abuse it, then it backfires.'

In Grey Hawk's tale, a little boy has gone missing. An elder is enlisted to find him, a 'smoke-reader' who sets a fire of cedar branches and tobacco, and follows the smoke to the shadowy figures of two large cats. When the cats are shot, they disappear, but the trail of spoor transforms into a set of human footprints. 'We got ourselves a couple of skin-walkers,' the elder declares. Listening in the community, they find out about somebody who's been mysteriously wounded, and that's how they track down the missing child, who hasn't aged a day since he was abducted.

Shapeshifters have a long history in Native American tales, fuelled by the close relationship between humankind and wildlife. As Grey Hawk put it: 'We see things differently. Remember, we have spirit animals, we call them nations. The eagle nation, the wolf nation. They're like us, part of the whole. But in European culture, they separate themselves. Look at the animals and you can learn everything you need. Follow a deer and that deer will teach you how to find water, what plants to eat, to listen. We learn from the animals.'

This doesn't stop the native stories from being macabre or scary.

Among the Algonquin people of Canada, stories have been told for centuries about the Windigo, man-eating monsters compared by a French writer in 1695 to werewolves. Exacerbated by colonial destruction of indigenous communities, a 'Windigo Psychosis' spread. In the nineteenth century, there were reports of cannibal activities and tribespeople cited fears of transformation. 'The Devil wants me, and will change me to a Windigo,' one young Cree woman was reported as saying.* Such stories, though poorly documented, suggest that in the development of the rougarou, the traditional French werewolf was one factor among many.

'All of the cultures that formed the Creolised culture of Louisiana have these legends,' pointed out Dr Rachel Doherty, author of a paper entitled 'The Loup-Garou in Louisiana'. 'You have Afro-Caribbean legends of shapeshifting, indigenous legends of shapeshifting. However, France is known for its werewolf legends.'

A huge influx into Louisiana at the beginning of the nineteenth century came from Haiti, where the revolution of 1791–1804 sent French-speaking merchants, former plantation holders, and slave-owners to Louisiana and caused a population boom in New Orleans. To this moment can be traced many stories involving possession, enchanted skins, and references to Vodou. In a tale recorded in the collection *Cajun and Creole Folk Tales* (1994), a man becomes a rougarou after drinking the blood of a black chicken at a crossroads at

---

*   In the nineteenth century, white settlers often remarked on the power of the 'Windigo Psychosis': 'They have such a dread and horror of this that it is constantly in their minds,' reported George Helsch; and a native known as Swift Runner was said to be possessed by the Windigo when he murdered his family in 1879. Stories of the Windigo made it down to Louisiana, where the Cajun scholar Barry Ancelet told me he heard such tales as a child. 'When I was growing up,' he said, 'we had a neighbour and she used to tell us stories about the Windigo, which came in the memory of people all the way through the exile and somehow survived. It's a malevolent spirit that could inhabit people who were lost in the woods and could cause them to become cannibals — which is similar to werewolves.'

midnight. In *Gumbo Ya-Ya: a collection of Louisiana Folk Tales* (1945), a loup-garou's transformation is attributed to 'some voodoo grease'. The rougarou stories that spread around Louisiana reflected the diversity of backgrounds behind them, with shapeshifters transforming into pigs, owls, cats, wild dogs, phantoms, and many other forms, and only rarely into wolves. What this suggests is that, rather than being a direct importation from France, the rougarou was stirred out of a mixture of ingredients. It's as idiosyncratic a stew as you could find — a monster gumbo.

Among the storytellers who Lanor and I interviewed on the Narrative Stage, there were many wonderful tales — of Vodou drummers, will-o'-the-wisps, and alligator attacks. But there was only one who had a heap of rougarou tales. I'd called on him a few days earlier, at his house in New Orleans, and now I met him in Houma.

'So here we are again!' said Glen Pitre.

Wild curls of white hair made an unruly halo around his face, his moustache always quivering on the edge of a laugh. Glen has travelled one hell of a journey through life, from a modest Cajun fishing community to the bright lights of Hollywood. In 1986, he took his movie *Belizaire the Cajun*, starring Armand Assante and Robert Duvall, to the Cannes Film Festival. His other movies include a World War II drama starring Tatum O'Neal and a documentary about Hurricane Katrina, narrated by Meryl Streep. Along with thirty or so movies, he's somehow found time to write half a dozen books. He's that kind of guy.

When I visited Glen's house in New Orleans, an old fire station near the French Quarter that also functions as a studio, we sat beside a mosaic he'd recently completed of a mermaid and a dragon before stepping inside the house, sitting under African tribal art, books on mythology and Cajun culture, and a remote-controlled drinks cabinet stocked with every liquor imaginable.

'The stories I remember,' said Glen, 'weren't told like a story, they just came out of the conversation. "Oh, you know so and so, he's a rougarou."' Folklorists call these kinds of stories 'memorates'. Among tales of shapeshifters, they are as common as wildflowers.

'Down in Cut Off, where I grew up,' said Glen, 'if somebody was a little strange, or an outsider, there'd be warnings. There was a guy who was a doctor from Europe, name of Dr Lenkowitz. I suppose he'd moved because of the war. And we were told not to go near his house because he was a rougarou. Some said he took the form of an ape, some said it was a bear, some it's a dog. Whatever it was, don't ever go past his house at night, and don't go alone. Of course, he wasn't the only rougarou. There was a tree — an oak, or maybe it was a hackberry — and there was an old woman who lived near us, a Mrs Bourgeois. They said she always went to that tree when she turned into the rougarou.'

Glen heard many of the stories on fishing trips, out on the bayous and lakes, harvesting shrimp or oysters, spending their nights in makeshift camping huts. 'Every night you'd clean your nets and the boat, you'd get your mosquito net ready, and you'd wake up at dawn to shovel the oyster shells. And in the evenings, you'd tell each other tales. One moment, somebody's telling how they caught some giant bream; next thing you know, somebody else is recounting how he knows Mrs Bourgeois is a rougarou. But there's always somebody with another mind about it. "Whaddaya talkin' about? The oak tree? Mrs Bourgeois don't hang around no oak tree — it's the hackberry tree where she's gonna get you." No question she's a rougarou, it's the tree that's in doubt. And then the conversation moves on, somebody's giving advice on the best way to rig your tickle chain so you can get the most shrimp.'

One of Glen's novels, *Advice from the Wicked*, features a rougarou as a principal character: a man in denial, refusing to acknowledge his lycanthropic nature. He experiences blackouts and memory loss, waking up with tell-tale signs about him: 'The torn clothes and feathers or muskrat entrails he'd sometimes find around him when he woke from his blackouts Jerome put off to cruel tricks played by mischievous boys.' But over time, he comes to terms with his shapeshifting ability: 'A dog's life holds certain satisfactions,' he muses while gnawing on a coq au vin. 'A dog lives moment by moment. Any morsel dropped off the table or impromptu scratch of the belly offers boundless joy.'

There's a theme here, repeated in one of Glen's most intriguing tales: you may not choose to be like this, but isn't it human nature to grow accustomed to things? Which is what happens in 'The Shadow Companion', a story Glen heard from his godfather. Another memorate, since it was reported as true.

A brave oyster-man, a certain Monsieur Playsance, hears a noise around the oyster pile, so he goes to investigate. When he returns to his camp, he claims he's seen a rougarou. Nobody believes him, but he sticks to his story, repeating it to whoever will listen. The rougarou keeps appearing, he tells them, it shows up in his home, sitting on the headboard, resting on his shoulder. Over time, fewer and fewer people are prepared to listen to his story. They cross the road to avoid him, pretend they can't hear his greetings from the other side of the bayou. Old and lonely, with no company other than the rougarou in his head, Monsieur Playsance is long past his fishing days, but he still goes out to meet the boats when they come into dock. Now he has a cane to help him walk, and one day he trips on a pile of oyster shells. His cane flips out of his hand and the sharp end strikes his nose. He's been cut, and according to rougarou lore, that means his connection with the beast is broken. But it's no relief for Monsieur Playsance, for that rougarou — whether or not it existed — was his only companion. Now he's truly on his own, and he dies shortly after.

Listening to Glen's tales, I thought of Mikey on the streets of Houma, his mind a little jumbled, yearning for something to take the edge off things.

'That's what the rougarou means to me,' said Glen. 'It's a parable for compulsion, for addiction. When you draw the rougarou's blood, they're happy to be free. The rougarou has to kill, like the addict has to score his drugs. It's the dark side of human nature, but it's also the possibility of release.'

There were many more stories. But Glen's friends from the film business had stopped by, so conversation turned to camera specifications, sound quality, the nitty-gritty of filmmaking. We sat at a long wooden dining table eating shrimp pasta, drinking gin and bourbon out of Glen's magical drinks cabinet. In between reminiscences about filmmaking high jinks, technical calamities, blundering through flooded New Orleans after being helicoptered in by a film crew, every so often another weird tale seeped through.

Most of those stories I heard in Glen's house, sitting back to soak them up like I was at an old-time veillée. I heard a few again at the festival.

'Now let's see, how about a storm tale? You ready for one of those?'

Glen finished his set with a flourish: a wonderfully mad old memorate. A hurricane had struck, and his grandfather's cousin was caught — blown out of his house and straight out to sea, clinging to his front door to save him from drowning, despairing for his life until he was revitalised by the surprising, soothing call of a mermaid's song.

As Glen reached the end of the tale, a rogue's gallery of faces was looking up at the stage. There was a fanged vampire in a collared cape, a swamp witch, a bolt-necked Frankenstein's Monster, a couple of rougarous, Alligator Girl (with a baby rougarou in her arms), and Freddy Krueger with his knife fingers splayed across his bloodstained chest. Hard to gauge their reactions to the tale, since most of their faces were sealed behind latex or fur, although Freddy did give a subtle tilt of his head at the end. The monsters were gathering and now it was time for the next item on the schedule: the costume competition.

'There's kids at the schools getting into the story,' Jonathan told me, when we bumped into each other later that afternoon.

He looked shattered, but satisfied, with hundreds of happy festival-goers queueing for gumbo behind his buggy.

'They make their own rougarou scenes, dioramas in shoeboxes. I've got a pile of them at home.' He smiled, shaking his head. 'I don't feel I can throw them away.'

This is how the monsters survive: the children who pinned a tail on the rougarou and made rougarou dioramas will conjure their own tales, and the rougarou will howl through another generation's imaginations. Because it isn't just a monster-of-the-week for the latest horror franchise. It's deeper than that — as I would discover when I made my way across state.

LE GRAND DÉRANGEMENT

The werewolf stories that flourished in sixteenth- and seventeenth-century France — real-life tales about serial killers like Jean Grenier as well as fables like 'Bisclavret' — travelled with the French emigrants who set out for the New World. Fleeing the famines and religious wars that had made life in France so hazardous, the emigrants settled on a peninsula of what is now Nova Scotia, and called it La Cadie, 'the land of plenty'. But no Eden lasts long. In 1710, France was ousted by Britain and in mid-century, the French-speaking residents — the Acadians — were expelled for refusing to pledge allegiance to their new overlords.

More than 10,000 Acadians were packed into poorly supplied ships, where half died of malnutrition, disease, or shipwreck. Those who survived were scattered across the Americas. Some went as far as the Falkland Islands, others to the French colony of Saint-Domingue (later known as Haiti), some even returned to France. The condition of the survivors was summed up by a report from the governor of Quebec in 1757: 'In a word the Acadian mothers see their babies die at the breast not having wherewith to nourish them. The majority of the people cannot appear for want of clothes to cover their nakedness.'

Dispersed across a range of sanctuaries, the Acadians found one dumping ground more accommodating than others. From 1766 to 1788, large numbers arrived in Louisiana, a region claimed by the French in 1682 but passed to the Spanish after the Seven Years' War in the mid-eighteenth century. Catholic, underpopulated, anti-British, Louisiana received the refugees, although hardly with welcome arms.

According to the Spanish governor, they would be 'good vassals who, when the time comes, will gladly take up arms and sacrifice themselves to his royal service, in defence of his dominions'.

While native-born, French-speaking Creoles claimed the top ranks in Louisiana society, and the urban real estate, there was land enough for the Acadians, as long as they could make ends meet in the swamps. They built houses on stilts, making the most of the plentiful timber; they dressed in knee-length braguettes and palmetto hats, hunting mink and muskrat, fishing for crabs and shrimp. So developed a culture that mingled the challenging Louisiana landscape with the folklore of the old motherland: strange lights sighted on the swamps were likened to the feux follets (will-o'-the-wisps) of earlier tales; old-time ballads were performed to fiddles, violins, and accordions, stirring dancers at the regular balls, while tales were told at veillées that echoed the storytelling evenings of rural France.

Cut off from the dominant Anglophone society of the nineteenth century, the Cajuns nurtured a culture that remained distinctive, patronised as 'primitive' by a correspondent for *Harper's Weekly* in 1887. Over the course of the twentieth century, the French-speaking communities of the south were corralled by the state, forced to speak English at schools, their language treated as suspect, 'held in contempt by many people as a pure patois', as the New Orleans–based writer Lyle Saxon put it, 'though some authorities insist it is pure seventeenth-century French'.

Even now, it's a world of its own — the area below the Interstate 10 highway is known as 'the I-10 Bubble'. But it's better understood as a bubble cluster — all through those three centuries of habitation in Louisiana, the Cajuns had other bubbles floating in their orbit — Creoles and Native American tribes, runaway slaves bearing traces of their ancestral African culture, Spanish privateers. They soaked up elements from each other's cultures (so okra, for example, introduced by African slaves, became a core ingredient in the Cajun dish of gumbo) and told each other tales.

What emerged was a cultural fusion, with the loup-garou as a symbol of the region's hybridity, a fitting mascot for the festival in Houma. Its resonance is underlined by a group of poets for whom it has become their unifying image. Indeed, they are known as the 'École Lycanthropique' — the 'School of Werewolves'. What a prospect, I thought, as I made my way across Louisiana. Might there be some way I could track down one of these werewolf poets, and hear their tale?

THE SCHOOL OF WEREWOLVES

A hundred miles north-west of Houma, Lake Martin is a picture in silver. Stand on the bank and the lake looks still, eerie in its brooding silence; but pole across the water and you see it bubbling with life. A blue heron swoops through a corridor of cypress trees, flying so low the water ripples against its beard. Under the trees, where Spanish moss dangles from the branches like wax dribbling down candlesticks, a turtle squats on a log and a frog jumps into the cane-brake, under the shadow of a turkey vulture. Further back in the reeds, yellow eyes gleam under ridged hoods, and a trail of scutes leads to a long tapering tail.

'We call that one Stella,' said my guide Jason, drawing his pole across the thwart to punt us along the bank. There were nine in her brood: the little alligators visible as yellow-and-black stripes, slashes against the reeds that provide scant protection from their predators.

'You got gators out there, snapping turtles — they can take a lump outta yer leg. But you know what's the scariest of all?'

Jason pointed his pole into a cluster of trees so close together the light between them appeared as blades of silver:

'That's where the rougarou lives. Y'all know about the rougarou?'

'Oh yes!'

A couple of hours earlier, I had been dropped at the edge of Lake Martin by the folklorist Barry Ancelet: 'You know what to do if an alligator chases you?'

'Run?'

'Yeah but how?'

'Um ... really fast?'

'In a zig-zag! It means the alligator keeps shifting its weight, slows it down.'

Three miles around the lake, stepping back from the boardwalk when a couple of rotten planks split beneath my feet, I followed a narrow bayou under the wingbeat of herons and black-backed 'devil birds', past an idly menacing alligator basking near a bridge.

Bryan Champagne had lived his whole life around these swamps: 'Oh, the stories I could tell you ...'

Broad-shouldered, thickly whiskered, he had something of the walrus about him. He was wedged behind the counter of a wooden shack, surrounded by drinks freezers and shelves stacked with bait. His southern drawl flowed like a folksy tune on a banjo, strumming one tale after another: the tornado that danced across the lake, picking up alligators and snapping turtles, and flinging them into people's backyards; the treasure buried in the civil war or hidden by the pirate Jean Lafitte when he nosed through the reeds in his strategically pointed shrimping skiff; Bryan's hapless uncle who dug up a treasure that had been jinxed by a willow-tree spirit.

'He was runnin' when he died, they say the spirits were chasin' him. Now I can't say if that's for sure, but somethin' got him *real* bad.'

My days in Louisiana were full of moments like that — tales passed around, like greetings. I didn't have long left in the state, and I was still processing all the stories I'd heard when a moment of pure magic swept along the highway.

There I was, walking up from the lake, past cans of Michelob Ultra and the cracked carcasses of run-over armadillos. I was trying to block out the roar of traffic and my frustrations at Louisiana's almost non-existent public-transport system — when a voice crooned in my ears:

'Get in the car!'

Leaning over the steering wheel, pushing open the passenger door, was a familiar face: Barry Ancelet, the folklorist who'd dropped me at the lake a few hours earlier. Now, by chance, he was driving home to Lafayette from a meeting with a fellow musician.

'As my father used to say, don't just hope for a miracle,' he told me, racing down the highway. 'Depend on it.'

Tall and rangy, his face alert as a fox, Barry had loped into the library of Lafayette that morning:

'So, whaddaya got?'

He'd been suspicious of my questions about the rougarou, and the email exchange preceding our meeting had left me unsure what to expect. Countless cryptozoologists, Barry explained, had badgered him for quotes about 'sightings'. If I was another of that kind then he'd rather not waste his time. But I had no interest in finding the rougarou, I assured him. It was the stories I was after.

'So I'll tell you how it all started.'

Back in the seventies, Barry was a student of French, a Cajun from Louisiana wandering around Nice. But he felt detached from the literature that was covered in the lecture halls of the university. Only when he passed a basement bar and heard 'the Crowley two-step' did he start to realise what he was seeking.

Back home, he set about recording Cajun and Creole music, noting down the tunes and the tales, and establishing a regular festival for Louisiana's French-speaking culture.

'There were stories passed around my father's barbershop,' he said, 'around the barbecue pit and the fishing boats. These were valuable expressions of cultural identity and they hadn't been written down.'

He found 'tall tales', anecdotes, memorates, most of them from everyday life, but some contained more magical elements about buried treasure in the bayous or about the feux follets or even the rougarou. Pulling them together, Barry established an archive at the University of Louisiana, publishing anthologies and studies of folklore, a dictionary of Louisiana French and numerous other works, and playing a leading role in what has been dubbed 'the Cajun Renaissance'.

'If you're looking for legend stories — three act structures, that kind of thing — they don't survive so well. But maybe, yeah ... maybe you'll want to hear some of this.'

A laptop was unzipped. Power hummed, keys tapped, a tune started. Guitar chords swam against a smash of drums: fast and lush and mesmerising, the polyrhythm anchored by a marvellously growling voice. I looked at Barry. His eyes were brightening, his lips curling under his thick, looped moustache:

Dans le creux de la nuit	In the heart of the night
Le loup entend des cris	The wolf hears cries
Du fond du grand bayou	From the depths of the bayou
Ouuuu	Ooooo
Ça le rend fou	It drives him mad
Et ça réveille le loup	And it awakens the wolf

That storm of sound! There was madness in it, a wonderful madness. In the tunes I heard that morning, acoustic and electric guitars spun around fiddles, harmonicas, magnificent drumming, and the mournful triumph of the sax. There was a song punning on the French term for fairy tales, 'conte de fées' respun as 'conte des faits' (tale of facts), with police sirens and wind snarling behind the guitar licks; there was a poignant tribute to the pioneering Cajun and Creole musician Amédé Ardoin, with a beautiful harmony between fiddle and guitar. The lyrics were by Barry, adapted from poems he'd written over several decades, sung by him and his musical partner Sam Broussard. The songs were part of an album called *Broken Promised Land*, for which they had been nominated for a Grammy.

I asked him to play 'Le Loup' again. I loved the harlequin richness of the instruments, the defiant growl rolling through the verses. That was the man sitting beside me. No longer Barry Ancelet, professor emeritus and ethnomusicologist. Now he was Jean Arceneaux, musician and poet.

As he tapped on the keyboard to bring up another tune, his fingers moved with the flourish of a zydeco bar pianist. Later, he'd pull out a stetson and twirl it onto his head. I'd met some remarkable people on this journey so far, but Jean/Barry was unique. A real-life shapeshifter.

On the CD sleeve, the cover art, the images printed over the lyrics, there it was. Not just a wolf — it was, more specifically, a loup-garou, a werewolf. Across the lyrics was a man's face, mutating into a furry muzzle.

'It's that double identity,' he said. 'That's what I connected with.'

Wolves hunt in packs — and so it has proven with Louisiana's music and poetry scene. Alongside Barry/Jean, there's Zachary Richard, Deborah Clifton, Kirby Jambon, David Cheramie, a circle of Francophone poets from diverse backgrounds who marshal their vulpine conceit with remarkable coherence.

'Every major Louisiana poet,' Jean explained, 'if they're writing in French, they've used the loup-garou in their writing.'

For Rachel Doherty, who wrote her PhD about the 'École Lycanthropique', the movement is implicitly political: 'The message of these poems is: we have this choice to transform, to use Louisiana French, which was looked down upon for so long; to talk openly about this generational trauma, where people stopped using French because they were made to feel ashamed, and now we can spread the curse of this forbidden knowledge, we can be the monster with the dual identity. So it's coming to terms with your Cajunness or your Creoleness, it's wearing your wolf-face on the outside, something that's taboo.'

Shapeshifters speak to the wildness in all of us, and our relationships with our shadow selves ('the dark side of his being, his sinister shadow', in the words of Carl Jung). The wolf, in particular, appeals to a civilisational yearning for the feral side of our natures, the wildness we've had to stifle in order for society to flourish. It also works, symbolically, as a representation of any suffocated culture raising its wounded muzzle towards the repressive mainstream. Which is why the loup-garou has such resonance for Cajun and Creole cultures.

In his poem 'Linguistic Schizophrenia', Jean Arceneaux evokes the oppression of French in public spaces: 'It becomes automatic. / And you don't *parler français* in the school grounds / Or anywhere else *non plus*.' But what language, he asks, do we cry in, or scream? The theme of a concealed, trampled-down culture ripples through these lyrics. 'Children of silence, let's cry together', he rallies, evoking the silence at the heart of tales of the rougarou: if you see the beast, you have to keep their secret for a year and a day, else you'll be the next rougarou. By speaking out, the loup-garous are basking in the curse, wearing their wolf-face on the outside, as Rachel Doherty put it: shouting back against the silence imposed for so many generations on Francophone Louisiana. We may try to repress our shadows, but sometimes, as Jung put it, the 'sinister shadow ... represents the true spirit of life'.

Here we see the wolf coming, if not full circle, at least back from round the bend: from shame to the shaman. A recognition that, in harnessing the beast inside, we can peel away the layers of lies we tell ourselves and strike at something raw and true.

*

That night in Lafayette, my last in Louisiana, I stood on the bank of a bayou. A palisade of trees shredded the moonlight to cottony rags. I thought of my own double life — the loose-limbed freedom of the road, which I craved and relished, a habit I could never quite kick; but alongside that, the love I had been lucky to find, a love that every so often I would recklessly leave behind, through some need I had never managed to quell. I've read enough travel literature to know this is hardly unique, scarcely unusual. Whether selkies with suppressed identities or loup-garous bursting with their wild alter-egos, there's something in the ambiguity of shapeshifters that speaks to a great many of us as we track our braided paths through life. Perhaps it speaks to you too.

Shapeshifters had pulled me between three continents, ranging across sea, mountain, and swamp. I had seen blood spilled, storms stir, jaws snap. I had come across tales of kindly or gentle beings, as well as fierce and bloodthirsty killers. I had witnessed the close identification people felt with these shapeshifters, helping them to understand the darkness inside themselves and in some cases to heal. The story was growing darker, the path more tangled. In the next few days, I would be heading across the Mexican Desert, delving among a different kind of monster. They would lure me to cemeteries in Mexico and a haunted mill in the Balkans, to Vodou dances and Aztec temples, to stories of ghostly encounters and revolutionaries defying the rules of death. In the process, they would lead us from the woods and mountains of the ancient monsters, through spooky graveyards and gaslit avenues to the edges of the modern world. These monsters often have the power to change their forms, but they differ from the shapeshifters we've looked at in one crucial aspect: because they are no longer among the living.

Wildness may stir our souls, but is there anything that chills our blood so much as this — a journey among the dead?

PART THREE

When the Dead Rise

'I do not think that all the persons who profess to discredit these visitations really discredit them, or if they do, in daylight, are not admonished by the approach of loneliness and midnight to think more respectfully of the world of shadows.'

Percy Bysshe Shelley, 18 August 1816

CHAPTER SEVEN

The Conquistador and the Ghost

THE SEVENTH TALE

Midnight in Mexico City. Iron-cased lanterns flicker on their pegs, gusts of wind sparking shadows on the volcanic stone. Near one of the old waterways, the pilings are mirrored by the hitching posts for horses, and a drunken lord sits over the water with a bottle to his lips. Behind him, his servant peers over his shoulder through the light of a taper, urging him to return to his coach.

'Señor, it is late, and you know what that means.'

'Surely I do. But tonight I will not run — tonight I will face her! Tonight I will ...'

The words are sucked inside him by a terrible wail. The noise howls across the fronts of the villas, reverberating on the iron gates. It sounds faraway, but Don Muño can feel her shadow, like an icy gust on the back of his neck. When he pulls himself to his feet, she is so close he could reach out and touch her — if there was a body to touch.

'La Llorona!' cries the servant. 'The Wailing Woman!' He drops his taper and runs.

Long-haired, long-gowned, the ghost approaches Don Muño. A pale face hovers inches over his own, and all his insides melt as its features transform: a fiery-eyed skull, framed in locks of frozen silver.

'Forgive me!' he cries, one last time.

Slipping backwards, he feels the crash of the water around him. He heaves himself onto dry land, sodden and sober, and peers in anxious relief, for the streets around are empty and silent.

Once her name was Luisa. Descended from an old Aztec lord, so they said. Well-born for Mexico, but hardly enough for the son of a conquistador. Still, Don Muño would have her. She had bewitched him, had she not? With the spells those native women were ever casting, the heady smoke they inhaled, the unguents they smeared on their tawny skin. And so things took their course. A child was born, then another; Luisa began to make demands. But Don Muño was pledged: to a true-born Spaniard nourished on the milk of Castile. How could he take a mestizo to wife when he had a noble-born virgin to share his bed? Luisa refused to understand. She burst into the chapel as the vows were being exchanged, stinking of burned copal, scandalising the guests. Enough! Don Muño sought her out, in the back street where he'd installed her — a decent-enough property overlooking a canal, with its own balcony and pretty shutters painted to match the piercing redness of the stone.

'She is gone, my lord!'

The maid pointed to the shutters. Swinging onto the balcony, he looked down into the canal. There she was: dark hair puddled under her white rebozo shawl, nearly covering the bodies she had already submerged in the water.

'You want your children? Then you must fish them out!'

That demonic laughter — oh, he would never stop hearing it, long after it had dissolved into a wail of grief, a mad cry that rang around her when she stood on the scaffold. Every night, when Don Muño stumbles home, every time he ventures out in the dark, that wail fills his ears. And in those outstretched arms, that mad figure tilting towards him, he recognises the woman he spurned. The Wailing Woman, whose curse is upon him: a stain that can never be cleansed.

THE BOY WHO SAW A GHOST

'I was nine years old,' said Jesus Ismail Castañeda, 'when I saw her.'

Chickens pattered around us, teetering on blocks of volcanic stone. Lizards shinned up a brick wall, like they were taking part in some high-stakes time trial. I was in the town of Tepoztlán, fifty miles south of Mexico City, sitting on a plastic chair on a yard of packed earth. Behind the iron gate, you could stand on the hilly lane where La Llorona had appeared to Jesus, under the green-tinged crags of Tepozteco Mountain.

'It was late, around midnight, and I had come out of the house for a pee.'

Jesus was sturdily built, with a moon-shaped face creased from eight decades of active living in a land where the sun isn't slow to burn. As I listened to him, I tried to imagine that round face on a little boy, looking out from this very yard at his first glimpse of the ghost.

'She came floating along the street, about thirty centimetres off the ground. I knew it was something not of this world. She was leaning forwards, her arms were reaching out, and the sound she made, it was horrifying. I felt as if somebody was pouring cold water down my back. I ran inside and hid under the bedsheets, but I could still hear her, screaming, all the way down the block. Even the dogs were scared of her — they all went silent until she had passed, then they started barking again as soon as she had gone.'

Over the years, Jesus had worked in factories and hotels, raised his children and seen the arrival of his grandchildren. A full life, unbroken by that childhood vision.

'Seeing La Llorona — it was a shock, I was very scared,' he said, 'but after a few weeks I recovered.'

Ghosts stretch back as far as stories can go: the spirit of the prophet Samuel, summoned by the Witch of Endor in the Bible; an Egyptian priest's spectral encounter, written on pieces of pottery from the Ramesside era. But few nations have identified with a particular ghost, so closely and for so long, as Mexico with La Llorona. 'The beginning of her was so long ago that no one knows what was the beginning of her.' So said Gilberto Cano, a nineteenth-century resident of Mexico City. Still, most interpretations today pin her to a specific point in time. More than just another ghost-of-the-week, La Llorona is a Mexican icon, a symbol for grief, sexual betrayal, and the culture that was pulverised under the hooves of the Spanish cavalry, all the way back in 1521.

HERNÁN CORTÉS'S LUCKY CHARM

The grey waters of the Mexican Gulf roll towards the low-down harbour of Veracruz, smacking the seawall and smoothing out inside the Wall of Rings. Trawlers teeter, ferries lie in dock, while men work the cables on the decks. Behind them are the coral-stone walls and bastions of the fortress of San Juan de Ulúa, a defensive islet that harboured the conquistadors in April 1519. Its rock-vaulted gunpowder stores, cannon emplacements, sentry boxes, and doors adorned in múcara stone testify to its long-term defensive significance, between the coming of the Spaniards and the US invasion of the mid-nineteenth century.

It was here that Hernán Cortés made landfall with around 600 men — misfits, criminals, ex-soldiers, disinherited noblemen, and adventurers in search of gold. Cortés was a fitting leader for such a gang — a smooth-talking street fighter with 'no more conscience than a dog', to quote a fellow conquistador, who charmed his followers with honeyed words and bore a scar on his chin from a long-ago brawl. 'If God helps us,' Cortés wrote, 'far more will be said in future history books about our exploits than has ever been said about those of the past.'

He founded a town near the current site of Veracruz, named after the True Cross, and 350 miles down the coast, he gave the local Mayans a drubbing. As many indigenous tribes were learning, it doesn't matter how many arrows you've carved and spears you've sharpened if you're up against cannons, muskets, and the novel sight of sword-wielding caballeros on horseback. Lining up in tribute, Cortés's vanquished foes presented treasure and food. 'And this present was nothing in comparison,' recorded the conquistador Bernal Díaz del Castillo, 'to twenty women, and among them a very excellent woman who called herself Doña Marina ... and truly she was a great lady and daughter of great lords and lady of vassals ...'

The Spaniards could hardly have been luckier: she was 'good-looking and mettlesome and self-assured,' del Castillo recalled, and 'never we saw weakness in her, but much greater effort than that of a woman'. Of more practical consideration, as the priest Bartolomé de las Casas pointed out, she 'knew the Mexican languages because she had been, as she said, stolen from her land towards Xalisco in that part from Mexico that is to the west and sold from hand to hand ...' A native of the land, with a facility for languages (initially she translated the local tongue into Nahuatl, which a castaway called Jerónimo de Aguilar parsed into Spanish); but also a noblewoman who had been stripped of her inheritance and owed no loyalty to the Aztec rulers. She was, as the Mexican scholar Fernanda Núñez Becerra has put it, 'the bridge over which the words of Cortés passed'; but as Malinche, the name by which Mexicans would remember her, she became a symbol of treachery — the native woman who sold her land to the strangers from over the sea. A woman who, in many of the folk tales, transforms into the vengeful ghost La Llorona.

'The Mexican people have not forgiven La Malinche for her betrayal,' wrote the Nobel laureate Octavio Paz in his seminal work on Mexican identity, *The Labyrinth of Solitude*. For Paz, as for many Mexicans, she remained an embodiment of historical trauma, vilified by succeeding generations. In the streets of Veracruz, they can pummel her with their boots, thanks to a series of pavement panels. Based on the 'Codices', sixteenth-century pictograms made by the native people on accordion-like folds of tree-bark, these decorated slabs show a series of episodes from the conquest. In one image, Malinche is standing behind Cortés, in a plain dark dress. One hand is raised as she transforms the local tongue into Spanish. Underneath and around her, the native people line up to present their tribute, or tumble under Spanish blades.

Her presence in these images is corroborated by native testimony collected by Catholic priests. 'La Malinche said to the guards "come forward",' one recalled, describing the Spaniards' activities in Mexico City (or Tenochtitlan as it was known). 'When the captain [Cortés] and La Malinche saw the gold, they grew very angry,' said another — the translator and her master tied not only in words but also in their emotional reactions.

The close working relationship that developed between Cortés and Malinche is further suggested by stories from the conquest, notably her key role in protecting the conquistadors in the lavish city of Cholula. Eager to be rid of the Spaniards, local leaders were plotting to do away with them. Hearing of their plan, Malinche passed it on to the conquistadors, leading to a pre-emptive assault and the sacking of a city that Cortés himself compared with Granada. Later, Malinche bore a child to Cortés, paraphraser doubling as paramour. Her child, Martin, would become a symbol of the nation that emerged from the conquest — the mestizo or 'mixed' race that accounts for the majority of the Mexican population today. Which is why Malinche is not only the great traitor but also, in a sense, the 'Mother of the Nation'.* How's that for a national enigma?

---

* In *The Labyrinth of Solitude*, Octavio Paz calls Malinche 'the Chingada in person', explaining that 'The Chingada is one of the Mexican representations of maternity, like La Llorona or the long-suffering Mexican mother'. For Paz, 'The strange permanence of Cortés and La Malinche in the Mexican's imagination and sensibilities reveals that they are something more than historical figures: they are symbols of a recent conflict that we have still not resolved.'

Sixty-six miles north-west of Veracruz, in a suburb of Xalapa, the historian Fernanda Núñez Becerra lives in a gorgeous yellow villa, cocooned in lush foliage and twisting trees, surrounded by red lobster-claw heliconia and knobbly wands of palito cactus. Elegantly dressed in a wrapped robe, her rich voice flowing like the French wine she poured into our glasses, Fernanda told me about her life investigating the woman at the heart of the conquest:

'She was so important in history, but so little had been written about her — from a historian's perspective. Of course, she was written about in stories — in romanticised novels in the nineteenth century, especially — but hardly anybody had troubled to find out who she really was. But I never imagined when I started my research how she would transform. Now she has become this icon — the star of telenovelas and films, an icon for the Chicanas in New Mexico.'

The past is never past, because the angle from which we observe it is always in flux. Hidden for centuries behind the men of the conquest, latterly Malinche has been dragged out of the shadows, to stand in the spotlight of a popular TV series and a novel by the acclaimed Mexican author Laura Esquivel. Reviled as a traitor she may have been, but revisionist readings see in her a figure of freedom, refusing to accept the blood sacrifices of pre-Hispanic Mexico, shrewdly perceiving an opportunity to regain the high status that was taken away from her when she was sold into slavery by members of her own family. As ambiguous as the ghost with whom she has become associated.

Fernanda has researched La Malinche over the course of several decades, and her book *La Malinche: from history to myth* is the most comprehensive scholarly account of this complicated figure. Behind the individual, she suggests, is a whole society, the women of that society — and it is through Malinche that we can glimpse them:

'She is seen as the first Christian in Mexico, the first convert, and because she had a child by Cortés, she is seen as the mother of the mestizos. But there were many other women taken by the Spaniards.

Malinche just happens to be the one whose name has survived. Her importance is symbolic.'

For Fernanda, Mexico's history is tantalisingly out of reach, its museums 'mausoleums of an anachronistic nationalism', but at the same time breathtakingly relevant to the nation's contemporary troubles:

'In the nineteenth century, when romantic writers were telling the story of Malinche, they made her into a beautiful princess, they made her white, in love with Cortés. They ignored her colour. And there is a connection with today, when indigenous people are suffering so much from poverty, from discrimination and police brutality. She is a symbol, but she reflects something real.'

Behind all our monsters, this earthy reality. Terrible things were happening, terrible things are always happening: wars between the police and the drug cartels, between different cartels, between special forces and the sicarios (hit men) who used to work with them, between indigenous communities and the gangs attacking them. A matrix of violence even more toxic than the inter-tribal rivalries that gave Cortés an added advantage all those centuries ago. History illuminates the background behind La Llorona; but to understand the story's enduring resonance, we have to reckon with the troubles of today. As the film archivist Viviana García Besné put it to me, in her garden in Tepoztlán:

'When I think of La Llorona, I think of the mothers weeping for their children in all these places where the violence is happening.'

A couple of days before I met Fernanda, newspapers had reported a dog running down a street in Zacatecas with a human head between its jaws. A few weeks later, another grisly dog was sighted, in Irapuato, with a human hand in its mouth; on following the dog's tracks, investigators found fifty-three bags full of human remains. For Fernanda, these incidents reflected not only the venomous nature of Mexico's drug wars but the 'dehumanisation' of indigenous people. Vulnerable to extortion and kidnappings, forced to labour on drug plantations and illegal mining operations, their makeshift self-defence groups chopped down by the violence of the cartels, their land seized or rendered uninhabitable by crossfire, their appeals for justice ignored or undermined by collusion between the cartels and corrupt officials, they have been sucked into an everlasting spiral, with thousands upon thousands of lives lost, unidentified bodies heaped together like the mountains of the dead at the climax of Cortés's conquest.

Malinche was a real-life woman in history, whereas La Llorona is a legend. But in many of the stories told about this avenging ghost, it is Malinche's spirit that transforms into the spectre. This isn't the historical Malinche so much as Malinche the 'symbol': poster girl for the hundreds of indigenous women who found themselves, usually without any choice, in bed with the conquistadors. Maddened with regret, loathing themselves as much as their conquerors, they represent the unresolved conflict (as Octavio Paz put it) that continues to beat at the heart of Mexican identity.

THE ART OF DEATH

West of Veracruz, fields of maize ripen with Mexico's staple diet. Desert engulfs them, yucca and maguey cactus twisting their branches in eccentric permutations, as if in a desperate bid to attract the attention of the threadbare clouds. A kestrel wheels over the steep brown hills, patiently scrutinising the desert's slim pickings. Wide and arid, the plateau links the western and eastern arms of the Sierra Madre, which thrusts above in dagger-shaped peaks of granite and slopes that flash with inky obsidian.

High in the Valley of Mexico, around AD 1325, an archipelago of artificial islands was built on a huge lake surrounded by mountains and volcanoes. The builders were the Mexica — the Aztecs — and they had chosen their site, so the legend goes, after their god Huitzilopochtli sent them a sign: a golden eagle devouring a rattlesnake on a prickly pear. The ceremonial centre of their city, known then as Tenochtitlan, remains the heart of Mexico City today — the Zócalo or 'base'.

After a bus to the outskirts, the Metro carried me into the city and I came out at the Zócalo. It was a little before dawn and I was almost alone with the ghosts. As light dribbled over the volcanic stone of the Palacio Nacional, street sweepers in hi-vis jackets moved around the square, and a group of indigenous demonstrators stood in front of banners showing the faces of their missing relatives. The strings of their demonstration tent were lashed to the bronze feet of a row of Aztecs in a monument to the city's foundation. Towering over the square were the Catrinas — giant skeletons twelve metres tall, bony faces offset by magnificent costumes. One was framed in an Aztec headdress, another in a bridal veil, another in a bonnet. It was the end of October, and the Day of the Dead was just around the corner. No better time to explore a tale about the returning dead.

Ofrendas were out on display — models of skulls and skeletons, often in humorous poses — along with food and drink and marigolds, the flowers of the dead in Mexican culture. Between Aztec headdresses and candles, under flights of colourful piñatas, behind sprawling depictions of Aztec gods made with coloured sand, was a written banner linking the remembrance of the dead, the Catholic tradition of All Souls and All Saints, with the belief in Mictlan, the underworld of Aztec cosmogony. 'In this day of the dead celebration,' a notice explained, 'death does not represent an absence but a living presence.' It is this entanglement of culture, mingling pre-Hispanic beliefs with Catholicism, that makes Mexico's heritage hard to pin down — but also gives it its uniqueness and power.

Traces of the Aztecs' world appeared all over the city — dancing warriors in jaguar masks and serpent garb, with skulls and seed pods rattling on their calves, performing on the Zócalo; a traditional ball game, played in the square outside a church, in which the ball has to be passed through a stone hoop; the ruins of temples, balustrades, and sculpture-work, spreading behind the cathedral in a ripple of limestone and stucco.

At first, the ruins are camouflaged by the broad shadows of the cathedral, much of which was constructed from the stones of the Aztec temples. But plunge into old Tenochtitlan and they rise around you. Statues of Aztec gods stand sentinel, near ofrendas containing the sacrificed skeletons of children and magnificent reliefs of deities. In one of these, the goddess Coyolxauhqui is surrounded by her own dismembered body parts, her breasts bared, girdled in a belt made of snakes, with a skull for a buckle, signifying her defeat by her brother — the patron god of the Aztecs, Huitzilopochtli. Cortés sent back treasures like these to his master, the Holy Roman Emperor and King of Spain, Charles V: 'a large gold wheel with a design of monsters on it', for example. But what Cortés saw as monsters, for the native people were gods.

*

Only in Mexico City can you queue in a brightly lit hall to take a selfie under a monstrous figure wielding a pair of human hearts, his tongue the shape of a sacrificial knife. Although known as the 'Aztec Calendar', this monumental disc has been identified as a sacrifice stone. Here in the Anthropology Museum — a full-on sensory overload of sculpture-work — motifs of death ripple all around. To one side of the sacrifice stone are skeletal heads hewn out of volcanic stone, chiming with the calaveras outside.

Step further back, past a stone jaguar and a circular frieze of spear-brandishing warriors, and you can pay your respects to the goddess of motherhood and the earth. Skulls and severed human hands adorn Cihuacoatl's neck like precious pendants, and more skulls pompadour her head, rhyming with the grisly bared teeth of her own skeletal expression. Cihuacoatl is believed to be at the root of the legend of La Llorona. On the eve of the conquest, it's said the people of Tenochtitlan heard her roaming the streets, letting out a terrible wail: 'My children, where shall I take you?' This was one of eight omens contributing to Emperor Moctezuma's fatalistic belief in his dominion's certain doom. It is the point of origin for the legend of La Llorona, the divine lament of Mexico's original 'Weeping Woman' synchronising with Malinche's 'betrayal'.

These vivid sculptures articulate the long-enduring Mexican art of death. Many of the nuances behind their ritual uses are lost. But something has survived, or returned — dredged from the traumatised hippocampus of a nation's tragic history, or reinstated by nostalgia and economic forces. Death reigns supreme, dominating Mexican artistic culture, from Mayan sculptures to the horror vacui of Diego Rivera's mid-twentieth-century murals.* More than two millennia earlier, Aristotle pointed out that 'we enjoy looking at accurate likenesses of things which are themselves painful to see, obscene beasts, for example, and corpses'. Monsters and the dead: the ancient Greeks may have worked Aristotle's principle to a spectacular pitch, but nowhere has made such a danse macabre out of death like Mexico.

AN EMPIRE FALLS

Cortés was amazed by Tenochtitlan, 'as big as Seville or Cordoba', a city of canals and lagoons and soaring palaces of volcanic stone, defended from the mainland by movable bridges and watered by a massive

---

* Artworks like Rivera's belong to a movement known as 'indigenismo', which flourished in the wake of the Mexican Revolution of 1910–20. The anthropologist Manuel Gamio argued that Mexican artists should seek inspiration from pre-Hispanic Mexico, especially the culture of the Aztecs. However, critics claimed the movement obscured the reality of indigenous life. While it is common in Mexico to link Day of the Dead and the representation of death images with pre-Hispanic culture, that view has been challenged. Its influences may 'include the artistic and religious legacy of Aztecs and Spaniards at the time of the Conquest', the American scholar Stanley Brandes has argued, but its motifs are driven by 'specific demographic and political circumstances' as well as 'commercial interests', such as the popularity of sugar figurines in colonial times and the satirical cartoonist José Guadelupe Posada's lively broadsheets of the early twentieth century, which were full of skulls and bones and especially popular during the Mexican Revolution.

stone aqueduct. People traded and gathered in a 'square twice as big as that of Salamanca, with arcades all around', using cocoa beans and feather quills filled with gold dust for currency, parading in masks and feathers, in the skins of jaguars and even human beings. With 200,000 packed into an area of twenty square kilometres, Tenochtitlan was more populous than anywhere in Christendom. But that wouldn't stop the conquistadors from tearing it apart.

Moctezuma gave them a royal welcome: a thousand chiefs thronged the emperor as he garlanded Cortés in necklaces made from snails' shells and gold. He lodged the Spaniards in the Palace of Axayacatl, attending on them with his jesters, dancing dwarves, and singers. But the spectacles disintegrated as Moctezuma found himself a prisoner of his guests, the inevitable loser in one of history's strangest clashes of character. On one side was a messianic and merciless gold-and-glory-hunter; on the other an indecisive ruler who no longer believed in his own empire.

With the conquistadors controlling Moctezuma's movements inside the royal precinct, an impasse developed. When Cortés left for Veracruz, to fend off a challenge from another branch of conquistadors, it snapped. One of the most prominent and treasure-hungry of the Spaniards, Pedro de Alvarado — known for his diamond ring and jewelled necklace — decided to pre-empt a rumoured attack by striking at the religious ceremony of Toxcatl. 'They ran in among the dancers, forcing their way to the place where the drums were played,' recalled an eyewitness. 'They attacked the man who was drumming and cut off his arms. Then they cut off his head, and it rolled across the floor. The blood of the warriors flowed like water and gathered into pools. The pools widened, and the stench of blood and entrails filled the air ...' By the time Cortés returned, the Spaniards and their hosts were at war.

What happened next gives an insight into the deep reach of Mexico's 'art of death'. Peering from the windows of their palace refuge, the conquistadors saw scenes from a nightmare: decapitated corpses rolling down the streets, dead men leaping around an altar. The Aztecs were presenting a warning in mime. With their minds cracking as much as their bodies, suffering from malnourishment and running out of ammunition, the Spaniards scrambled out of Tenochtitlan on the so-called 'Night of Sorrow'. Many of them didn't make it — hundreds were drowned in the canals.

But giving up wasn't Cortés's style. 'I would not abandon this land,' he declared, 'for, apart from being shameful to myself and dangerous for all, it would be great treason to your Majesty.' So, shaking off his latest setback, Cortés regrouped and realigned his relationship with the local tribes, deploying his chief translator, Malinche, and manipulating collective resentment towards the Aztecs.

The conquest of Tenochtitlan took place over seventy-five days and saw the deaths of a quarter of a million of the native people. 'We have chewed dry twigs and salt grasses', declared an Aztec elegy; 'we have filled our mouths with dust and bits of adobe; we have eaten lizards, rats and worms ...' It's a testament to their efforts, and in spite of their technological inferiority, that the Aztecs managed to hold off the siege for so long. Chanting war-songs and beating their drums, they captured many prisoners from the Spaniards and the tribes allied with them, sacrificing them in the temples and arranging their heads on pikes. The water was their salvation — for there the horses were vulnerable and the Aztecs slid out in ambush. So the conquistadors filled in the canals with rubble, beginning the process that would transform Mexico City into the earthbound city of today. 'The cries of the helpless women and children were heart-rending,' a native reported. 'The anguish and bewilderment of our foes was pitiful to see. The warriors gathered on the rooftops and stared at the ruins of their city in a dazed silence, and the women and children and old men were all weeping.'

The conquistadors had bemoaned the Aztecs' human sacrifices, which certainly seem gruesome to the modern eye. But how many bodies were trampled under the conquistadors' horses? In one of his most revealing letters, Cortés expressed both his regret at the scale of death and the self-righteousness that enabled him to bear what he'd done: 'we could not but be saddened by their determination to die'. So a mighty empire was reduced to rubble, its statues and bas-reliefs knocked to pieces, the walls of its temples repurposed to build the churches and mansions through which 'New Spain' would be administered.

As for his most significant translator: Malinche was passed on to one of Cortés's commanders. His Spanish wife was on her way across the Atlantic; the newly self-appointed Regent of New Spain could hardly be seen to cohabit with a barbarian (his wife would die in mysterious circumstances only a few months after her arrival in Mexico, freeing the ever ambitious and newly ennobled conquistador to marry, a few years later, the daughter of a count). The house where he set up Malinche is still standing, a couple of blocks north of the cathedral. Look behind the signs for a primary school, half-torn flypapers, and scrawling graffiti, and there it is: a commemorative plaque on a peeling red wall. Should more be made of it? This depends on your perspective on Malinche: the traitor who abetted the enemy and shared his bed, or the mother of the mestizos? A goddess or a monster, or a human making the best of things in a time of frantic change?

AT NIGHT IN THE FLOATING GARDENS

Death in technicolour: wading around the Zócalo, I was never more than a few inches from another macabre snapshot. Sugary pan de muerto, 'bread of the dead', gulped down with hot, bitter coffee, strolls around the parks between lovers in calavera make-up, stripy black-and-white lips fusing their bleached white skull-faces together; groups of young women squeezing together on the pedestals of lampposts, make-up kits on their knees, embellishing their skull foundations with flamboyant butterflies and the feathers of tropical birds, in teal and blue, canary yellow and blood red.

In the neighbourhood of Coyoacán, where Cortés's grand villa was raised out of blocks of volcanic stone, the ofrendas were matched for visual flamboyance by the costumes of the people wading between them — vampires and werewolves, creepy scarecrows with straw pouring out of their sleeves, an Aztec warrior in a jaguar headdress. Plain clothes were taboo — they marked you out, a breach of etiquette. So I bought myself a glittery skull T-shirt and popped my head inside the werewolf mask I'd taken to the Rougaroufest in Louisiana. Now I was one of the crowd.

By the cemetery of San José Panteón, a few stops further down the Metro, burritos and pulque were sold from stalls around a stage. Following a ring of Aztec death-spectres performing a salsa with the skull-wigged goddess Cihuacoatl, a banshee wail announced the arrival of La Llorona, warbling through a much-loved folk-song to the passionate strumming of a six-string:

Ay que dolor, que penas, Llorona, Llorona, que penas las mias
Ay que dolor, que penas, Llorona, Llorona, que penas las mias

(Oh what pain, what sorrows, Llorona, Llorona, what sorrows of mine
Oh what pain, what sorrows, Llorona, Llorona, what sorrows of mine)

Wailing goddesses and weeping women: this was their season. Outside Coyoacán's Church of San Juan Battista, a skull-faced variant in a white rebozo was holding two plastic baby corpses on a string — generously slathered in fake blood — posing for photos. But nowhere did La Llorona float as magnificently as in Xochimilco. It was time to take to the waterways, where the Wailing Woman is in her element.

The canals and chinampas (floating gardens) of Xochimilco offer a glimpse into Tenochtitlan at the time of the Conquest. Braziers puff out copal smoke, stalls sell elote flan and sweet pan de muerto, and your nose is massaged by the delicious perfume of red poinsettias and marigolds, the flowers of the dead.

'I am La Llorona,' read a poem hung inside a sixteenth-century courtyard house near the market. 'I invite you to the flower market. Let's go eat some food and taste the flowers.'

Sunlight lit up the floral displays and flashed on the sugary beakers in a pulqueria (a bar specialising in the sweet cactus beverage brewed since Aztec times) where revellers were strutting their stuff to a band, arms around their shoulders, legs kicking out. Sleeping dogs sagged in front of iron gates, and piñatas straddled the labyrinth of knotty streets like rainbows. Through a narrow gap between the houses, I reached a canal. A band of black-clad mariachis was climbing onto a raft, so I jumped in beside them. The pilot pulled on a rope strung from the trees on the banks, sliding us to the spit of land on the other side.

A mile up the bank was the embarkation known as Cuemanco. Arches flanked an alley of boutiques and snack stalls where Mexican holidaymakers were draining sugary, pint-sized beakers of pulque. The boats moored along the canal were even brighter than their drinks. To take in all those colours was the visual equivalent of swallowing a packet of Smarties. But amid all the brightness, there was space for the grim: a long-haired, skull-faced La Llorona adorned the entrance arch, silhouetted the stonework of the trajinera dock, and appeared on a brightly painted boat beside an image of the goddess Cihuacoatl. In Cuemanco, the Wailing Woman was inescapable.

'I grew up with this story, those of us who live here, we all did.'

Eduardo Ordoñez was one of the producers of a stage show about the legend. He met me at the box-office kiosk, and we walked along the canal, discussing the show and its background.

'When I was a kid, my older brothers used to creep me out with stories about La Llorona. I never imagined I'd end up producing a show about it!'

Re-imagining the story was a way for Eduardo to engage with

the suppression of indigenous identity, to peel back the pre-Hispanic roots of the tale:

'This is our culture. It is good to perform it, and celebrate it. The Spanish tried to destroy it, but it survived in spite of everything they did, and this story is a way for us to show that.'

How Mexican — to celebrate your culture through a ghost story; but how true of Mexican history.

The elements were just right for such a tale. Wagons of cloud rolled overhead, growing ominously dark, faster than the draining of the light. Assigned to a trajinera, I queued up with my fellow spectators to step into one of the boats, swapping small talk with a bubbly Bolivian lady and a young Mexican called Giovanni. Coloured awnings and painted headboards blazed with colour until the falling light turned them to ashy vessels floating between inky poplars and ahuejote willows. The shadowy wetland sucked us between widening canals, past artificial islands constructed by the Aztecs in the fifteenth century using reeds and stakes as underwater fencing. The watery thoroughfare gaped open, revealing a lake, flanked by bamboo and ahuejote. Out of the darkness, gleaming with lens flares and fizzling LEDs, appeared a stage installed on an islet.

Trajineras sculled around us, selling beakers of pulque, tacos, and burritos. Embers glittered out of cooking pots, illuminating the sellers' folksy dresses. But gradually, the noise of the loudspeakers muted the chatter of trade and our own mutterings of anticipation. Time to settle into the story, another variation on the national legend: the native girl who makes love to a conquistador and the terrible fate that engulfs her.

In this telling, she is a young woman in sixteenth-century Xochimilco. She falls in love with an iron-clad Spanish commander, but he refuses to admit their love in public, not even when she has borne two children by him. In a powerful scene, the commander has the babies hurled from a wall to prove she means nothing to him. An anguished invocation — 'Oh Mother!' — reels in the goddess

Cihuacoatl, and in a remarkable pièce de théâtre, the heroine is circled by masked spirits. Her rainbow-like indigenous dress is stripped away in favour of a ghost-white gown, her luxuriant hair smothered by a rebozo. In this pale shroud, she descends into the lake, disappearing under a patina of bubbles.

'There she is!'

Gasps all around and a mass grab for phones. Here's something you don't get at the Old Vic — floating a few feet away was the Weeping Woman. She was gliding on a kayak, arms outstretched, her scream reverberating against the prows of the trajineras.

I needed a few moments to process it all, but the heavens had other ideas. As if in some kind of celestial protest against all the pizzazz on the water, they let rip — dragon-like growls of thunder and flashes of lightning powerful enough to act as interplanetary smuggling signals. Rain rattled on the canopies over our heads and formed rising pools around our feet. There was a mad dash to punt out of the lake and back to the canal. Our pilot, David, tugged on his pole, his jaw set in a determined grimace. Too many trajineras, too little vision: thump, and the boats were jammed in a rain-sodden tangle. It took all of David's punting prowess to pull us free and slide towards the dock.

'You want a lift?' asked Giovanni.

'That would be amazing!'

We'd been sat next to each other during the chaos, helping each other lift our bags out of the wet. Giovanni peered through a pair of smart specs, under long, drenched locks. Sitting in the back of his friend's car, he told me about his adventures: travels to Germany and Ireland, where he'd pursued an interest in Celtic folklore.

'People call me Malinchiste': a traitor to Mexican patriotism like Cortés's translator — a commonly used term for anybody seen to kowtow to foreign influences. But Giovanni was as Mexican as any. He'd even witnessed La Llorona for himself:

'I was six years old, and I was walking with my mother, we were trying to catch a bus in Veracruz. It was watery, exactly the kind of place where La Llorona is supposed to haunt — that's what my mother said. I don't know, I just saw something blurry, but my mother was sure it was her.'

The play was testament to the resonance of La Llorona — not only its popularity with Mexicans like Giovanni, but the passion of the people behind it, like Eduardo. Giovanni's was the first memorate I heard about La Llorona. But soon I would be heading to a place that buzzes with stories about her. For the next day would find me in the mountain town of Tepoztlán, where it could well be said there is something in the water.

A NEIGHBOURHOOD OF HAUNTINGS

The legend has many forms. In 1585, Bernardino de Sahagún, one of the Franciscan monks who accompanied the conquistadors, chastised the Mexican converts: 'Your ancestors also erred in the admiration of a demon whom they represented as a woman, and to whom they gave the name of Cihuacoatl. She appeared as a lady of the palace. She terrified, she frightened, and cried aloud at night.' Within another century, according to the politician Vicente Riva Palacio, the wailing goddess had been mingled with a real-life tragedy from the colonial Spanish period. In Riva Palacio's version, Luisa, the jilted lover of a high-ranking ranchero called Don Nuño de Montes Claros, kills their three children and staggers around the city, before a crowd gathers to witness her execution.

Riva Palacio was writing during the nineteenth century, the story's primary period of development. Tales of revenants were sweeping across Europe and the New World, triggered by Romanticism's obsession with the past. Gas lights enabled people to frequent the streets more regularly at night (and imagine what they contained) and the spread of magazines increased demand for sensational tales, inspiring a boom in supernatural storytelling.* While authors like Edgar Allan Poe and Sheridan Le Fanu were raising neck hairs in the Anglophone world, a newly independent Mexico was stirring up its own ghost stories, among which La Llorona would become the most iconic.

The earliest known published version is an 1849 poem by the polymath and poet Manuel Carpio ('Full of deadly terror for all, / By the river in heavy darkness / Weeping she goes, wrapped in her mantle'). Riva Palacio's telling followed in 1885, about doomed Luisa and Don Nuño. In 1910, the American journalist and traveller Thomas Allibone Janvier quoted a Mexican called Gilberto Cano in his *Legends of the City of Mexico*: 'many bad things come out by night in the streets of the city, but this wailing woman, La Llorona, is the very worst of them all.' In Cano's lurid account, the spectre haunts deserted streets, preying especially on lustful nightwatchmen. 'Throw off your rebozo that I may see your pretty face,' one of them implores her, only to be faced by 'a bare grinning skull set fast to the bare bones of a skeleton!'

If the nineteenth century was the engine room of the story's formation, the twentieth provided opportunities to peddle it to the masses. There was a 1917 play by Francisco C. Neve, in which a mestizo woman called Luisa is jilted by her lover Ramiro (a fictional son of Cortés) and madly murders their child. In 1933, there was a novel by Antonio Guzmán Aguilara, who storylined a movie about La Llorona the same year — one of Mexico's first talkies, in which a woman is coaxed to the edge of madness by the whispering spirit of La Llorona. Like the unmasked villain in an episode of *Scooby Doo*, an indigenous nanny turns out to be the nemesis, disguising herself as the ghost to fulfil the long-ago curse of Malinche. As the century progressed, there would be many more versions in Mexico — dramatic movies

---

* In *The Ghost: a cultural history*, Susan Owens argues that 'supernatural tales proliferated' in this period. 'Victorian ghosts were shaped by the demands of the magazine format: stories had to be brief, gripping and sensational.'

like the 1947 *Inheritance of La Llorona*, or a 1960 *La Llorona* from the golden age of Mexican horror, or a 1974 luchador (wrestling) movie, *The Vengeance of La Llorona*. More recently, there have been chilling variations in the USA and a profoundly political version in Guatemala (*La Llorona*, 2019, in which the spectre forces recognition of the genocide of Mayan people by the US-backed military government of the 1980s).

Even more disturbing are the real-life cases: delinquents recorded by the psychologist Bess Lomax Hawes at a juvenile centre in 1960s California, for example; or a woman suffering postpartum psychosis in 2001 who drowned her five children in a bathtub in Houston. 'Yo soy La Llorona,' she told the police when they arrived on the scene: 'I am La Llorona.' The story's ambiguity gives it undiminished resonance in the twenty-first century. On the one hand, it's a patriarchal tale about an infanticidal madwoman. But, like the counter-image in a Rorschach sketch, another interpretation blazes through. Implicitly, the tale dramatises the damage inflicted on women by the callous men who use and discard them — and it offers them a chance for revenge.

The legend abounds in so many versions that none is definitive. But the 1933 movie can make a strong case for having the greatest impact in Mexico. It was the nation's first sound horror film, produced by José Calderón, whose entrepreneurial family had sewn up the film business around the US–Mexican border with a chain of thirty cinemas and their own studio. *La Llorona* was one of their first hits, produced only two years after Hollywood's huge success with *Frankenstein* and *Dracula* (a Spanish-language version of the latter was filmed at the same time and on the same sets as Tod Browning's classic, but at night and with different actors). 'She was not a European monster who was merely transplanted to Mexico,' as the film scholar Emily Masincup points out: 'this was her territory, and this was Mexico's story to tell.'

Big banner newspaper adverts and press articles anticipated the release, which was praised as 'spectacular' in the newspaper *El*

Universal, especially for its production values, with 'proportions on the screen not imagined until now'. But over time, the film tumbled into neglect and the original print was lost. It was the producer's great-granddaughter Viviana García Besné who tracked down a sixteen-millimetre print, full of star-shaped 'cue marks', with a corrupted soundtrack, a print so damaged she called it 'the weeping Frankenstein'. She managed to restore it, putting the movie back in circulation.

Now Viviana lives in the town of Tepoztlán, fifty miles out of Mexico City. When I contacted her, she invited me over for lunch. So I wandered past murals of Aztec warriors and stalls selling flowery calaveras and painted pulque jars. Marigolds and bunting hung around the gates of a cemetery, opposite a lane wriggling towards an iron gate guarded by a pair of noisy dogs. Inside was a bustling family home, with teens on screens and a flurry of craft-making for a Day of the Dead party. Viviana was wide-eyed, chatty, and welcoming, her arms sweeping the air to gesticulate to one of her children or to point out some feature of her garden. She had just the kind of humour you'd expect of somebody who's lived so much of her life with a ghost story. Within moments of my arrival, she sat me down at an outdoor dining table and told me about the black widow spiders she'd found crawling out of the woodwork:

'Look at your face — but it's true!'

She also mentioned the scorpions she sometimes finds hiding in her shoes.

'So tell me, Viviana,' I asked, keen to move the subject on from potential sources of fatal venom, 'why did your family choose La Llorona — why this story for Mexico's first horror movie?'

'Why? Because this is *the* story, Mexico's greatest legend. It's the most popular Mexican story, the one everybody knows. What is our greatest monster, our biggest legend? It's La Llorona.'

As a child, Viviana recalled playing games about the ghost — looking for her in the cemetery near where she grew up in Mexico City.

'I didn't know anybody who didn't play La Llorona as a kid. What games did you play?'

'Hmmm, to be fair, I did a lot of monster-chasing too!'

Restoring the 1933 movie, for Viviana, was a personal form of raising ghosts. In those cleaned-up frames, she was able to see her loved ones again, in a charming children's party scene early in the movie — her grandmother refusing to sit down, her great-aunt scratching her head. But it was Neri, Viviana's friendly cook, who suggested a more direct link to the ghost story.

'You know my brother-in-law Jesus?' she said. 'He saw La Llorona when he was a boy.'

I had to concentrate to stop the pozole soup from dribbling down my T-shirt.

'When you say he *saw* her ... ?'

That afternoon, accompanied by Viviana's son Aliex, I stepped through an iron gate on the other side of Tepoztlán's market, and sat down with Jesus Ismail Castañeda. It was then that I heard about Jesus's experience of La Llorona, my spine growing distinctly colder as Aliex translated Jesus's words.

For Jesus, La Llorona was part of the nightscape, a chilling spectre associated with water, an ever-present reality. He had plenty of other stories — the sound of rattling chains at one of the hotels where he'd worked; a figure in a wide white hat sitting on a black horse who had ridden away when he made the sign of the cross and who Jesus had believed to be the devil. His experience of La Llorona — the boyhood vision with which this chapter began — had taken place eight decades ago, but he had no doubt about its truth, and he told it with a matter-of-fact sincerity. He admitted to his fear but denied that La Llorona had adversely affected his life. But as I would learn, not all the ghost's witnesses found closure so easy.

The Day of the Dead was upon us. Glowing skulls clung to the belfry of the Church of the Holy Trinity like they were trying to imitate the lizards. A trail of marigold petals led towards the stained glass behind the altar, the statue of Christ in the transept, and a cigarette-wielding, black-hatted skeleton, loitering alongside a Catrina in a black dress trimmed with purple lace.

I stayed at a hostel behind the cemetery, and the next day I wandered between the lushly decorated tombstones. Candles glowed under coloured piñata, hung over the graves like bunting. Marigolds were scattered at the edges of the graves. There were offerings of fruit, brandy, sweets, even liquor bottles. It was All Saints' Day, when Mexicans traditionally remember those who died before reaching adulthood. In the cemetery, people were sweeping and tidying, filling up buckets to wash the gravestones. A family was gathering around a burial kiosk, a little boy clambering over the gravestone while his father swigged on a bottle; a young couple gripped each other's hands before a child's grave; an elderly couple made their way to the grave of their granddaughter.

'You are visiting?' asked the grandfather.

He gestured for me to follow, introducing himself as Francesco. I held back, wary of trespassing on something so personal, but he coaxed me along with a smile.

'Today is the day of the "little angels",' he explained. 'This is when we visit the graves of the children. She was only twenty-seven days old when she died.'

'That is sad, I'm very sorry.'

'No, we are not sad,' said his wife, Theresa. 'We come here to celebrate.'

She was laying down marigolds and golden baubles to brighten up the tomb, to make it a happy place, where the spirit might feel at home. Others were decorating the tombs around us — a wreath over a headstone, a coloured piñata, a plate of food left on a gravestone as an offering.

'This is for my mother,' explained a woman setting down a bowl with tamales, the spicy meat tucked inside corn husks. 'It was her favourite dish. We leave the food here and then tomorrow we'll come back to dine with the dead. We'll eat mole and rice, we'll have a feast!'

I thought of the sombreness of cemetery visits back home, the passive politeness with which I had stood, head bowed and hands clasped, over the memorials to my father, my grandparents, aunts, uncles, the scores of loved ones we all lose to the tidal pull of the years. Surely the Mexican way is healthier? I thought of how sad I had been, and lost at times, knowing I could never again speak to those who had gone. To believe in ghosts, in the Mexican sense, is to believe these regrets can be eased. For every year, for a couple of days at least, the dead are not remote.

Darkness, as everywhere else, is their time. All over town, people visited the ofrendas — the displays of skulls and flowers and food that some people had taken to extraordinary creative lengths. I went along with Meg, a friend of Viviana's from the US, and a local lad called Diego. Strolling down from the market, squeezing between figures in skull paint and Aztec-style headdresses, we reached an artist's home, the Tlalmanco House, which had been transformed into a skeletons' circus. Antics of the dead were displayed in life-size dioramas: a skeletal trapeze artist floated overhead, a skeleton clown was knocked down by a skeleton strongman holding a dumbbell, a couple more skeleton clowns beamed hollow-eyed from inside a clapped-out van. Out in the alleys, children swung by with buckets for sweets. In the doorways they passed, young women in black Catrina dresses, their faces transformed into shining skulls, posed in arresting tableaux vivants. Light streamed around them in waves of gold, piercing the blackness of night.

On one of these streets, we dropped in on Liliana and Hilario, Meg's homestay hosts when she had studied in Tepoztlán a couple of years before:

'Welcome! Welcome! Come inside, have something to drink!'

Warmth oozed from their voices, and smiles flashed as they led us across a courtyard. We sat in the ofrenda room. A table was laid with fruit and bread, tamales, rice, and tequila. There were dahlias and other flowers, and a blanket of marigolds trailing between the table legs.

'These are the things our loved ones enjoyed,' Hilario explained, 'their favourite dishes, their favourite drinks. Tonight we leave it all for the dead, then tomorrow we eat it.'

'Look,' said Doña Socora, one of the family's elders, standing beside the offering table: 'the candles are flickering.'

This meant one of the dead had arrived. After all, Doña Socora pointed out, there wasn't much wind in the room. The doorway to the other world had been opened, oiled according to tradition by the burning of copal and the trail of marigolds. If ever there was a night for ghost stories, this was it, so it seemed an appropriate occasion to mention my interest in La Llorona. Not that I ever imagined the torrent of stories this would unleash.

'Oh yes, La Llorona!' Hilario rubbed his hands, nodding to Liliana. 'Of course, I saw her once. Shall I tell you?'

He was in his twenties when it happened. He'd been drinking and was stumbling back home. 'I stopped at a well to wash my face, and when I turned I saw a woman, very beautiful, in a long white robe. She was floating a little way off the floor. She was combing her hair, as if she'd been bathing. Then out of her mouth came this ... wail. I was so scared, I sobered up straightaway. I ran straight home and crawled into bed between my parents. My mother said, "What are you doing? You're twenty-five years old." But when I told her, she understood.'

The experience had shaken Hilario. After several weeks of anxiety, he sought help from a traditional healer, 'to bring the fear out of me'. Herbs were placed on his arms and his head was 'tapped'. He had faith in the healer: like victims of the jinn under the influence of a raqi, he believed in the traditional remedy, so he was able to recover. Culture as catharsis: the same folk beliefs that enable people to credit traditional phantasms can also cure them from their effects.

'You know there have been many sightings of La Llorona around here,' said Liliana. 'She's been down the high street many times. They even caught her on the security cameras.'

It was a night for storytelling, and Hilario and Liliana offered the perfect hearth-place. They told of the naguals, shapeshifters who transform themselves into cows, pigs, or other animals, with telltale signs of abnormality, such as crossed legs. They talked of a magical dog (another nagual, Liliana was sure) that leaped over a wall and sent the other dogs scurrying for shelter. There was a story about vampiric witches, a mother and daughter who could magically separate their feet to fly away and suck people's blood. At least, until the husband of the younger witch killed the elder by burning her feet and threatened his wife with the same if she ever did it again. And there was Hilario's late uncle, renowned for his magical powers, visited many decades ago by the president and presented with Tepoztlán's first motor car. Magic and reality were tangled up, inseparable (as Liliana pointed out, she'd grown up without a TV and what was there to do in the evenings but tell stories?), a fusion of worlds in which I could happily have spent the rest of the night. But the night wasn't for the living. It was time to let the spirits have their feast.

Another barrage of rain. When we stepped outside, the streets were foamy, the slope transformed to a rapid, glistening and gurgling under the streetlights. Picking our way towards the marketplace, it was like trying to ford a river. I said goodbye to Meg and Diego, and skipped back towards my hostel, long-jumping over puddles, ducking out of the splashdown from the roofs. On the edge of a plaza, revellers were draining the last of their pulque. Skeleton make-up dribbled down their faces and soggy marigolds slid out of their hair. The flowers fell to the ground to be trampled underfoot, remnants of a magical evening, like Cinderella's pumpkin. I thought of Gilberto Cano, the nineteenth-century witness of the legend: 'her loud keen wailings, and the sound of her running feet, are heard often, and especially on nights of storm.' Water, La Llorona's element, was seeing in the day when the spirits come back.

Inside the gate of the cemetery, the lights of phones were visible, twinkling against the wet. Devotees were sitting with their loved ones, with cans and bottles, generously sized rollies and tubs of food, settling in for their all-night vigils, people like Francesco and Theresa, like Hilario and Liliana. Looking up to the heavens, I thought about my own loved ones, the people I had lost, the people I missed. It was only when I made it back to the hostel that I realised I was soaked all the way down to my socks.

CHAPTER EIGHT

The Age of Vampires

THE EIGHTH TALE
'You stay away from here — or I'll skin you alive!'

'Dushman', they call him, 'the enemy', because he loves brawling even more than he loves drinking rakija. But he's the headman of his village and nobody can boast so many sheep. Standing up to Dushman is no easy task, especially for Strahinja, a hard-working, flute-playing lad whose happiness is in the gift of 'the enemy'.

How much simpler life might be — if he hadn't fallen in love with Dushman's daughter! But how could Strahinja resist Radojka's beauty? Her eyes gleam like chestnuts, and long dark tresses of hair dangle over her blossoming chest like the willows that lap the waters of the Rogačica. Strahinja has pledged his heart to Radojka, and he has reason to believe she loves him back, but every time he so much as approaches Dushman's homestead, he's chased away by the crackle of gunshot and the relentless barking of the ever-hungry hounds. The lovers are in despair. What could possibly bring them together? Strahinja will have to do something remarkable — something to convince the villagers of Zarožje to plead his case and force Dushman to accept him as his son-in-law.

Near the village, in a gorge crowned by jagged rocks, a mill squats over the fast-flowing Rogačica. Villagers used to go there to grind their flour, but lately they have been avoiding it, for it is said to be haunted by a vampire. Without a miller, the villagers are aching with hunger. So Strahinja volunteers to be their miller — for one night, at least.

The shrieking of owls, the churring of nightjars: to these and other eerie sounds, Strahinja pours the villagers' wheat into the hopper. He lights a small fire, fits the millstones onto the spindle, and checks the catch tub. Rotating the runner stone, he watches the grain sliding down the chute. If talk of a vampire is true, he will need to be ready. He finds a man-shaped log and sets it down beside the fire, draped in a blanket to give the impression of a sleeping figure. With this decoy in place, he climbs into the loft. There, he lies over some boards, holding two pistols loaded with steel and coins.

Silence, except for the beasts skulking in the woods, the rustle of leaves under their claws, the thumping of Strahinja's heart. No matter how hard he tries to keep himself calm, he can't stifle it. But now another sound, the one he's been anticipating all through the evening: the whine of the door on its hinge. Inside the mill steps a man draped in a linen shroud. He sits down by the fire. With a darting move, he thrusts his arms around the log and proceeds to choke it. But there's no blood in a log and he wails in disappointment:

'Oh, Sava Savanović! For ninety years you have been a vampire, but never did you have to go without your supper as you have tonight.'

As soon as Strahinja hears these words, he blasts with both pistols. Below him, there is a billowing of smoke. But when it clears, the vampire has disappeared.

The song of skylarks and the distant crowing of a cock are the signals *that Strahinja is safe. That morning, the villagers are startled to see him alive. But he has done more than survive — he has learned the secret to bring about the vampire's destruction.*

'His name,' he tells them, 'is Sava Savanović.'

None of the villagers recognises the name ... except for one, a blind and nearly deaf relative of Strahinja's called Mirjana, so old that she still remembers the scandal from nine decades earlier:

'Sava Savanović ... there's a name I haven't heard in years. I was only tiny, but I remember people talking about him. He killed a woman who refused to love him, and the people of the village beat him to death with their mattocks. They buried him in a place near the murder ... now, let me see if I can remember ... It was under a spreading elm tree ... they called it the Crooked Ravine.'

One ravine after another is explored, a posse of villagers scouting out the grave. At last, they find the elm tree, the river twisting below. They dig into the earth until a coffin is uncovered. The corpse inside is as bloated as a wineskin, the face as red as blood. It's nearly dusk and the gunshot wounds on Savanović's hand are already nearly healed. No time to lose! Holy water is splashed over his face, a hawthorn stake is thrust into his chest. Eyes flash, burning with hate; his lips burst open, exhaling his final breath, along with a butterfly. Hands reach out to catch it, but the butterfly is too fast. That, they say, is the vampire's soul.

The next day, a group of villagers accompanies Strahinja to Dushman's farm. While her father is busy, Radojka hurries out with her lover and runs down the hillside. Dushman's hounds race in pursuit, guns crackle like thunder, but Strahinja has too much support for 'the enemy' to stop him. He's brought about the vampire's demise, the whole of Zarožje is on his side. So Radojka and Strahinja begin their life together with a blissful wedding and three days of merry feasting. Flour is ground at the mill once again; bread is in plentiful supply. And as for those butterflies fluttering around the hawthorn bushes ... well, people keep their mouths closed and pray they won't be the cursed spirit's next host.

THE FIRST VAMPIRE

Glasses full of beer, smoke in the air, and heavy metal on the jukebox. I was in a café in the Croatian capital, Zagreb, and I couldn't have hoped for better company. Across the table from me was Boris Perić, a scholar and author whose novel *Vampir*, published in 2006, was a bestseller across the Balkans. He is so bound up with vampires that he's even been depicted in a play about them:

'It was our oldest vampire story — the tale of Jure Grando.'

Boris held up his glass, waving a Winston, the smoke curling across the beams of light darting between the heavy curtains. A big man, he filled the banquette, a subversive strand of ponytail curling over his shoulder:

'I appeared as one of the characters, explaining the action for the audience. They acted out the story, how Grando murdered people in the village of Kringa, and every so often I would appear to comment on the events. I have to say, it was strange to see myself on the stage. Afterwards, I introduced myself to the actor who had played me. "Boris Perić," I said. He took my hand and replied: "The same."'

Kringa is Croatia's original vampire village. I'd visited a couple of days earlier, taking a bus through the furred mountains of Istria, tunnelling inside the limestone massif of Učka to the old provincial capital of Pazin, walking a dozen miles across sun-tormented hills. Coming here in high summer was a questionable decision. I staggered towards Kringa like an ant on a griddle, aching under the weight of my tent, watching the instant drying of the sweat that rolled down my T-shirt. The road was twistier than it had looked on Google Maps, only intermittently shaded where the forest loomed. I had filled up with water in Pazin, but my flask was already warm; it felt like I could pluck a few juniper leaves and turn it into tea. Whenever there was tree cover, I sought shelter, but there were long stretches of uncanopied asphalt, so scalding that I was starting to empathise with vampires. I too was afraid of the sun.

Tall oaks and chestnut trees peeled behind me. I put on my

headphones and switched on my tunes, humming along for the last couple of miles. Backhoe loaders and other construction machines were flashing between metal gates and piled blocks of Istrian stone — the honey-white limestone so highly prized it was used to build the palazzi of Venice. Money had been pouring in from tourism, viticulture, and construction. The region gleamed with gated villas. But they only reinforced the abiding impression when I reached the dusty, curving street of Kringa — abandonment.

'Legend of the Vampire Jure Grando 1672,' proclaimed the village sign, under a reproduced sketch of the village from 1689. There used to be a bar — a stone house tangled with grape vines and glowing apples, now derelict, its vampiric theme visible in a wreath of garlic around a window.

'There weren't enough customers,' said Maria, a former resident visiting her grandmother, who I met outside the church and who gave me a lift out of the village. 'They thought the tourists would come to Kringa, but they never did. Maybe it's too far from the beach.'

Still, Jure Grando's killing spree was testified on the wall of the village school, a stone plaque inscribed with the names of the nine residents who put him to death. History tends to relegate supernatural activity to hearsay, so here is a rare thing: official recognition of a monster attack.

The core of the tale was set down by the Slovenian author Johann von Valvasor, in his three-volume *Glory of the Duchy of Carniola* in 1689: the earliest known historical report of a vampire's rampage. 'There was no doubt about the certainty of the events,' von Valvasor declared, 'for I myself spoke to people who were there.'

By the time the residents of Kringa became aware of the vampire in their midst, so von Valvasor reported, Jure Grando had already been haunting the village for several months. Father Giorgio, a local priest, was shocked when he visited Grando's widow and saw the dead man 'sitting behind the door; and went away completely frightened'. With increasing regularity, Grando prowled the village at night: 'He walked back and forth in the streets, and now here, now there, banged on the front door: in whichever house he knocked on, somebody died soon afterwards.'

Sharing a bed with your spouse is one thing, but it's a whole different matter when he's been in the grave for several years. Grando's widow 'bore an abhorrence for him', von Valvasor narrated, 'and begged [the mayor] to help her against her deceased husband.' So a group of villagers came together, under the leadership of Mayor Raditić. He plied them with drink and led them to the graveyard, armed with lanterns and a crucifix. They managed to dig up the corpse, but Grando's flushed red face was more than they could bear. Chivied by the mayor, they came back a few days later, this time armed with a sharpened hawthorn stake. Not sharp enough: Grando's chest resisted the stab, so one of them tried to smash through his neck with a hoe and another 'who had more heart ... jumped in and cut off his head'.

As von Valvasor recorded, there were similar cases elsewhere: 'something like this happened in Lindar and also, just recently, in an Austrian village in the province of Venice.' So it's no wonder the villagers knew exactly what to do. The year 1689 isn't the beginning of vampires but the moment when the world began to take them seriously: an incident in a little-regarded village, recorded by a well-connected outsider, spreading to the wider world. And oh, would the story spread ...

By the time von Valvasor published his account, Isaac Newton had distributed his universal laws of motion, William Harvey and Andreas Vesalius had scrutinised human anatomy, and Otto von Guericke had invented the electrostatic generator. For writers like von Valvasor, this was the Age of Enlightenment. Which made tales of vampires even more intriguing. They echoed the magical beliefs that were being left behind, but also underlined how much this brazen age had yet to learn.

Downhill from the plaque, under a stone archway, I stepped into a graveyard so beautiful and bright in colours, it seemed like the secret garden in a fairy tale. Beyond the perimeter wall was the forest of

Draga, its trees bursting like giant broccoli over a sky of pure azure. Flowers garlanded every headstone, their petals catching the light from the candles set beneath them. Gold lettering spelled out names and dates, over faces outlined in greyscale. Beauty and death — it was almost a match for the festive graveyards of Mexico. But in this case, it was the very graveyard where, to quote Boris's novel, 'the first recorded case of vampire beheading in the history of our troubled lands had taken place'.

For Boris, this was vampirism's ground zero. In *Vampir*, a modern-day private investigator roams around Zagreb, following a trail of clues in search of the original seventeenth-century vampire, Jure Grando, which lead him inevitably to Kringa. The deeper he wades into the case, the more corruption and foul play swirls around him: murdered prostitutes, tampered medical testing, strange behaviour in a sanatorium.

'It's about capital,' Boris explained. 'The exploitation and corruption under the surface of society. Of course, this is nothing new — many of the classic vampire stories are about the breakdown of borders and empires.' He pointed out that some of the enduring themes in the most famous of all vampire tales, Bram Stoker's *Dracula*, include then-modern concerns. Fears of racial and sexual pollution shadow Stoker's 1897 classic, dramatised not only in the movement of a bloodsucking foreigner to England but also in the vampirisation of his victim Lucy, who receives blood from four different men (three of whom have already proposed marriage to her). Like Stoker, Boris drew on the anxieties and hidden desires of his milieu — the selling of blood through black-market operations, the rise of drug addiction, anxieties around migration, the sexual exploitation of a photographer's model. Contemporary fears: but they fit the old tale, following a line back through Stoker to the old vampire story from Kringa. After all, as Boris explained, the old story was deeply tied to the anxieties of its age.

'I've been to Kringa many times,' he said. 'Let me tell you what I learned.'

Glugging his Staropramen in the café in Zagreb, he ordered another and swept the air with his cigarette:

'I learned that these are old beliefs. There were people I talked to, older people. They were uncomfortable about these stories, they didn't like that I was researching them. They remembered the legend, from being told it by their grandparents, and they didn't like to talk about it.'

In Istria, there is a tradition of vampires — a 'strigon' in the local dialect — and also the 'krsnik', shamans who are able to defeat them (that old mirroring of evil spirits and exorcists we encountered in Japan). 'The legends say that the vampire was a living being who did evil through his lifetime, and he was born under certain circumstances that made him a vampire. There are different ideas about this. For example, they say if the placenta of a newborn baby is black, they will become a vampire.' Assembling the various strands of local folklore, Boris searched around Kringa, looking for traces of Grando. On the outskirts of the village, he found a pile of Istrian stone inscribed with the name 'Grando Stantsiya'. 'This means a house, a property with fields, gardens, cattle. The Grandos were a wealthy family. Perhaps they were not very popular in the town of Kringa, perhaps they were too wealthy.' Reading between the lines in von Valvasor's account, Boris gleaned a tale of complicated local politics:

'Kringa used to be a significant town. It had a fortress, surrounded by walls and towers. But they collapsed in the seventeenth century, during a war between the Austrians and Venetians. They didn't fight each other directly, they set the local communities against each other, and Kringa was ruined. This is how the cemetery was built — the walls of the fortress were used to build the terrace.'

The conflict was known as the Uskok War, after the pirates on the Dalmatian Coast, mercenaries co-opted by the Austrians in their battle for supremacy with Venice. Slovenes, Spaniards, even English troops were pulled into the fracas, cannons fired from sea and land, fortresses besieged, villages plundered. The result: fever spread, so did famine, and in their misery people sought a scapegoat.

'Personally,' said Boris, 'I call it political propaganda. Remember, the one who led the villagers was Raditić the mayor. He took the credit for defeating the vampire, and he had a stronger position after Grando's killing.'

As for the Grando family, the name can still be found, Boris told me, in several villages fifteen miles from Kringa, but not in Kringa itself:

'Either the family died out, or they left in shame to make a new life for themselves.'

THE DARK SIDE OF ENLIGHTENMENT

Demonic bloodsuckers go all the way back. We can line up Lilith, apocryphal ex-wife to Adam, demon queen, and sucker of babies' blood, alongside the blood-drunk Sekhmet of ancient Egypt, the vetala of Indian folklore, the undead draugur of the Icelandic sagas and walking corpses reported in twelfth century England. But none combine the full set of qualities we expect from vampires today: previous human existence, occupation of a burial-place, appetite for blood, allergy to daylight, and susceptibility to wooden stakes or symbols of religious orthodoxy.

'In this century, a new scene has been presented to our view, for about sixty years past ...' wrote the French monk Dom Augustin Calmet in 1746: 'it is common, we are told, to see men, who have been dead several years or, at least, several months, come again, walk about, infest villages, torment men and cattle, suck the blood of their relatives, throw them into disorders, and, at last, occasion their death ... It is certain that nothing of this sort was ever seen or known in antiquity.' As Calmet wrote, 'the name by which they are known is that of oupires, or vampires.'

Mention vampires and the mind goes straight to Transylvania. But the soil that nourished the stories — and, so it's said, several undead bodies — is a little to the west. To quote the folklorist Alan Dundes, 'the first occurrences of the term vampire in European languages all refer to the Slavic superstitions; the wide dissemination of the term and its extensive use in the vernacular follows the outburst of vampirism in Serbia.' Jure Grando may have been the starting point, but over the ensuing decades it was on the other side of the Danube and Drina that the most significant episodes occurred: a series of mysterious deaths sending shockwaves back to the imperial court in Vienna, a phenomenon that became known as 'the vampire craze'.

In 1725, in the Serbian town of Kisiljevo, a man called Petar Blagojević had reportedly risen from the dead and murdered nine of his neighbours; an account was published in the *Wiennerisches Diarium* that July. Although other cases had been recorded in earlier years,* it was the Serbian cases that penetrated the murky barrier between Europe's east and west, aligning with the ever-expanding reach of the printing press to spread the 'vampire' across the continent.

The most significant episode (as far as the vampire's trans-European reach was concerned) took place in the Serbian village of Medveđa in 1731. A former hajduk (an irregular soldier), Arnaud Paole, had recently come back from border skirmishes in Kosovo. He was killed by the accidental overturning of his hay-cart, but forty days later, local people claimed he had risen from the dead and started attacking them. Before his demise, he had spoken of being bitten by a Turkish vampire in Kosovo, and this was assumed to explain his reawakening.

In the shadow of the Paole case, commissioners representing the Habsburg Empire were sent east. The subsequent reports were so

---

* As well as von Valvasor's account of Jure Grando, the English diplomat Paul Rycaut described Greek and Armenian revenants in 1679 ('they feed in the night, walk, digest, and are nourished, and have been found ruddy in complexion'); cases in Poland and Russia were mentioned in the French publication *Mercure Galant* in 1693 and 1694; and in 1718, Louis XV's botanist, Joseph Pitton de Tournefort, described the disembowelment and cremation of a revenant in Greece.

lurid, they were quickly translated into multiple languages, and it was from these accounts that the word 'vampire' entered the lexicon of Western Europe. The first English use of the word appeared in the 11 March 1732 edition of *The Illustrated London News*. Within a couple of months, accounts had also been published in *The Gentleman's Magazine* and *Applebee's Original Weekly Journal*.

Here is Sergeant Johann Flückinger, reporting to the Belgrade High Command on 26 January 1732: 'As they saw that [Paole] was a real vampire, they drove a stake through his heart as was their habit, during which he ... bled a great deal of blood. Whereupon they burned the corpse to ashes the same day and threw them into the grave.' Whoever Paole had killed might become vampires too, so their corpses were dealt with in the same way. Not only were they burned, Flückinger recorded, but 'the heads of the vampires were struck down by the local gypsies and the corpses were cremated, their ashes thrown into the Morava River'. Even this wasn't enough. 'They also add,' Flückinger continued, 'that this Arnold [Arnaud] Paole attacked not only the people but also the cattle and sucked their blood.'

When even their meat could turn them into vampires, what hope was there? In a three-month period, seventeen fatalities were attributed to vampirism, several 'without having previously had an illness'. Individual cases enable us to reckon with the human cost of the craze and offer grisly reading. Take Miliza, a sixty-year-old woman who died after eating infected mutton. Her grave was opened, revealing 'much liquid blood' in the breast, according to Flückinger: 'the remaining viscera were in good condition ... During the dissection, all the surrounding *hajduks* were very surprised about her fat and perfect body, unanimously saying that they knew the woman from their youth, and all her life she looked thin and desolate ... that she had reached this astonishing plumpness in the grave.'

Investigating alongside Flückinger was a medical officer called Glaser, a specialist in contagious diseases. His report was sent to Vienna's Collegium Sanitatis and to his father, who was also a physician. Glaser Senior described these events for the new medical weekly *Commercium Litterarium*, although in language conspicuously less scientific than his son's: 'A magical plague has been rampant there for some time,' he wrote. 'Perfectly normal buried people are rising from their undisturbed graves to kill the living.'

The corpus of documentation was swelling like the bloated skins of the so-called vampires, leading to attention from the highest ranks. In the wake of the Paole case, the commander of the Austrian army in the Balkans, Duke Karl Alexander, turned his attention to vampires, and on a trip to Prussia he presented a copy of Flückinger's report to King Wilhelm I, who ordered the Royal Prussian Scientific Society to investigate. They were sceptical, pointing out that 'we have found no traces of it in history' and concluding that 'no coherent conclusion can be drawn about the vampire creation, for the first phenomenon measured has natural causes, but the [rotting] smell and the [creaking] sound [of the buried corpses] may have happened because of the air that had erupted in the cavity of the heart'.

Scientific scepticism, however, runs a slow second behind the broadcasting power of bloodcurdling storytelling. The secret was out, and these new-old Balkan monsters were penetrating Western Europe faster than the high-society fad for velvet beauty spots. In periodicals published across the continent, the Serbian vampire outbreak became one of the most popular subjects, leading the French satirist Voltaire to comment that, 'From 1730 till 1735 nothing was heard of more than vampires. They were waylaid, their hearts torn out, and they were burned.' Vampires were being discussed not only in coffee shops and literary salons, but at the highest levels of government. King Louis XV of France commissioned his special envoy in Vienna, the Duke of Richelieu, to report on the deaths; while George II of Great Britain held an 'implicit faith in the German notion of vampires'. According to the prime minister's son, the writer Horace Walpole, the king 'has more than once been angry with my father for speaking irreverently of those imaginary bloodsuckers'.

So glamorous was the vampire grip that Western Europe became the dominant field of operations. It's telling that Walpole associated vampires with Germany rather than their point of origin. More than a century later, Bram Stoker would set his earliest draft of *Dracula* in the Styrian Mountains of Austria. But in the Balkans, a less exoticised and less eroticised folklore continued to develop, intimately connected with ordinary life in the region's villages.

One of these tales had fascinated me when I read it in translation: a novella by the Serbian writer Milovan Glišić, *After Ninety Years*, published in 1880 and inspired by events reported from a village on the Serbian–Bosnian frontier in the eighteenth century. Over the course of many retellings, the vampire said to haunt this village had become Serbia's most iconic bloodsucker, featuring not only in Glišić's novella but also in a much-loved horror movie in the 1970s, *Lepterica* ('The She-Butterfly'), and an award-winning novel published in the twenty-first century, Mirjana Novaković's *Fear and His Servant*. Sava Savanović may have been staked out of existence long ago, according to the legend, but his haunting place was still intact. Although only just. When the roof collapsed in 2012, a tongue-in-cheek warning was issued by the local authorities: the vampire was on the move.

Like the ill-fated Lucy in *Dracula*, I couldn't resist the lure of the bloodsucker. I crossed the border from Zagreb and climbed into a bus in Belgrade, rolling under karst mountains where the ash-coloured cliffs poked out like the angular features of vampiric giants, bearded with spruce and juniper pine. This isn't travel-writing hyperbole — it's local folklore. I was heading for a valley where the overhanging mountains have been named for the fangs of a giant vampire. My adventure in this neglected hinterland would involve butterflies, a river mill, and a night of what I can honestly describe as sheer terror.

FRIGHT NIGHT

Straight off the bus and I was already facing the dead. A handsome-looking old lady, a bullet-headed man. They were peering behind a vegetable patch and tufts of grass tall enough to make hay, their faces outlined on a pair of marble headstones. The bus out of Belgrade had been packed; but here, ninety miles south, I was the only one to disembark. The road snaked into heat haze and a wispy flourishing of forest.

Zarožje — the village from the tale — wasn't much to speak of: a garage, a couple of cafés, a sprawl of homesteads fenced off with chicken wire. At one of the cafés, men were sitting under a veranda with glasses of rakija, occasionally tapping their fingers on the local paper. One of them made a stab at conversation, but there's only so far you can go when the scruffy-looking outsider hasn't even a dozen words in your language. Another put a couple of plums on the table before me. I asked him about the mill. He clawed his hands and bared his teeth, a pantomimic grimace.

'Sava Sa...vanović!'

He was imitating the macabre figure depicted inside the café, on an advert for a locally brewed rakija — Serbia's most famous vampire advertising its national drink.

'The mill — going there — easy?'

He narrowed his eyes: '*Povratak je teži* — coming back is harder.'

The best part of a day would have to pass before I understood what he'd meant.

Apples glistened on overhead branches, juice sliding out of cracks in their skin. Blackberries and elderberries reflected the sunlight, embedded in the brambles like jewels. Passing a shrine with a hose hanging under an icon of the holy family, I doused myself in spring-water; then carried on past a vineyard and the occasional homestead. Every house had its own vegetable patch, and its own graveyard — a cluster of headstones at the edge of the garden, shiny red peppers and green zucchinis counterbalanced by the grimness of grey slate and illustrated marble. It was a feature of the area — the dearly departed laid in family plots, rather than a communal graveyard. It means the dead are always nearby, in the sight-lines of the living.

The road dived down a corkscrewing dirt track where the forest had been pared back, oak and hornbeam hemmed around homesteads and pasture fields. The tree-line loomed above the limestone cliffs of a gorge. Great pointed boulders clawed at the sky ('rog' in Serbian, from which comes Zarožje — 'the place behind the horns'), traditional climbing targets for daredevil youths. According to local folklore, these are the fangs of a giant vampire turned to stone by the Serbian patron saint, Sava; whose name, in the way of monster lore, had been twisted back, doubled into the local vampire's: Sava Savanović.

Flies smudged the air like thumbprints on a painting. Shafts of light poked between the trees. Butterflies somersaulted inside them, as if they were auditioning for the circus in Pixar's *A Bug's Life*: yellow-banded skippers, poplar admirals, and varieties that neither I nor Google Lens could name. I remembered the end of the tale: Savanović staked in his coffin, his lips parting to let out a butterfly, the incarnation of the vampire's spirit. There's science behind this piece of folklore — butterflies are attracted to rotting corpses (photographers often use animal flesh to lure them), uncoiling their proboscises to slurp the salts and amino acids found there. With the storytelling in mind, I kept my mouth closed, swatting at the lepidoptera whenever they drifted near.

I had my feet halfway inside the story — the butterfly, the gorge, and now the river Rogačica ('the little horn stream'), throbbing ever louder in my ears. Below a whitewashed Orthodox chapel, the road plunged to a bridge, where I hailed a couple of bikers, their faces hidden by visored helmets. A stony path dropped behind them, sinking through flowers and thick grass towards a wooden building squatting over the rush of water. Climbing down to the bank, I pulled off my shoes and socks. The water frothed like shampoo, bursting between a pair of mossy rocks, making my toes disappear. It was marvellously refreshing.

Above me was the mill: box-shaped with a slanted roof, patched up with concrete posts but originating from the eighteenth century. Its man-made construction stood out against the forest like the magic cottage in a fairy tale. A sanctuary, or a chamber of secrets. In this tale, it's a death-trap but also a trump card. By surviving his night of terror, Strahinja discovers the vampire's secret, and the chance to marry his beloved Radojka.

Inside, two bluntly grooved millstones rested against the wooden slats of the wall; the high roof arched over the grinding hopper and the spindle onto which the stones would be lifted. A garlic bulb had been left on the hopper's edge, and a hawthorn stake rested against one of the posts. Nearly everything you need to fight a vampire.

'What are you doing here?'

One of the bikers had stepped across the threshold. Stripped of his racing suit, he was now bare-chested, a muscular figure in combat trousers. The question was so direct, it felt like a challenge. As I took in his sinewy physique, his shaven skull, and square jaw, I couldn't help thinking of Serbian squaddies in war reports from the nineties. But as soon as we started talking, the cliché evaporated. We were just a couple of guys sharing the thrill of this strange, beautiful place. He was here with his girlfriend — his name was Miroslav, hers Yasmina.

'We live across the valley, but we've never been here before,' Miroslav explained, while Yasmina offered a bag of crumbled Domaćica biscuits. 'We thought of coming before, many times, but ...'

'The vampire?'

'It's a spooky place, huh? That's why we're here in the daytime.'

They weren't sticking around, but I wished they would. Miroslav asked me to take some photos and they posed around the mill, holding up the hawthorn stake, modelling themselves as vampire-hunters to entertain their friends on social media; but they had more hills to ride before nightfall.

'Give yourself plenty of time to walk up to the village,' warned Miroslav. 'It's a steep climb back, and you don't want to do it in the dark.'

During the course of the afternoon, there were others — a couple of guys who sat on the rocks with beer cans; two grandparents with a child. The grandfather greeted me, rattling through a narration that I slowly realised was the tale of Sava Savanović. Although I couldn't follow his speech, I felt soothed by the flow of story, matching the turns of the plot to his granddaughter's widening eyes. *Stay a little longer, oh please stay.* But human visits were fleeting, even more than the butterflies. When they were gone, I listened out for birdsong. Even that was fading, giving way to a nauseous silence.

One by one, the features around me were snuffed out: the bridge, the rocks where I'd washed my feet, the river, finally the mill. The only enduring sound was the churning of the water over the rocks, splashing and frothing between the fallen branches. Otherwise, the sounds were new — or, perhaps, I hadn't been listening out for them: the rustling on the other bank, the scratching and shifting of leaves in the undergrowth. When I stepped on a scree of pebbles, there was a comical plopping in the water. Silence fanned around me like a nervous intake of breath; then an explosion of scraping sounds under the trees. I backed up the slope above the river, and as the last of the light shrank between the trees, I pulled myself inside the mill.

'Please God,' I wrote in my diary, 'let me pass through the night in peace.'

At half past eight — deadly dark by now — the valley filled with a blaring of engines. Through the crack of the door, I could see headlamps flashing on the bridge. Bikers? The floor of the mill was scattered with bottle caps and cigarette butts. I imagined night-prowlers, Satanists, some Balkan version of the Lost Boys. I feared how they might react to a lone foreigner in their den. But on they rode, engines gunning, motors grinding up the hill. Relief poured out like a leaking of my veins. Nervous as I was of wild animals, of creatures crawling out of the dark, of the wolves and bears successfully reintroduced into the Povlen mountains in recent years, there was nothing I feared so much as humans.

Still, the sounds of nature were scraping at my nerves. What was that whining in the ceiling? A bat? Hardly a comforting thought when your mind's full of vampires. No ... it was high-pitched, but too repetitive. I zoomed in on the sound, trying to make the cheeping tangible, to separate it from the spectres in my imagination. A sparrow chick, perhaps, trapped in the roof of the mill.

Fatigue was making my body limp. I rested my back against the bed-stone, shuddering when it banged at the wall. Sleep wasn't on the cards tonight. Who'd even want to sleep in a place like this? Better to sit it out, and move off at the first glimmer of light.

At last, that moment came. It was 4.00 am, dawn a pale promise on the crest of the gorge. I'd lasted eight hours of dark — surely that counted for enough? I tiptoed out of the hut and climbed up to the bridge. The sky was as clear as a star chart. Orion was drawing his bow, and the Plough looked as if it was ready to scoop up the Pole Star. Shooting stars dived through the sky, scratches of gold against velvety black. Looking up at that spectacle of light, I felt a swelling inside me. I bounded forward, throbbing with the joy of being alive (or, at least, not undead).

But I wasn't out of the woods yet — in every sense. Rustling in the trees; worse still, the snarling of dogs. Alerted by unfamiliar steps too early in the day, the growls developed into a volley of barks, picked up by other dogs, turning into a mob chant of canine accusation. I thought of Strahinja in the tale, chased by Dushman's hounds; and blinked out nightmare visions of being dragged, bloody and mangled, into some angry farmer's front room. 'The way back is harder,' I'd been told. That guy was right, but at least it was a matter of gradient, and nothing more sinister. At last: a tarred road under a canopy of hornbeam. Beyond the trees, Zarožje's cluster of buildings spread around the main road, promising a way out.

Nobody was around. I sat on a wall, relieved to take off my backpack. For several minutes, my only company was a pair of butterflies. They were dancing around each other above a tuft of grass, like ballerinas trying out their moves in the rehearsal room. I watched them from the wall, a little less repelled with each passing moment, while I waited for the day's only bus.

An elderly woman in a patched gown and headscarf shuffled over to the garage, a tracksuited teenager carrying a rucksack beside her. The arrival of the bus prompted an urgent hug. From my seat inside, I could see the woman waving a handkerchief in emotional farewell. Sunlight flashed on the tears rolling down her cheeks, like a cascade of pearls.

Here was a reminder, here in a place associated with death and the macabre, that ordinary lives were being lived, people were being loved. And isn't that the beating heart of the story of Sava Savanović? Not the undead miller with his bloated cheeks and linen shroud, but Strahinja and Radojka — two lovers yearning for a life together, away from the creepy spectre of a bloodsucker. Vampires may be bringers of death, but good stories remind us why we want to live.

THE CRAZE MUST END!

This is what my night at the mill taught me: you think you're rational, you don't believe in vampires, but your incredulity will be tested when you're alone in the dark. I never believed a vampire would come to puncture my flesh, but I wasn't sure that nothing would. To the Viennese officials of the Enlightenment, the Balkans must have seemed like Sava Savanović's mill did to me that night: a place where anything might happen, every valley uncanny, every mountain a stronghold for spectres.

But the Habsburg Empress Maria Theresa, safe among her wall hangings and her lyre-shaped crystal chandeliers, never sat in a dark mill. And as far as she was concerned, enough was enough. It wasn't just the stories of hajduks and villagers east of Belgrade. Like a contagious disease, the stories were drawing uncomfortably close. Reports emerged of vampire killings in the Banat, Moravia, and Wallachia. In

Paris, there were riots when a rumour spread that children were being seized from the streets so that ailing aristocrats could be revitalised by their blood. Gossipers passed the story that Princess Eleonore von Schwarzenberg, who had died in Vienna in 1741, had risen from the dead as a vampire. With each passing year, the vampire craze was widening its sphere of operations. When a female 'vampire' was decapitated and burned on the Moravian–Silesian border, the empress called on her closest advisers. This vampire obsession must end.

The Austrian officials had tried to understand the craze in terms of the science available to them. For the physician Georg Tallar, the symptoms associated with so-called vampires — pallor, sudden death, blood flowing out of long-dead corpses — could be attributed to long winter fasts, imbalanced diets, and anaemia. Others suggested premature burials, plague, or the conditions of the soil; some pointed to clerical corruption (Orthodox priests profiting from the fees for multiple burials) or deferred to local beliefs. Scientific societies queried the reliability of the witnesses' statements, and the empress's personal physician, Gerard van Swieten, dismissed the entire phenomenon: 'All these occurrences are only to be found in areas where ignorance still prevails.'

Issuing an edict on 1 March 1755, the empress complained that 'some of our country's inhabitants go so far in their credulity as to take what a dream or imagination presents to them, or what is presented to them by other fraudulent people ...' Therefore, 'such sinful customs are not to be allowed in our states in the future, but rather are to be treated with the most severe penalties ...' And so the mania for digging up bodies, driving wooden stakes through their hearts, and chopping off their heads with hoes was outlawed. 'Enlightenment' prevailed; Austrian rule was fortified. At least, until the Habsburg forces abandoned Serbia to the Ottomans in 1791, a couple of years before the empress's daughter Marie Antoinette had her own head cut off, for very different reasons, courtesy of a French guillotine.

When monsters are snuffed out of everyday fears, storytelling becomes the bottle in which they are stored. Vampires were so current in popular consciousness in the 1760s that Voltaire included a lengthy chapter about them in his *Dictionnaire Philosophique*. They tended to appear 'in Poland, in Hungary, in Silesia, in Moravia', he pointed out, in places distant from the hubs of power. Hence, there had been no vampires sighted 'in London, not even in Paris'; although, the satirist added with his characteristic bite, 'in these two cities there were speculators, tenderers and merchants who sucked the blood of the people in broad daylight; but they were far from dead, rotten though they might be.'

Here was the powerful subtext behind vampirism — the same material that would fuel Bram Stoker's *Dracula* and Boris Perić's *Vampir* — society's rot. Acerbic commentators like Voltaire and the English writer Charles Forman (who lambasted a seventeenth-century tax revenue as a device 'to indulge the luxury, and gratify the rapine, of a fat-gutted vampire') were pioneers of a satirical fad that has rarely gone out of fashion.

'Brokers, Country Bank Directors, and their disciples — all whose hunger and thirst for money ... has preyed on the heart and liver of public confidence, and poisoned the currents of public morals, are they not all Vampyres?' So wrote Uriah Derick D'Arcy in *The Black Vampyre: a legend of St Domingo*, published in 1819, hot on the heels of the British writer-physician John Polidori's *The Vampyre*. D'Arcy's remarkable tale — in which corpses are raised on the island of 'St Domingo' (Haiti) and a court of 'immortal bloodsuckers' joins forces with an army of black slaves in the cause of 'universal emancipation' ('Our fetters discandied, and our chains dissolved') before the vampires are mown down and staked by bayonet-wielding soldiers, 'the whole infernal fraternity securely disposed of' — has been mostly forgotten. But it reflects the popularity of these themes on both sides of the Atlantic in the opening decades of the nineteenth century.

Of all these early narratives, the one that had the greatest impact was Polidori's *The Vampyre*. It was this telling that established the cynical, sensuous vampire as its anti-hero, inspired by the author's former employer, Lord Byron. 'The contribution of this stereotype', as the scholar Christopher Frayling has written, 'was decisive'. Byron had conceived the storyline himself, on the same famous night of storytelling that spawned Mary Shelley's *Frankenstein*; indeed, the popularity of *The Vampyre* was partly due to its being attributed, initially, to the 'mad, bad, and dangerous' poet. Byron had written himself about vampires, a few years earlier, in his 1813 poem 'The Giaour':

> But first, on earth as vampire sent,
> Thy corse shall from its tomb be rent:
> Then ghostly haunt thy native place,
> And suck the blood of all thy race

These early vampire-tellers weren't schlock artists peddling cheap scares for the masses. They were among the most vital and influential voices of their age. In 1797, Johann Wolfgang von Goethe had described a vampire-like revenant in 'The Bride of Corinth'. Samuel Taylor Coleridge's 'Christabel' (conceived in the same year) echoed some of the genre's emerging motifs. They tallied with the necrophiliac obsessions and fascination for the past pouring like poisonous blood through the veins of Romantic literature. By harnessing the vampire as a spirit of the past, Byron and his ilk were expressing the spirit of the present: the zeitgeist.

Later in the nineteenth century, that power had decayed, and vampires were being mobilised for penny dreadfuls like *Varney the Vampire* (serialised from 1845–47) and Sheridan Le Fanu's popular serial *Carmilla* (1872), which put the lesbian vampire trope on the map ('with gloating eyes she drew me to her, and her hot lips travelled along my cheek in kisses ...'). All these versions would be bleached into near invisibility in 1897, however, with the publication of Bram Stoker's *Dracula*.

It was a question of timing. The British publishing industry was in full swing, the popular taste for morbid tales at its peak, and the story mixed exotic Eastern European settings with a milieu familiar to its educated Victorian readership. Everything that followed would do so in *Dracula*'s slipstream. For all the variety and ingenuity of the many earlier vampire stories, it was in the wily Romanian count that vampirism found its definitive form. From Count Duckula to the Muppets' Count von Count to Mavis's dad in *Hotel Transylvania*, there's no monster more easily lampooned. Polidori's *Vampyre* had established the Byronic, upper-class, sexually predatory vampire trope. In the wake of *Dracula*, there was no going back: vampires, in the Western imagination, became the snobs of monsterkind, sneering at the riff-raff below. And their association with the Balkans was blurred. Appropriately enough, for a story that begins with a question of land sale (Count Dracula enlisting young solicitor Jonathan Harker to negotiate his property portfolio in England), Stoker's novel installed Transylvania as vampire lore's primary real estate. But in the Balkans, the old stories were never forgotten. They continued to be told, continued to provide fantastical outlets for exploring the traumatic pathway between the living and the dead.

THE BORDER OF UNKNOWING

To learn more about the storytelling the craze inspired, I travelled north. Along the highway from Zarožje, down from the karst cliffs and furred peaks of the Dinaric Alps, across the Pannonian Plain between ripples of sunflowers and fields of wheat. A landscape of sharp edges and bright colours, teasing the imagination with vampiric possibility.

The Petrovaradin Fortress preens over the Danube like a shelf of viennoiserie in a baker's shop: a bulwark of mediaeval defensive architecture made-over by the occupying Austrians in the eighteenth century, splashed custard-yellow with a sugar-white clock tower on which the black dials appear like a pair of Oreos. Below the fortress, stucco cherubs and clusters of grapes adorn the pastel-painted house fronts and neo-gothic church façades, bombarding the Old Town of Novi Sad with the rococo confidence of the old occupiers. It feels like 400 miles have been squeezed out and you're magically stepping over the Ringstrasse of Vienna.

I crossed a bridge over the brown Danube and strolled down a pedestrianised parade. Boutique shops and canopied cafés flanked me either side. I'd arranged to meet Mirjana Novaković — a bank clerk by day, who also happens to be one of Serbia's most celebrated authors. She'd suggested one of the cafés, where young couples were sitting under the pavement parasols, tapping their phones between sips of Jelen beer, ignoring the vaping businessmen with their bottles of Bermet, the local vintage favoured centuries ago by the Viennese elite.

Mirjana looked a little more jaded than the cool kids around us. Drawing on a cigarette filter, she glanced across the table, humour bubbling in her sceptical smile, heavy eyelids drooping under a mop of grey hair.

I'd contacted her after reading her spellbinding novel, *Fear and His Servant*. It's a comedy horror, spiky with satire but dripping with atmosphere, revolving around the devil's escapades in eighteenth-century Serbia. Accompanied by a heavy-drinking Serbian sidekick called Novak, the devil embroils himself in the political machinations of the Austrian occupation, crossing paths with real-life historical figures such as the military commander Duke Karl Alexander, and investigating the old tale of a vampire haunting a mill by the river. There are costumed balls, discussions about the pleasures of art and the meaning of mortality, renditions of Serbian epic poetry, an encounter with vampires in a Belgrade cistern, and a scene in which Sava Savanović is stabbed in his coffin. As with Milovan Glišić's tale, a butterfly escapes with the vampire's dying sigh.

'I like Glišić's story,' explained Mirjana. 'It's actually a very funny story. There is a lot of humour in it about rural life, and I wanted to use this horror genre, the suspense and fear when you have to sleep at the mill.'

I thought of my own night at the mill. An involuntary shudder from me, a smile from Mirjana. She'd found her way into the subject after reading *How to Quiet a Vampire*, a 1977 novel by the political agitant Borislav Pekić. In the course of his narrative about a mediaeval scholar who used to be a Gestapo officer, referencing Nietzsche, Freud, and Saint Augustine along the way, Pekić pointed out that 'vampire' is the only significant Serbian word used around the world.

'Isn't that an interesting thought? The only word we have given to the world — and it is this one! And the more I looked into it, the more it seemed important: the story about the vampires and the Austrian Commission, how Europe came in contact for the first time with these kinds of stories, a hundred and fifty years before Bram Stoker. And the next idea I got was why not put the devil in it? So I had this story of the Serbs and the Austrians, vampires and the devil, and it went from there.'

The novel had been translated into several languages, including English, Arabic, and Russian, and awarded one of Serbia's top literary prizes.

'Well,' said Mirjana, self-deprecatingly, 'people like vampires, don't they? The otherworldly ...'

But she also wanted to emphasise the real-world situation out of which she'd carved her story:

'It was the late 1990s when I was writing it. There were bombings in Belgrade, there were refugees coming in from the fighting in Bosnia, there was war going on around us. I remember I was working in the bank when a woman came in. She was shaking. She had been at a wake. The dead woman had suddenly risen and said, "The bombing will end in ten days." Then she had lain down dead. Maybe it's just a crazy story, but the point is that people on the other side know things we don't. These ideas are still alive, people still believe them. This is why vampires mean something. I think they are a version of the most important border you can cross, the border into what we don't know.'

Listening to Mirjana, I thought of another writer, across another border: Boris Perić talking about the villagers of Kringa, their fear of vampire tales, their discomfort with the legend. As long as the stories make people squirm, they're still alive.

High heels click-clacking on the cobbles; mobile phone ringtones blasting the air with snatches of turbo-rap; roars of greetings and bellowed laughter: the sound caul over our morbid mutterings. Mirjana sipped her coffee and outlined the plot for the new novel she was working on, about a flamboyant Serbian spy from World War II. But the spectre of vampires lingered, like the smoke drifting over our heads.

As I walked through the darkening streets to the bus stop, I could feel it, pressing against me, in the gravestones peeking through the iron bars of a churchyard, in a death notice pasted onto a shop shutter, in the old man bent nearly double, hacking into a crack in the pavement, eyes discoloured under the glare of a lamppost. For a moment, I was in the pages of Mirjana's novel, peering through the darkness at the coach carrying the devil, and back in the mill, arms around my wincing heart, praying for dawn. I blinked against the light, shifted my backpack over my shoulders, and made my way to the bus.

Vampires, like ghosts, enable us to play around with death and the life beyond. Science may not have discovered any sign of life beyond our mortality, but doubts remain (questions over consciousness, for example, and how to define it), vents in human knowledge through which imaginations are able to breathe. Which is why monsters of the dead span the globe — counterparts to the myths spun by the world's religions.

So now for a twist on this theme. This one takes us to a different kind of revenant (indeed, it asks if they are revenants — returning dead — at all). It also connects to one of the most significant uprisings in history, albeit one that has long been overlooked. If ghosts and vampires tend to be willing agents, preying on their victims by choice (at least in the traditional tales), there are other monsters, far less eager to be hauled out of their graves, forced to toil for sorcerers of the dark arts.

CHAPTER NINE

Revolution of the Undead

THE NINTH TALE

Under the jagged mountains, over tangled jungle and vast fields of sugar cane, night has fallen. By the light of the lantern, the bokor — the priest who deals in magic — stands beside an open grave. In one hand he holds a whip, in the other a govi jar, containing a potion to raise the dead.

'Hurry!'

Silently, his minions dig into the soil and pull up a body, wrapped in a white shroud. Under the cadaver's nose, the bokor passes the jar. The corpse's eyes flash open, breath wheezes out of his lips in long creaking sighs. He is alive — in the physical sense at least.

'You work for me now,' says the bokor. 'Come on, zonbi, there's plenty to do!'

With a rope attached to the man's shroud, he leads him out of the cemetery, his labourers following behind.

Across the dark plain they walk until they reach his lakou, the compound where his family lives. There, the new zombie is pushed into the sleeping shack to lie, silent, alongside the others. In the light of morning, the bokor performs his spells, forms a vèvè cross out of cornmeal in front of the temple where his prayers are performed, and initiates the new zombie in his retinue.

'Make sure there's no salt in the broth,' he tells his wife.

She steps forward to feed the slaves. She tries not to think about them, about their lives before the mysterious illnesses that snatched them away, about how they were deposited in their graves then reawakened after the mourners had left the cemetery. Oh, she tries — but sometimes she feels for these silent creatures, and wonders how she might soften the unholy pain of their existence.

'I'm off to the cockfight,' her husband tells her next day. 'Mind you watch the zonbis, there'll be work to do as soon as I'm back.'

'But what about the fair?' she says. 'All those cloths for sale — didn't you say you wanted me to make some new clothes?'

'Very well. Take the zonbis with you, they can carry the cloths. But mind you follow my rules. Bring them back as soon as you've bought everything.'

All the colours of the fair! The bokor's wife inhales the smells from the snack stalls — all those sweetened plantains and pork eggrolls and sugar-dusted beignets — and tussles with the vendors over the prices of the cloths, coming away with a stack of materials. She'll be able to sew herself a new karabela dress and a gown for the bokor. But under their heavy burdens, the zonbis are a pitiful sight. With all the laughter ringing around her, it doesn't seem right to lead them away without a treat. Surely a nibble of plantain wouldn't do any harm? She buys a bunch and distributes them.

'There,' she says, 'that should keep you going.'

But no sooner have the zombies tasted the salt than a change ripples through them. That hallucinatory glow fades from their eyes. In its place, *she can see real human eyes, swivelling and staring with the dawning realisation of what has happened. They throw down the cloths and open their mouths, letting out anguished groans and cries.*

'Come on, zonbis!' She raises up the sisal whip to keep them in line. 'Pick up the cloths! We need to get back.'

But those faces are creased with fury. She flinches from their hands as they reach down to strike her. Peeking out from the shelter of a vendor's cart, she watches them lurching, life coursing back into their veins. Against the red sky, they form a dark chain, limbs jerking as they learn to control them again, a group of men dwarfed by the mountains soaring overhead.

Some are seen, so people say, burrowing back into the very graves from which the bokor disgorged them. But others have disappeared, and occasionally there is talk of a lonely figure, mumbling in a marketplace, struggling to remember where he came from or what terrible crime he committed to end up in this state. People shudder when they see these pitiful figures, and ask each other:

'Is that a zombie? Is it a living person — or a walking corpse?'

DEAD MEN FIGHTING

Living cadavers labouring for their overlords: so it was for the slaves of Saint-Domingue (now Haiti), the Caribbean island where the story of the zombie developed. In the folk tales, the zombies are freed by the taste of salt or sugar, the spells cast by their masters broken, and they come together to turn the tables on their oppressors, or shamble across the plains to the freedom and dignity of their graves. This is a folk tale, but it's also an imaginative retelling of history. As the great Haitian writer René Depestre put it: 'The history of colonisation is the process of man's general zombification.'

Monsters may be fictions, but how often does that tell the whole story? Just as the vampire broke out of the occupied Balkans, something comparable happened, a few decades later, in the Caribbean: the idea of the zombie, rooted in West African mythology, inspired dark stories of the undead, passed around the lakous or homesteads of rural Haiti before being transported across the sea, evolving into the cliché of Hollywood movies and emerging, in the words of cultural historian Roger Luckhurst, as 'the dominant figure of the undead in the twenty-first century'.

Let us start with what we know: the misery of the Africans transported to a rocky island of marshes and jungles, mountains and plains, 4,000 miles from home. When France established its colony of Saint-Domingue in the course of the 1600s, white labourers outnumbered black. But over the subsequent century, as sweet sugar flavoured the desserts and drinks of the well-to-do, a million Africans were shipped over to work the plantations. By 1781, the colony had more than eleven black people for every white person, and was exporting more sugar and coffee than anywhere else in the world.

'The sun beat straight down on their heads,' wrote an eighteenth-century French naturalist called Justin Girod-Chantrans, 'sweat ran from all parts of their hides. Their arms and legs, worn out by excessive heat, by the weight of their picks, and by the resistance of the clayey soil become so hardened that it broke their tools ... A dead silence reigned among them. In their faces, one could see the human suffering and pain they endured, but the time for rest had not yet come.'

For many slaves, conditions could be even worse. They were flayed with whips, forced to wear tin muzzles if they were caught eating cane, buried alive, crucified on planks, roasted on open fires, dropped into cauldrons of boiling cane syrup, coated in sugar to draw the flies, had burning logs rammed between their legs, their anuses filled with gunpowder and set alight, were lashed to stakes in swamps to be devoured by mosquitoes, rolled down mountainsides in barrels studded with spikes. Under these conditions, the birth rate failed to rise above a pitiful 1 per cent. Many took their own lives, and few desired to bring new ones into such torrid conditions. 'Last night,' recorded an eighteenth-century slave-owner, a Monsieur de Gallifet, 'a slave choked himself to death with his tongue while his master was having him whipped. This happens quite often, as there are slaves who are desperate enough to kill themselves in order to inflict loss upon their masters.'

From this perspective, slaves are not people: not for their masters, not when economic prosperity depends on their abjection. They are monsters — 'savage people, habituated to the barbarities of Africa', as one slaver expressed it. So narrow was the planters' focus — fixated on profits, whining about the heat and the insects, grumbling about the social scene — they only stopped to notice what life was like for the slaves when they were complaining about conditions for themselves.

'From morning to night,' one French planter moaned, 'wherever we turn, their faces meet our eyes ... Add to this the fact that our conversation has almost entirely to do with the health of our slaves, their needs which must be cared for, the manner in which they are to be distributed about the estate, or their attempts at revolt, and you will come to understand that our entire life is so closely identified with that of these unfortunates that, in the end, it is the same as theirs.'

Equality for all: so proclaimed the revolutionaries of France. Their arguments, their speeches and pamphlets, made it out to the colonies, where they were distributed among the plantations and the people working in the towns. But if freedom is something you're keen to restrict, it's probably best not to broadcast the literature. Toussaint Louverture, the revolutionary leader, read widely in French literature, and not only did other leaders of the Haitian Revolution, but so did many of their foot soldiers.* And when it came to storytelling, there was a mingling of ideas in both directions.

---

*   According to a 1799 feature in the French newspaper *La Gazette Nationale*, it was reading the writings of the Abbé de Raynal that kindled Louverture's 'enthusiasm for general liberty. He often had his eyes on that page where Raynal seems to announce the liberator who would tear off the shackles of a large part of the human race'. An insurgent captured in 1791 was found with a Vodou fetish around his neck, while his pockets contained 'pamphlets printed in France, filled with commonplaces about the Rights of Man'.

*

On 14 August 1791, more than 200 slaves gathered at a ceremony in the wood known as Bois Caïman. Led by a Vodou priest called Dutty Boukman, they shared their grievances and vowed to fight for their freedom. 'Throw away the image of the God of the whites who thirsts for our tears,' declared Boukman. 'Listen to the liberty that speaks in all our hearts.' The priestess Cécile Fatiman danced, possessed by the spirit of the lwa, the gods of Vodou,* and spread the blood of a black pig among the participants, who swore to kill their overseers and break the chains that had held them so long.

Many factors divided the rebels (among them, languages, tribal and regional affiliations, experiences on different plantations, and the sliding scales between freedmen and slaves), but one unifying force was Vodou. Forbidden by the colonists, resonant of Africa, this ancient code for living glued people together, and the revolution's leaders made canny use of it. As the Haitian sociologist Laënnec Hurbon has written: 'The slaves strove to be reunited with their lost origin, to retrieve the essential components of the African world from which they had been denied.' To the French and their allies, the revolutionary leaders were monsters.† But to a great many of their followers, they were on the other side of the spirit world: shamans and sorcerers, freeing an oppressed people from those who had chained them. Jean-Jacques Dessalines, leading general of the revolution, was considered

---

* The lwa number many hundreds, and they are intermediaries of the supreme creator god of Vodou, Bondye. Damballah is one of the first and most important of them all, credited with using his coils to form the cosmos, and moving between earth and water to generate life.

† Contemporary writings about the revolutionaries are rife with what the historian Marlene L. Daut terms 'monstrous hybridity', in keeping with the period's fascination for the overlap between monsters and humans. To give one example, the Baron de Vastey wrote about the military commander Alexandre Pétion, 'never before has any monster stained himself with the type of crime as horrible as that of which Petion is guilty'.

a houngan (a Vodou priest) and covered himself in magical talismans before going into battle. A reputation for magic was key to his power, which led to him emerging as the first head of state of independent Haiti in 1804. It was said he could make himself invisible to spy on the enemy camp, and transport himself through magic portals. 'Dessalines is coming to the north ...' his troops sang, 'he is bringing new magic. / New magic.'

This aura of supernatural favour was far from unique. One of Dessalines's generals (and later ruler of northern Haiti), Henri Christophe, possessed a talisman that allegedly kept him safe from all weapons except for silver bullets. Another leading fighter, Capois-La-Mort, was said to have his own magical resistance to bullets. At the climactic Battle of Vertières in 1803, his horse was killed, but he carried on charging the French, despite being shot twice through his hat. Stories like this flourished, driven by the unforeseen momentum of the first successful mass slave uprising in world history.

Among all these dramatic figures emerged another, who gained a fearsome reputation in the months after independence. Under Dessalines's orders, white inhabitants of Haiti were rounded up and massacred, 'crime for crime, outrage for outrage', in the governor-general's words. One of the killers was known as Jean Zombi. He was a man 'noted many times for his cruelty', according to the Haitian historian Thomas Madiou, writing in the 1840s. In one incident, Jean Zombi 'left his house full of fury, arrested a white man and stripped him naked. He then led him to the steps of the government palace and plunged a dagger into his breast. This deed horrified all the spectators, as well as Dessalines.'

Those were the tumultuous early days of a nation born out of the torment of slavery, a period that matched the darkness of France's own post-revolutionary Reign of Terror. European powers had sent not only French but also Spanish and British troops against the revolutionaries, and would demand reparations for the plantation owners' financial losses before even the most limited trade deals could be agreed (entailing a cycle of debt from which Haiti has never been freed — another chain to replace the ones that had been broken). Much would be regretted, as successive Haitian leaders fell in the bloodbath, but Jean Zombi remained in the hearts of the people, elevated to the status of a lwa, a divine spirit in the Vodou pantheon. 'The dead-alive Zombi, recalled in the name Jean Zombi,' to quote Joan Dayan's classic work, *Haiti, History, and the Gods*, 'thus became a terrible composite power: slave turned rebel ancestor turned lwa, an incongruous demonic spirit recognised through dreams, divination, or possession.' And the idea of the living dead — remorseless as the men who exacted their revenge on their oppressors, or vacant as the dead-alive slaves toiling for so long in the fields — would resonate throughout the twists and turns of Haiti's national story, ready to be reimagined by each successive generation.

TALES IN THE YARD

Of all the lands I'd marked on my map when I was planning my travels, Haiti was the longest bet. I never made it closer than New Orleans. On my way to hearing tales about the rougarou, I passed by the Vodou stalls of the French Quarter, wandering under skull-faced neon zombies advertising zydeco bars and strip joints. I met an artist on Royal Street, Jared Osterhold, who painted golden-eyed zombies carrying jazz instruments behind the black-clad psychopomp Baron Samedi ('Vodou zombies', he called the lwa's retinue, 'they're very different from the ones you see in Hollywood') and a Vodou mambo (priestess) who sat me down under a painting of the lwa Damballah in her consultation room, fielding phone calls from clients looking for help in their lives while she talked about the fluidity between life and death.

I wasn't going to make it to Haiti, not when the country had been ripped apart, by the president's assassination the previous summer, an earthquake that killed more than 2,000 people and an explosion of chaos that was showing no sign of abating. A few months earlier, all of Haiti's elected officials had left government after repeated failures to hold elections. There had been outbreaks of famine and a resurgence of cholera (first introduced into Haiti in the wake of the devastating 2010 earthquake, when UN peacekeeper troops dumped septic tanks into a river), and the streets were being ruled by powerful gangs whose leaders had names like 'Barbecue' and whose followers were being busted out of the prisons of Port-au-Prince. Following events from New Orleans, I read about the closure of foreign embassies, riots and lynchings, random executions and civilian massacres. Not exactly an auspicious time for an outsider to wander around asking about stories of the living dead.

What I hoped for was a glimpse of Haitian storytelling life. Political chaos — there are plenty of reports on that. But who tells us what it's like to listen to the tales? To sit down and hear about the lougawou (or loup-garou), or the monstrous Diablesse? I might not be able to make it to Haiti, but in the world of zombie lore, national borders have limited powers. Haiti might be out of reach, but Haitians were certainly not — and so I made my way to Fèt Gede, the Haitian Day of the Dead.

A barrel-roofed studio in Brixton, South London: painted skulls and vèvè crosses decorated a cloth-covered altar, and paintings of the lwa hung against the brick walls. Expat Haitians were drumming powerful beats on tanbou drums, dancing in purple and black and sipping beakers of rum. I'd contacted Guilaine Brutus, head of the UK's Haitian Heritage Group, and she'd suggested I come along. That night, people talked of their childhoods on the sunbaked plains, by the sea in towns like Jacmel, or in the crowded bustle of Port-au-Prince. There was Anne, half-Irish, half-Haitian, a social linguist whose grandfather had developed the orthography for Haitian kreyòl (Creole); a guy in a skeleton mask who remembered how 'people would say "stop acting like a zombie" if you were letting someone screw you over'. There was Max, who in between conjuring beats on a drum reminisced about 'sitting around the fire listening to tales — man, some of them were really scary, zonbis, all that sort of thing!'; and Leah Gordon, a British photographer who'd been visiting Haiti over three decades and had directed a powerful documentary weaving the nation's history around the carnival in Jacmel (where, among the horned devils, winged angels, and caricatures of historical figures parading the streets, she'd filmed a group in white shrouds, bound with ropes, play-acting as zombies).

Women in white quadrille dresses, heads ringed in purple bands, their faces transformed to grinning skulls, floated around each other in spidery dance moves, twirling their skull-headed canes to the rhythms of the drums. It was as surreal as Day of the Dead in Mexico, and certainly no evening for bystanding. Tugged into the dancers' circle, I misstepped with my two-left-feet in a storm of rhythmic bodies, my psyche split in a fifty-fifty division between embarrassment and euphoria. Later, I was participating in a call-and-response in kreyòl, sipping rum over discussions about the Haitian Revolution, listening to Aurélie Gerbier, a former employee of Haiti's Ministry of Finance, enthusing about the konts of her childhood — the folk tales of Haiti.

'You'd sit in the backyard, and there were always plenty of mosquitoes,' Aurélie recalled, 'so to get rid of them we made a fire. Or sometimes we'd spray things inside the house, so we had to sit outside for a while. We'd gather around the fire, drink tea or hot chocolate, and what else would you do? You'd listen to an elder telling a kont. Sometimes it was an aunt, or my grandmother, or a neighbour perhaps. But mostly it was my mother — she really loved telling stories.'

The ones Aurélie remembered were tales of transformation and magic, like the story of a shapeshifting fish called Tezen and the girl who falls in love with him, singing to him by the river and escaping her jealous family to live underwater with her magical merman. Zombies too 'are part of our history and culture', Aurélie reflected, recalling how 'some of the stories were really scary.' The magical powers in these stories 'express our Vodou culture. If you go to a river and find a golden comb, you're gonna get rich. Everyone in Haiti knows somebody who went away and came back with power like a Vodou priest.'

Talking to Aurélie and others reminded me that the zonbi tales are part of a wider tapestry. Across the Caribbean, among stories of the trickster Ti Malice and the greedy Uncle Bouki, or the many variations on mermaids, stories of zombies are echoed in different forms — in ghostly duppies, spine-chilling jumbees, and eerie moon-gazers. At a gathering for storytellers, a few weeks earlier in Gloucester, I had met the Anglo-Guyanese storyteller and author Wendy Shearer, who told me about the Lagahoo of Trinidad, a shapeshifter that prowls the night with clanking chains, dragging a coffin behind him. 'Of course these are the chains of slavery,' Wendy pointed out, 'he's attached to the spirit still walking the earth. That trauma is carried down, from generation to generation, and folk tales carry it.' For Wendy, these eerie monsters are told 'to hide the truth and the trauma', expressing the pain that people have endured, but at the same time obscuring that pain behind the comfort blanket of stories. We find this in monster tales all around the world: the magnificent ambiguity of storytelling itself, which exorcises the suffering that feeds it.

PHANTOMS AND PHARMACOLOGY

The stories I heard from Aurélie, Wendy, and others had been handed down orally over the course of centuries, and while specific dates cannot be fixed to them, they shine some light on the rich trove of storytelling that existed in the Caribbean, undocumented but very much alive. When it comes to written, dated sources, we depend upon European texts. The earliest of these is a book published in 1697 by a Frenchman called Pierre-Corneille de Blessebois. Judging by the events of his calamitous life, he was something of a rascal. After libelling most of his acquaintances with provocatively titled works such as *Modesty Extinguished*, jilting his fiancée and trying to sell her to a fellow prisoner, killing a mistress's husband, and assaulting the wife and daughter of a Parisian wigmaker, de Blessebois was shipped off to the Caribbean island of Guadeloupe with orders never to return to France. The book he produced there, *Le Zombi du Grand-Pérou*, is a purportedly autobiographical tale about a lustful Creole countess and an equally lustful marquis, and the 'cunning spirits' the countess deploys to aggravate the latter, in which the author acts as a spell-casting go-between until he is seized by the colonial authorities and thrown into 'the dirtiest and deepest ditch in the castle'.

De Blessebois didn't invent the word 'zombie', nor did he understand it. Whether it comes from the word for a dead person's spirit in Congolese ('nzambi'), a corpse in the Tsogo language of Gabon ('ndzumbi'), or another derivation altogether is a subject of continuing scholarly dispute. What is clear is that its roots were African and it travelled across the Atlantic along with the slaves.

A century after *Le Zombi du Grand-Pérou*, the French naturalist Michel Étienne Descourtilz provided a tantalising glimpse of how zombies were imagined by the slaves themselves. During the revolutionary fighting, he reported, a black soldier on leave had come across his sickly, half-naked mother, marked by signs of venereal disease: 'He repulsed her in saying that this old zombie had never been his mother.' The old woman was left rolling on the ground, biting the earth, and praying for death. She may not have been a supernatural being, but the figurative association is clear enough, and more than de Blessebois's mischievous spirits, Descourtilz's account evokes the tangible figure of the undead the zombie represents today.

These early glimpses of zombie lore may be filtered through the eyes of the Europeans who wrote them down, but 'zombi' appears in odd places among the revolutionaries — in the name of the fighter Jean Zombi, for example, or a rock known as 'La Roche à Zombi', near to which a small body of revolutionaries repelled an 800-strong army of Frenchmen in April 1803. As Haiti settled into its post-revolutionary independence, anxiety around zombie culture manifested in the legal measures taken to restrict them — a reminder that the zombie isn't just a bogeyman in fireside stories but a living phenomenon. A provision in the Haitian Penal Code, made in 1864, prohibited 'the use that may be made against a person of substances which, without causing death, has produced a more-or-less prolonged state of lethargy'. Long before independence, the slave population had been known for its expertise with mysterious substances, and many of the planters feared their ability to inflict fatalities when they served their masters at table.* This interest in pharmacopoeia would continue, aided by the island's rich supply of toxic vegetation and marine life, and during the twentieth century, researchers theorised about the poisons deployed.

Among the case studies that emerged was the story of 'Marie M.', a well-born woman buried in 1909, spotted by a schoolmate five years after she had died, whose opened coffin revealed a different skeleton, in different clothes from Marie's. There was a man in the city of Jacmel, around 1912, found in a catatonic stupor, tied to a tree, identified by the priest who had buried him several days earlier. There was Felicia Felix-Mentor, a young mother and grocer from the village of Ennery, buried in 1907 but said to be alive twenty-nine years later, when a woman going by that name was visited in a hospital in the city of Gonaïves by the American writer Zora Neale Hurston. 'That blank face with the dead eyes,' Hurston wrote. 'There was nothing that you could say to her or get from her except by looking at her, and the sight of this wreckage was too much to endure for long.'

No proof of dark arts surfaced in these cases, and Hurston was ridiculed for her account. But the stories kept coming. In 1919, in the cane-fields of the Haitian American Sugar Company (HASCO), it was said that a headman called Ti Joseph had turned up with 'a band of ragged creatures who shuffled along behind him, staring dumbly, like

---

* Poisons were widely used by the rebel leader François Mackandal during a failed but inspirational insurrection in the 1750s. A French official in Port-de-Paix, Monsieur du Millet, declared: 'This colony is swarming with slaves, so-called soothsayers and sorcerers who poison and who, for a long time, have conceived the plan of insensibly wiping out all the whites.'

people walking in a daze'. This story was recorded by the American author William Seabrook, in his travel book *The Magic Island* (1929). The zombies were unable to give their own names, he wrote. They stood vacant as cattle and were fed on unsalted plantains. But one day, Ti Joseph's wife wanted to attend a festival in a local market, so she took them along and gave them sweets of brown sugar. Salt or sugar, so the folklore says, gives zombies back their understanding. Suddenly the men were alive, crying out in horrified awareness of their post-mortal condition. They ran back across the plain to their graves, clawing at the earth to lie themselves down. Their relatives, discovering what had been done to their loved ones, paid a bokor to make a deadly ouanga (a fetish housing a spirit) pierced with pins and needles, and hacked off Ti Joseph's head with a machete. Only a few years later, Seabrook visited the plain where this had happened, and was shown three labourers 'plodding like brutes, like automatons'. Looking into their eyes, Seabrook wrote, 'They were in truth like the eyes of a dead man, not blind but strong, unfocused, unseeing.'

What Seabrook witnessed was, in all likelihood, a corvée gang of indentured labourers, a common sight during the US occupation of 1915–34, when toiling for the colonial overlords had uncomfortable echoes of slavery times. Along with other contemporary accounts, *The Magic Island* helped to drive the image of Haiti as a backward land of barbaric rites, a reputation that fortified the occupation (which is why Seabrook is often mentioned with distaste by commentators today).

But if we nudge Seabrook to one side, there was still a story doing the rounds, a folk tale reflecting a widely held belief. Over the decades, similar stories would be repeated by Haitian storytellers and novelists such as Frankétienne, René Depestre, and Edwidge Danticat — stories of the zombie gang liberated by salt, returning either to their homes or their graves. And accounts of the risen dead were sufficiently widespread for a Haitian doctor called Lamarque Douyon to assemble files about the recorded zombie cases in the 1960s.*

When 'true-life tales' do the rounds, they feed the fiction; just as the fiction provides fuel for the 'true-life tales'. As with ghosts, so with tales of zombies. I sought them in Haitian folklore collections, and found them in abundance. When it comes to sinister subject matter, the tellers of the konts have plenty of material to work with. There's the child-snatching Tonton Macoute, who goes around with a bag full of the heads of the children he's murdered, the shapeshifting lougawou, and the Diablesse, whose monstrous face is hidden by a brimmed hat, while her hoofed foot is concealed under her long dress (shades of La Llorona and Aicha Kandicha, reflecting the universality of the 'monstrous feminine'). Among these macabre characters, 'zonbis' have their own sinister place. In one tale, skeletons clamber out of their graves to perform infernal tasks for the bokor. In another, a taxi driver looks over his shoulder, to see dead men coming to life after a pick-up from a cemetery. In another tale, a man wonders who has been stealing the plantains, corn, and peas from his plantation, only to find out the thieves are zombies, working under the cover of night and their own ostensible lack of existence.

If there's one Haitian zombie tale that's stuck in my mind, it's 'The Case of the Key' (retold by the storyteller Liliane Nérette Louis in a bewitching collection called *When Night Falls, Kric! Krac!*). It tells of a village girl working for a wealthy woman, ordered never to enter a

---

* Among those who consulted Douyon was the scholar Wade Davis. He was investigating in particular the story of a so-called zombie named Clairvius Narcisse, who reappeared eighteen years after his death had been recorded in an American-run hospital in 1962, and who told of being exhumed, beaten, bound and forced to serve as a slave on a plantation in the north of Haiti. What Narcisse shared with many of the lesser-documented cases was not only the dark arts involved in his experience but also his status as a social outcast (he had fallen out with his brother over a land dispute and was spurned by his community for failing to take care of his children). Becoming a zombie isn't just a curse. In the local law administered by secret societies operating in rural Haiti, it is also a punishment. To quote Wade Davis: 'the fear in Haiti is not of zombies, but rather of becoming a zombie.'

certain room. Curiosity inevitably drives her there, and she finds the room 'full of dead people who had been made into zombi.' She drops the key in a pool of blood, which she is unable to clean off, and when the mistress returns she is told she will be locked in the room with the zombies.

This story mirrors the seventeenth-century French classic 'Bluebeard' (not only in its structure but particular details such as the girl's struggle to wipe the blood off the key). Which is hardly surprising: house slaves heard such tales in the nurseries of their masters' children, or during the old storytelling evenings, the veillée. They also learned the steps to French dances, overheard their masters reading revolutionary pamphlets, and absorbed other aspects of French folklore such as the loup-garou (mixing French terms into their own long-standing folklore around possession and shapeshifting). Just as French plantation-owners carried elements of Vodou with them when they fled the revolution (elements that would fetch up in Louisiana's tales of the rougarou), so it worked the other way round.

Stories like 'The Case of the Key' hint at the antiquity of zombie tales. If the idea of the zombie came out of Africa, it stands to reason that slaves were telling these stories long before the revolution, stories that found literary echoes in the writings of de Blessebois and Descourtilz. 'The zombie is a beast of burden that its master exploits mercilessly', wrote the anthropologist Alfred Métraux in 1972. 'The existence of zombies is, projected onto the mythical plane, that of the former slaves of Santo Domingo.' An African concept, fused with the collective trauma of slavery to conjure an idea that has resonated throughout Haitian history: which is why it features in many of the nation's seminal literary works.

'Blows, knuckle raps on the head, karate chops, double-handed slaps across the face'. In the first novel written in Haitian kreyòl, Frankétienne's *Dézafi* (1975), a colony of zombies is forced to labour in brutal conditions recalling the violence of slave plantations. The author wasn't simply evoking Haiti's troubled past, he was writing during the dictatorship of 'Papa Doc' Duvalier, who drew on Vodou and Haitian folklore, appointing a Vodou priest as minister of education, naming his terrifying paramilitaries 'Tonton Macoute' after the folk-tale child-snatcher, and adopting the nasal voice, the stiff, zombie-like body language, the dark suit and glasses associated with the lwa of the dead, Baron Samedi. Franketienne's novel isn't just a re-imagining of Haitian folklore: it's part of a political contest over that folklore, a contest that continues today.

In *Dézafi*, the hero, Klodonis, is mocked by the bokor for his intellectualism, his interest in French philosophy and ideas, compared to a 'Parisian salon rat'. But it is this multicultural figure who saves the other zombies. When the bokor's daughter, pitying and a little in love with him, feeds Klodonis salt, she initiates a spree of liberation. Sickles, machetes, pickaxes, chair legs — the captives grab any weapons they can lay their hands on, knocking down the bokor's henchman and hanging his guts on a fence, trampling the bokor into 'tiny bits and pieces'. This exhilarating climax takes the old tale of the zombies let loose, liberated from their bondage, and turns them into a radical challenge to a regime that was silencing intellectuals like Klodonis. It's thrilling to read because it operates on multiple levels: a folk tale retold, a cri de coeur against the corruption of the Duvalier regime, when the president profited from the mass sale of Haitian people's body parts. But the narrative hinges on a crucial feature that Americanised zombies have lost. The Haitian zombie isn't a dead person brought back to life. In this respect, they are very different from other revenants like ghosts and vampires. The zombie is a living person who appears to be dead. Or, put it another way: the Haitian zombie has the potential to be freed.

THE GREY ZONE

The revolution made Haiti an independent nation, an inspiration to slaves in the USA and a thorn in the side of white governments across the West. Over the nineteenth century and into the twentieth, Haiti would inspire revolutionaries and succour them, from slave revolts in the antebellum south to revolutionaries in Cuba. But in 1915, the USA began its two-decade-long occupation. It was in this period that William Seabrook visited, writing about the zombies in the HASCO fields, and that Zora Neale Hurston met Felicia Felix-Mentor. Many others came, inspiring a glut of books and transmitting stories of zombies into American culture.

The result was the early zombie movies such as *White Zombie* (1932), in which Bela Lugosi (star of the previous year's box-office hit *Dracula*) zombifies a bow-lipped blonde on the night of her wedding to add her to his collection (which includes a minister of the interior, a police chief, a brigand leader, and a witch doctor); and the haunting, ambiguously written *I Walked with a Zombie* (1943), which reimagined *Jane Eyre* with Vodou ceremonies and a bug-eyed Carrefour, the Vodou spirit of the crossing-point. The accuracy of these films has rightly been questioned, and the reduction of 'native' characters to little more than props behind the central white characters. That said, the eerie and ambiguous atmosphere of *I Walked with a Zombie* continues to draw praise from many film critics.

In these early films, the zombie still expresses the horror of individual enslavement, but in the revival of zombie tales in American filmmaking later in the century, the individual swelled to a horde, leached of poignancy. The motherlode of the modern zombie flick is George A. Romero's *Night of the Living Dead*, released in 1968. Romero's relentlessly hungry, flesh-eating monsters inspired the snowballing storm of zombie flicks and series that followed, from *Dawn of the Dead* to *The Walking Dead* to *The Last of Us* to *Scoobie Doo on Zombie Island*. In the feedback loop of twenty-first-century globalisation, its influence can be traced in zombie films from Africa, including the Senegalese classic *Atlantics* (2019), which won the Grand Prix at the Cannes Film Festival for its tale of drowned migrants returning home as zombies.

Once more we find a thorny cultural lineage. The word 'zombie' is never mentioned in *Night of the Living Dead*, and the director insisted that wasn't what he intended: 'To me, zombies were still those boys in the Caribbean doing the wet-work for [Bela] Lugosi', he said in an interview, referencing *White Zombie*. The appeal of Romero's film was that it brought the monsters into a recognisable setting — the suburban streets of America. The age of the Caribbean-set zombie movies, or the Eastern European settings of early horror talkies and the later Hammer Horror series, was coming to a close. Hollywood had de-globalised its monsters, narrowing their sphere to middle-class cul-de-sacs with white picket fences.

For the scholar and translator of Caribbean literature Professor Kaiama L. Glover this is no less disturbing than what went before. 'What we're really grappling with,' she told me, 'is shoring up our borders. We can see the discrepancy between what we have and what people in the global south have. Our most common images of these people are overflowing crowds in refugee camps or tent cities or migrant boats. If you watch *World War Z* or *The Last of Us*, what we see is our anxiety about the sub-human horde swarming to consume our civilised spaces. It's quite an outlet when you can look at another human being and kill them with impunity because they're not really like you. You can go take a blowtorch or an AK-47 or a semi-truck and mow them down.'

Is it the monsters we're afraid of — or other people? (I thought back to my night in the vampire's mill in Serbia; what — or who — was it that really chilled my blood that night?) If monster movies have matched — and mapped — the patterns of geopolitical reality, from colonial-era 'exploration' to the more defensive 'base-under-siege' tales of the immigration age, it suggests these storylines reveal more than we would like to admit.

But it is in Haitian storytelling that we can see the zombie's roots. It remains a vital image, depicted by many artists and authors in Haiti.* In René Depestre's acclaimed novel *Hadriana in All My Dreams* (published in 1988 and winner of the prestigious Prix Renaudot in France), the splendour of carnival sets the scene: half-naked werewolves, multicoloured Pierrots, Caribs in brilliant plumage on parade, along with a 'zombie car', and a creole heroine called Hadriana, who drops dead at the altar at the very moment she declares 'yes' to marry her Haitian fiancé. She rises again, 'lost in the paralysing void known in Haiti as zombification', set aside for use as a sex toy — her body separated from her soul, which is locked inside 'an old, oversized champagne bottle'. Hadriana escapes, fleeing the graveyard during a storm, joining a refugee boat to Jamaica.

Depestre wrote the novel from his own political exile in France, a lament for his 'zombified' country. Whereas Frankétienne stayed in Haiti, imagining revolution on home soil, for Depestre, living in his own Villa Hadriana in the south of France, salvation is individual. The 'zombified' nation is doomed, but the heroine has the possibility of escape, like the author himself.

'For me,' said Kaiama L. Glover, who translated the novel into English, 'knowing Depestre very well, much of what he's trying to do with the Haitian zombie is show it isn't limited to Haiti, that it has value outside the island. So making this white, European-descended woman susceptible to zombification is a way of thinking about alienation, it's a way of showing that anyone can become a zombie.' Here is a powerful contra-flow to the relentless direction of globalisation. A world refracted through the folklore of Haiti.

The zombies in these modern novels are linked to the folk tales by mundanity. Zombies can appear in a taxi, working in a wealthy

---

* Among numerous examples in Haitian art, one of the best-loved is the 1946 painting *Vol de Zombis* by the Vodou priest Hector Hyppolite: a pair of shrouded zombies are led out of a cemetery by a bokor, his paraphernalia scattered on the ground below. Another is Wilson Bigaud's 1953 oil painting *Three Zombies*, in which the straw-hatted bokor grips a govi jar in one hand, holding his tied-up, skull-faced zombies with a rope in the other.

woman's house, toiling on a plantation; the neighbourhood baker can be turned into a zombie; so can a Francophile intellectual or a Creole heiress on her wedding day. They reflect a land whose restless psychogeography allows for the strange and magical to be happening under our very noses. They celebrate Haiti, turning a source of external vilification into what the anthropologist Franck Degoul has called 'a privileged marker of Haitianness ... Zombification is Haitian, uniquely Haitian, exclusively Haitian.'

How far we have travelled from the dragons and giants of ancient stories! The monsters no longer announce themselves with earth-quaking roars and spectacular dimensions. If you can't see a vampire's fangs, if you miss the light in a zombie's eyes, how are you to know you're dealing with a monster at all? Hollywood's zombies might signpost themselves with dripping flesh and creaky sounds, but the Haitian zombies are better camouflaged. They underline the porousness between the living and the dead, as well as between dreams and reality.

Names like 'Jean Zombi' and the 'Roche à Zombi' show that zombie tales existed in the period of the Haitian Revolution, and these dark tales made their way into Western culture long before Hollywood absorbed them. Zombies are referenced in Robert Southey's *History of Brazil* (1810–19), for example, and, indirectly, in the Jamaican slave-owner Bryan Edwards's *History, Civil and Commercial, of the British Colonies in the West Indies* (1793). Coleridge annotated Southey's zombie reference in his copy of *History of Brazil*, and scholars have speculated that Edwards's account (with its Caribbean tribe whose 'narcotic potion ... occasions a trance or profound sleep of some duration') influenced 'The Rime of the Ancient Mariner'. The impact of stories from the Caribbean on Mary Shelley's monster novel is all the more likely when we consider her interest in abolition and the theme of enslavement in *Frankenstein*. Writing about the origins of *Frankenstein*, H.L. Malchow suggests 'it may be valuable to bear in mind that the black Jacobins in Saint Domingue [i.e. the Haitian revolutionaries] and the parliamentary struggle in England to abolish the slave-trade guaranteed that issues of race played a significant contemporary role in the larger political debate surrounding the capacities and rights of mankind.' Shelley certainly read Edwards's *History* (only a year before she first told the story of Frankenstein). What this suggests is that, when they came to inventing their own macabre beings, the increasingly prevalent stories of the living dead — of vampires, certainly, of ghosts no doubt, but also of zombies in the Caribbean — were part of the lore that fed European writers' imaginations. And the relationship tilts back round, so that we find John Polidori's *The Vampyre* inspiring Uriah Derick D'Arcy's Haiti-set *The Black Vampyre*.

Romantic, gothic obsessions coaxed the mass audience for such stories, but the monsters themselves emerged out of societies suffering from large-scale oppression. It is the same across these stories of the undead. La Llorona was conceived by Mexicans under the power of the conquistadors, tales of the vampire flourished at a time of military occupation in the Balkans, the zombie was developed by Caribbean slaves under the vicious rule of colonial planters. Tales of the dead can be throwaway and fun, but they can also be profoundly connected to history. By their very nature, they are asking us to reconsider how we see the past. The stories of the dead recounted here express the emotional heritages of people whose trauma was passed down, generation after generation, articulated through macabre tales of ghosts, vampires, and zombies.

For Mary Shelley, inventing her own monster of the undead — a patchwork figure culled from graveyard parts — the theme of political dispossession resonated. Her tragic 'being', with his 'yellow skin' and 'black lips', and his fraught relationship with his former master, has much in common with the vampires of the Balkan tales and the zombies of Haiti. Like the zombies, he is a social outcast, spurned by society, characterised by inordinate physical strength (which many observers have compared with contemporary depictions of Caribbean slaves). Considering Shelley's reading, this is a striking connection, and it reinforces the significance of the Haitian zombie in global culture. For the zonbi stands at the threshold of modernity, representing an ambiguous approach to monsters, the hard truth acquired by people whose freedom could only be claimed through violence. In this sense, rather than being the 'primitive' island of so many clichés, Haiti was ahead of the curve, foretelling what the rest of the world would take a little longer to catch up on. It is this ambiguity that has come to define monsters in the modern age, and has made them more disturbing than ever.

PART FOUR

When the Future Beckons

'He felt as though he were wandering in the forests of the sea bottom, lost in a monstrous world where he himself was the monster. He was alone. The past was dead, the future was unimaginable. What certainty had he that a single human creature now living was on his side?'

George Orwell, *1984*

CHAPTER TEN

Mary Shelley's Monster-Making Circle

THE TENTH TALE

Robert Walton, ship captain and explorer, has seen nothing like it. Pincered with his crew between sheets of Arctic ice, he peers through his telescope. Muscling through the blizzard is a giant on a sledge, 'a savage inhabitant of some undiscovered island'. Walton has barely recovered from this sight when onto his ship comes another — an exhausted traveller from Switzerland. His name is Victor Frankenstein and he tells Walton his tale.

How promising his life was! For Victor came from a kindly and prosperous family, and he was devoted to his studies. Here lay the issue. He became so fascinated by the mysterious processes of life that he explored them to an unparalleled degree. Studying in Ingolstadt, he secretly collected body parts from cemeteries and charnel houses, and in a garret far from human scrutiny, he assembled a patchwork being. But as soon as he brought it to life, he was repelled by what he had done and shunned the very place of invention. When, days later, he looked into the garret, there was no sign of his creation. Only on learning of the murder of his brother William, blamed on an innocent family servant, did Victor recognise the tracks of the monster he had brought to life.

At the Glacier of Montanvert, the creature leaped down the icy cliffs to confront him, revealing how he had lived: feeding off fruits, learning human language by eavesdropping on an unsuspecting family, who shunned him in horror as soon as they saw his hideous form. Isolated but articulate, recognising his difference from humankind, the creature desired a mate, a female companion. Reluctantly, Victor agreed, and travelled to a remote island in the Orkneys to fulfil his macabre pledge. But he could not bear the sight of the repulsive creature, who was spying on his work, so he tore the half-made companion apart. Enraged, the creature wreaked his revenge by murdering Victor's friend Henry, and Victor found himself accused of the crime, imprisoned by a community convinced he was a murderous fiend. It took the intervention of his father, travelling all the way from Geneva, to release him.

Returning home, he determined to lead a simpler life, spurning scientific research and marrying his childhood sweetheart, Elizabeth. No more thoughts of the monster, no more vaunting ambition. But a grim visit was paid on their wedding night. Pacing through the house in anticipation of a fatal tussle, the new bridegroom heard a sudden scream. The creature had found the perfect way to stab his heart: Victor returned to the bed chamber to find Elizabeth had been strangled.

What did he have to live for now? Only the destruction of the monster — and not even that could quell his troubled soul. Morbidly bent on his dark quest, Victor has pursued the creature across the wastelands of Europe, all the way to the Arctic. There, he spills out the last of his tale to Walton, but his quest has sucked his ruined life to the marrow. He breathes his last, and soon after, the creature swings into the cabin, bemoaning the twisted fate that has doomed them both to misery.

Pledging to cast himself into flames, the creature sets off on an ice raft, towards his own demise.

THE CASTLE OF THE CORPSE-RAISER

Out of England they sailed, leaving Dover's cliffs behind on a reckless night crossing to Calais. She was Mary Godwin, sixteen-year-old daughter of two radical authors. He was Percy Bysshe Shelley, a promising twenty-one-year-old poet, avowed atheist, and heir to a baronetcy, who'd left his pregnant wife behind in London, as well as a baby daughter and a string of creditors. They had neither the support of their families, nor society at large. But society be damned! For this was the summer of 1814, the age of the Romantics.

First, there were practicalities to deal with. Revolutionary ideals are all very well, but if you're planning on skipping across nineteenth-century Europe, you need to be sure of your funds. They'd overspent on the first leg, rashly hiring four horses instead of the customary two out of Dartford and requisitioning a night boat rather than waiting for the morning packet. Even when Percy had pawned his watch and chain, they barely had enough to pay for a single ass to carry them across France. Nor were they quite as alone as they might have wished. Mary's stepsister, Claire Clairmont, was their gooseberry, indispensable for her linguistic skills and occasionally appreciated for her musical gifts, but liable to irritate Mary with her emotional flare-ups and her constant flirting with Percy.

Those early days of travel were a bitter disappointment — utterly failing to meet Mary's romantic expectations. France, wrecked by the Napoleonic Wars, was an 'uninteresting tract of country', she recorded in her journal. The hospitality was no better. At one of the inns where they stayed, Claire 'wasn't able to sleep all night for the rats who as she said put their paws on her face' and had to share the lovers' bed to escape the lustful attentions of the innkeeper. But as the gradient rose, so did Mary's spirits.

On sighting the Alps, Mary's prose turned to rhapsody: 'Their immensity staggers the imagination, and so far surpasses all conception, that it requires an effort of the understanding to believe that they indeed form a part of the earth.' Responses to landscapes are necessarily subjective. For Mary, it was Switzerland, its 'spots of verdure surpassing imagination', its 'verdant isles, and snow-capt mountains' that would hold her in its icy grip. Nature outstripped imagination itself — although she would make a fair go of reversing the pattern when she came to writing her most celebrated novel.

Frankenstein is many things: a foundational work of science fiction, the most influential monster novel ever written. Less famously, it's also a love letter to Switzerland. The monster is an urban creature, surely — constructed in a garret in the German university town of Ingolstadt? But it is in the Swiss mountains that he finds his voice, sheltering near a mountain hut and eating the fruits and berries he harvests. It is no coincidence that Mary would choose a mountain slope — at Montanvert just below Mont Blanc — for the crucial encounter between her monster and his maker. As the literary scholar Daisy Hay (author of a captivating biography about the Shelleys and their circle) put it to me: 'That summer, they [Percy and Mary] are developing a shared, secular register of the sublime. They're doing a lot of thinking about how the sight of the Mont Blanc glacier might allow you to understand geological cycles of decay and destruction.' This is more than aesthetic. It overlaps, Hay suggested, with political thinking: 'It's the only way they could think through the failure of the French Revolution — if you understood this destruction as generative of a political future you couldn't yet see. This is filtered through the sight of the mountains, and you can see it in *Frankenstein*, when she chooses to stage that encounter on the mountain.'

Wandering around the Swiss lakes that blissful summer, the young lovers floated in their bubble of mutual absorption, revelling in the landscapes and the stories they heard in the villages. Near Brunnen, where 'Nothing could be more magnificent than the view from this spot', they were told about a pair of lovers buried in an avalanche whose spirits were said to howl through the storms. There would be other tales — of buried treasure, a fountain of gold, and an alchemist trying to raise the dead. But tales would have to wait. Their money was running out, so they took a series of low-budget boats down the Rhine back towards the English Channel.

Spirits sinking with the landscape, Mary deplored their uncouth fellow passengers: 'nothing could be more horribly disgusting than the lower order of smoking, drinking Germans who travelled with us,' she wrote in high dudgeon. 'They swaggered and talked, and what was hideous to English eyes, kissed one another.' Still, there was interest to be had from the surroundings.

Of the many castles they passed, the one that stands out to any follower of Mary Shelley's life is the wind-battered thirteenth-century schloss above the beechwoods near Darmstadt. Not only would its name resound across literary history, but so would its story. For in this castle, a century and a half before the Shelleys' journey, there lived a scientist who committed himself to bringing the dead to life. The castle was known as Burg Frankenstein.

These days, it's best approached from the woods. I'd come from Bavaria, following my visit to Furth im Wald and the Drachenstich. A train carried me out of Frankfurt, and a tram out of Darmstadt, depositing me at the sun-pooled base of the Odenwald. A steep path wriggled between the beech trees, across mounds of mud sprinkled with sand. Pink paint slashed the trees, along with white circles and blue turrets, the coding of German woodland. Huge boulders jostled under the outer walls, like monsters snapping at the man-made defences. A wooden walkway teetered between the contents of a herb garden — apple mint, lady's mantle, lavender, and many others. The path tunnelled between the rocks, bursting open under a bastion tower and a weathered parapet.

Before I had reached the portico, Mary Shelley's novel was already bleeding out of the castle's sombre grey: Boris Karloff's matt-black, slab-like grimace silhouetted on a blood-red banner for a music festival. The roar of tractors, the knocking of hammers. No entry for visitors, I was told, so I pressed an ear to the stone to glean what I could — and when the gate creaked open for the tractors, I ghosted inside.

Floodlights and amplifiers were being installed around a stage in the inner bailey, under the parapeted walkway between the round stone towers of the donjon. How very *Frankenstein* (albeit more James Whale's than Mary Shelley's) — electric sparks flying under a mediaeval backdrop! The highest tower soared over a loopholed walkway, wooden-floored and stone-walled. Below the keep, a cavernous opening gaped around stone steps plunging down to a hidden cellar.

Here, suggests local lore, a scientist called Johann Conrad Dippel conducted scientific research. He ransacked nearby graves and charnel houses for body parts, grinding the bones into an elixir to pour between the lips of his dead wife. Well, that's the legend, at least. The truth happens to be even weirder.

Dippel was born in Castle Frankenstein in 1673, when refugees from the wars with France were granted asylum inside its battlements. After spending his early years in the burg, he retained a strong attachment, and when he completed his doctoral dissertation at Giessen University, he signed his name 'Franckensteina' (that is, the one from Frankenstein). But life, and his unorthodox scientific interests, hurled Dippel all over Northern Europe. He experimented on blood and bones in Berlin under the patronage of the Prussian king, Frederick I (the product he developed would become known as Dippel's oil, used effectively as an anti-spasmodic and stimulation for the nervous system); fled to Holland after being accused of spying for the Kingdom of Sweden; found his way to Denmark, where he was imprisoned and his works burned, before regaining favour by assisting the recovery of the king; and later returned to Germany, ending his life with a foaming mouth and his face half-blue, a mysterious fatality in the castle of his patron, the Count of Wittgenstein.

In the meantime, Castle Frankenstein fell into the hands of a German soldier who had defected to the French, whose widow assembled a circle of lovers and almost burned the place down. When she died in the 1740s, the castle was abandoned, a roosting place for eagles and owls. Treasure-seekers trawled around the rocks, following rumours of hidden stashes of gold and silver, and by the turn of the century, it had become a popular tourist spot, an atmospheric ruin for the Romantics, visited by Goethe among others.

A scientist experimenting on dead body parts, possibly foraging in graveyards, hailing from a castle called Frankenstein, a castle that was on the route Mary, Percy, and Claire took on their way home in 1814. Easy enough to see why researchers have been slotting these pieces together over the last century or so. For the Romanian scholar Radu Florescu, who researched the link with Dippel in the 1970s, 'It seems, then, that the impact of the castle, with its strange legend and mysterious alchemist, were brooding in Mary's receptive mind from her journey down the Rhine in 1814, awaiting the shock of a Genevan thunderstorm to launch the most powerful horror story of all times.' But Mary never mentioned Dippel in her journals, nor in any of the multiple prefaces she composed for Frankenstein. The association remains a matter of speculation.

What is certain is that the Rhine journey informed *Frankenstein*, for passages from Mary's 1814 journal were transplanted into the novel, along with descriptions of the mountains. Multiple seeds, waiting to ripen. But there were more conversations to be had, about consciousness, electrolysis, and materialism, and a storytelling challenge to be posed by Lake Geneva. In the meantime, Mary and Percy applied for parental approval and money — with limited success. Mary had been writing since she was small, and she was certainly composing fiction during the journey down the Rhine. Although the contents have been lost, we are left with the tantalising title of the story she was scribbling down, when she wasn't grimacing in her cabin, 'sick as death', moaning about her fellow passengers or gazing at the woodlands and bubbling waters of the Rhine. The story was called 'Hate'.

'NO COMMON PERSON'

What does it take to create a monster — an entirely new 'Being' in the world of fiction? Others have tried, and some succeeded, but none compares with Mary Shelley's achievement because none has become so tangled in world folklore. A proof of sorts was the costume parade in Louisiana. There were werewolves, vampires, even a boy on an inflatable dragon, but the only 'authored' monster was the bolt-necked 'Frankie'.

Much of the background behind the monster can be found in Mary's own story — in the traumas of an unconventional childhood, later experiences, and the company she kept. 'Mrs Shelley is very clever, indeed it would be difficult for her not to be so,' wrote Lord Byron. 'The daughter of Mary Wollstonecraft and Godwin ... could be no common person.' Her parenthood hung over her like the heavy clouds over Lake Geneva. Her mother was a figure of enduring influence, who travelled through France in the Reign of Terror and wrote the groundbreaking *Vindication of the Rights of Woman*, which was published in 1792. Five years later, she gave birth to Mary. In the process, she contracted puerperal fever from the unsterilised hands of the doctor who removed the placenta. Puppies were brought to drain her milk and she spent her last five days on a wine diet. The grotesque image of this remarkable author languishing on her deathbed, a ball of living fur at each breast, underlines just how new was much of the scientific thinking underpinning her daughter's novel two decades later.

Mary was hardly the only creative child born from her mother's death. But few had a mother so admired, and the guilt haunted her, reinforced by the vision of her mother's portrait in her father's study and regular visits to Wollstonecraft's austere tomb in St Pancras Churchyard. Mary's father, William Godwin, was a well-regarded author and publisher, and the family home in London was a literary haven. Mary recalled hearing, at the age of eight, a reading by Samuel Taylor Coleridge from his 'Rime of the Ancient Mariner', one of many texts that would influence her own tale. So frightened were she and Claire by Coleridge's reading, they hid themselves behind the sofa, anticipating generations of future story-shocked children. For his part, Coleridge was a little disturbed by Mary and her sibling, writing of 'the cadaverous silence of Godwin's children'.

The search for *Frankenstein* offers many paths, most of them well-trodden. Original as Mary's 'abhorred monster' may have been, he didn't arrive out of a void. From John Milton's revolt against the creator in *Paradise Lost*, to philosophy by Rousseau and Locke (whose thinking about the innate goodness of 'natural man' and the effects of experience in *An Essay Concerning Human Understanding* aided Mary in developing her creature's psychology, the evolution from early hopes to a bitter soul bent on destruction); from the creepy motifs of the emerging gothic genre (including *Caleb Williams*, a novel about a guilty secret by her own father), to contemporary stories about automatons and other artificial beings* — there is, to quote the scholar Chris Baldick, 'a fund of literary sources upon which *Frankenstein* cannibalistically feeds'. But another path takes us to the places that touched Mary Shelley, and if we track our way between them, we can draw closer to the emotional machinery that made her monster tick.

---

* One such tale was 'The Automaton', published by the fantasy writer E.T.A. Hoffmann in 1814, which features a 'Talking Turk' able to make uncanny predictions. Another, published in 1790, is *The Looking-Glass of Actuality* by a French courtier called François-Félix Nogaret, which strangely enough features an inventor of an automaton who goes by the name Wak-wik-vauk-on-son-frankésteïn. As the scholar Julia Douthwaite Viglione has pointed out (in *The Frankenstein of 1790*), this nonsensical-sounding name combines two historical figures: a French engineer called Vaucanson and the scholarly title taken by Johann Dippel. Mary may not have come across Nogaret's novella, but it underlines the alchemist's reach and the period's fascination for the subject of artificial life.

Early life first. Researching at the British Library in London, I often walked up to eat my sandwiches in St Pancras graveyard, which Mary regularly visited in her youth, learning to write by tracing out the letters on her mother's tomb. There, where visitors still leave tributes — flowers, coins, paperclips, pieces of fruit — Mary read poetry and canoodled with Percy in the shade of the willow trees. Here is a glimpse of the author who would send her 'hero' into charnel houses and cemeteries, a truly 'gothic' personality, at home among the dead.

Now for a crucial teenage influence. Windswept tidal water sprayed the viewing point at Broughty Ferry in Dundee, as I stood there on my way back from selkie-seeking in Orkney. Across the grey waters of the Tay are the rocks known as the Three Graces and a fifteenth-century keep. A three-masted wooden ship, with iron-shod bows and a massive hull to withstand the polar ice, floated nearby (in this case, Captain Scott's famous *Discovery*, but it echoes the polar expedition with which *Frankenstein* begins — and its design was based on the great Dundee whalers). Sent to Dundee to stay with family friends in 1812, Mary often walked the shoreline to 'commune with the creatures of my fancy'. It was in Dundee, she wrote, 'that my true compositions, the airy flights of my imagination, were born and fostered'.

Dundee certainly suggested details for the frame story about Robert Walton's venture into the Arctic, but it may also have begun the thinking behind Mary's creature. Walking along the banks of the Tay, she would have seen the longshoremen bowed under their burdens, disembowelling the whaling ships of blubber and oil. Across Britain to another port — Bristol now — Mary found herself, three years later, living in a house on the Avon Gorge, prickly with melancholy and missing her too-often-absent Percy. For a socially conscious woman who was reading Bryan Edwards's book on the West Indies and criticising the 'prejudiced' views in Mungo Park's *Travels in the Interior Districts of Africa*, the social impact of slavery was raggedly visible, only eight years since the Abolition Act. Her father had written passionately against slavery, while Mary and Percy were boycotting sugar because it came from West Indian plantations. As her novel would demonstrate, she was profoundly alert to the damage society did to those it monstered.*

There are other pathways into Mary's extraordinary creation, but here we have the core of her early years: her mother's death, the literary vitality of her home life, her early journeys and emerging libertarian outlook. If there is one place that made *Frankenstein*, however, it is surely the country in which most of the action is located (a country long associated with artificial life — famed for its clockwork automatons). In the spring of 1816, Mary set off once again for Switzerland, accompanying her beloved Percy and her stepsister Claire, just as before, but more alert to the injustices of the world, and to the bitterness of a father's disapproval (anger, to paraphrase Frankenstein's creature, against the one who had called her into being). Some of these ideas would feed into *Frankenstein*, and yet the girl who travelled to Geneva in 1816 wasn't mired in misery. She was reading voraciously, her mind fizzing with ideas. A morbid tale *Frankenstein* may be, but it was, as Mary reflected, 'the offspring of happy days'. And so, if we are to seek her monster anywhere, it is in the famous idyll that arose one strange stormy summer on the banks of Lake Geneva.

A STORM ON THE LAKE

The sour perfume of communal breathing, the sound of people snoring, as if leaking air-mattresses were hanging over all the seats. I could see myself in the window, the straggly cleft of my chin, my pointy nose. I'd been travelling for several weeks, and my eyebrows looked as if they were growing out of the cracks in the cliffs, while my cheeks were sprouting tussocks and there were bristlecones tumbling

---

* 'The alienated condition of black people,' Miranda Seymour writes in *Mary Shelley*, 'must have preyed on Mary's mind during her lonely weeks at Clifton, forming a significant contribution to the social intention behind the celebrated creature she brought to life in *Frankenstein* the following year.'

out of my lips. After so many nights outside, on buses or slumbering on station benches, I could feel a moistness in my nerves. When your mind has certain tendencies, and you've been on the move for a while, it's easy to muddle your reflection with a monster's grimace.

Dawn sparked between the pine trunks of the Jura, oozing light in spidery lines like electric jolts rippling down to the glassy surface of Lake Geneva. Here, where the Jura meets the Alps, huge mountains soaring over the passes linking travellers for millennia to France and Italy, you are plugged into Europe and protected from it, the combination of interconnectedness and isolation that suited Mary Shelley.

Down at the Quai du Mont-Blanc, I boarded a mouette, passing the morning bathers who leaped off the jetties or sunned themselves on the piers. With my back to the Jardin Anglais and the misty shaft of the Jet d'Eau, I climbed up the shaded hills of Coligny. Up, past a nail salon, a picture-framing store, a chocolaterie. In Mary's day, Coligny was a village, a refuge from Geneva; now it's a chic suburb. But in terms of who it attracts — the well-heeled, the elite, the expats — it hasn't changed so much.

Something was pressing on my mind that day. I thought of the selkie gazing at the sea, the troubled soul who turns into a werewolf. I'd walked too far, all the way past a golf course. Cussing at my misorienteering, I backtracked past a beautiful gateway with a stone tower. It turned out to be the headquarters of the Swiss Oil and Gas Trading Company, which only made my mood worse. I tried to distract myself with other charms — gargoyles jutting over the mosaics on the porch of an eighteenth-century church, a bronze figure in a park called *Grande Rimbaud*, who appeared to be cobbled out of discarded metal like some steampunk Frankenstein's monster. But I couldn't shake away the dark cloud that had settled over me.

A road snaked into shade and carried me past a gateway carved with the name 'Diodati'. On a scruffy slope of tall grass, box hedges framed the three-storey house where Mary first told her famous tale: a mansion of yellow stucco, buttoned with slatted green shutters, belted around the waist by a large protruding balcony. From here you could peer at the lake and watch the boats gliding by. But you had to be in the club. The hedge, along with the 'Private Property' signs, remind the visitor the house is closed to the curious. No need for axe-bearing guardsmen. All it takes now are CCTV and signs warning 'Attention au Chien'.

I felt like the Mariner in Coleridge's poem, peering in on the feast from outside; or Frankenstein's creature, listening at the mountain hut. Downhill I trudged, side-eyeing the villa, down past the spot where the Maison Chapuis once stood, where Mary, Percy, and Claire stayed, down towards the lake. Beside the main road was a lido, framed in a wooden walkway, and I dropped into the water, hoping the coolness would wash everything away. It was a hot day in August; perhaps I was struggling with the heat and the weight of my backpack on the steep roads. There was at least a promise of cooler weather ahead — a clot of clouds darkening over the Jura, as if the angels were trying to manufacture a dragon out of cirrus curls and sheets of altostratus.

Mary, Percy, and Claire came to Coligny in the summer of 1816. Once again, they had fled London's tattling society. Once again, they had set out for the liberal climate of the continent. 'To the warm sunshine, and to the humming of sun-loving insects,' Mary wrote in a letter on 17 May. 'From the windows of our hotel we see the lovely lake, blue as the heavens which it reflects, and sparkling with golden beams.' It was Claire who had instigated the adventure. Only a few weeks earlier, with extraordinary pluck, she had written to Lord Byron: 'An utter stranger takes the liberty of addressing you, sir ... my folly may be great, but the Creator ought not to destroy his creature.' Her words anticipated the narrative of her half-sister's novel, suggesting the nature of creation was a recurring theme in conversations that year. If the club-footed poet was the rock star of his age, Claire Clairmont was positioning herself as his groupie, offering herself 'with fond affection and unbounded devotion'. What developed was brief, but decisive. By the time they reached Geneva that summer, she was already pregnant.

After the collapse of his marriage to Annabella Milbanke, after accusations of abuse and rumours of an incestuous relationship with his half-sister Augusta, after the glittering success of his poem *Childe Harold's Pilgrimage*, Byron was at the peak of his fame and notoriety. He chose to flee the scandals and the negotiations over his failed marriage for the more liberal climate of Geneva. At Claire's instigation, the Shelley party preceded him, and they all gathered in the Hotel d'Angleterre. But the expat scene was far from convivial. Their fellow guests swerved between prurient disapproval and fascination for these literary celebrities, harassing them with their relentless gazing and indiscreet whispering.

So they crossed the lake to Coligny. Byron took up residence in the Villa Diodati, while Percy rented a smaller residence on the waterfront, the Maison Chapuis. Their mutual scandals bonded them. Percy and Byron enjoyed poetry discussions and boating; Claire made neat copies of the latest canto of *Childe Harold* and late-night visits to Byron's bedchamber; while his companion and personal physician, Dr John Polidori, fawned over Mary. No wonder the rumour mill was spinning at the Hotel d'Angleterre. Interest was so high the owner charged for use of his telescope so guests could spy on the goings-on. Typical was the view of a clergyman called John Pye Smith, who 'passed the house in which Lord Byron lives, in a sullen and disgraceful seclusion. Besides his servants, his only companions are two wicked women.' Or, as Byron put it himself, 'I believe they looked on me as a man monster.'

Sadly for the gossipers, the increasingly murky view was a blight on their recreational espionage. The summer of 1816 was as intemperate as you could get: the month of their arrival in Geneva registered the fewest sunspots on record. Storms lashed the sky, which was drained of light by the eruption of Mount Tambora, 8,000 miles away in what was then the Dutch East Indies — the largest explosion for the last 10,000 years. 'An almost perpetual rain confines us principally to the house,' wrote Mary. 'The thunderstorms that visit us are grander and more terrific than I have ever seen before.' Boating was out of the question, so the literary quintet rifled through Villa Diodati's library, sifting German ghost stories in French translation (in particular, a book called *Fantasmagoriana, or Collection of the Histories of Apparitions, Spectres, Ghosts, etc.*, translated by Jean-Baptiste Eyriès and published in 1812). When they weren't reading, they listened to Polidori's accounts of the anatomy lectures he'd recently attended in London, experiments by Dr Erasmus Darwin on electrolysis and Dr Galvani's earlier observations on 'animal electricity', which led to discussions about the nature of the soul. Mary didn't welcome these conversations: she worried about 'the effect of any human endeavour to mock the stupendous mechanism of the creator of the world'. Radical she might have been, but she had a conservative streak and hadn't abandoned herself entirely to Percy's atheism, nor his philosophy of free love. For the creation of her famous tale, this was a potent combination: an intrigue for matters of death alongside a genuine anxiety about the new science.

Locked inside Villa Diodati, here we find our monster-making party — prisoners to darkness and rain; gathered before a large fireplace, their faces reflected back from the mirror hanging over it. Time now to light the spark — for which the honour went to (who else?) Lord Byron.

Or did it? The challenge he famously posed was already set out in the ghost-story collection they had been reading: 'Everyone is to relate a story of ghosts, or something of a similar nature ...' With his trademark wit, Byron quickly developed an outline, a tale about an apparently dead man who is found alive and well, making love to his friend's sister; while Polidori related a story about a Swiss patriot's incestuous affair. Percy's story was about a depressed man exploited by his friends. Ever prone to flights of fancy, he came up with a more memorable image on one of those eerie evenings, when he suddenly rushed out of the room with a cry. He claimed that, on looking at Mary, he had seen a pair of female nipples flash open suddenly as a pair of eyes. Polidori splashed his face and made him inhale ether (later he'd call it a 'fit of fantasy', one that sufficiently affected the doctor to include in the story he ended up writing — *The Vampyre* — which took Byron's outline and turned the monster into a version of his then ex-employer).

Mary wasn't as quick at summoning her own story, but none could match the originality or force with which it eventually struck her. Later, she claimed it arrived in a dream: 'My imagination, unbidden, possessed and guided me, gifting the successive images that arose in my mind with a vividness far beyond the usual bounds of reverie. I saw — with shut eyes, but acute mental vision, — I saw the pale student of unhallowed arts kneeling beside the thing he had put together. I saw the hideous phantasm of a man stretched out, and then, on the working of some powerful engine, show signs of life, and stir with an uneasy, half vital motion.' Scholars have disputed her recollection of events, suggesting this may have been an attempt to disassociate herself from the supposedly unfeminine act of literary craftsmanship. In any case, she had a tale — a man who creates a monster, who acts like God and brings a being to life. While the celebrated poets soon lost interest in their stories, and Claire never got anywhere with hers, it was Mary and Polidori who worked their tales into readable form. Polidori's *Vampyre* would become a milestone in the history of literary bloodsuckers; while Mary's *Frankenstein* would become the most influential monster novel of them all.

How do you connect with somebody from two centuries ago — with a sparklingly imaginative woman of the Romantic Age, whose morbid depressions shared the same head space as her flights of fantasy? Riding the mouette back across the lake, I looked up at the darkening sky — hardly as foreboding as 1816's ash-laden vault, but eloquent enough. A rumble around us, turning all eyes to the Jura, its piny crest bristling on the far side of the water. Seconds later, another rumble, and a flash. The engine of the mouette was a match for the thunder, and it had a roof to shelter under. But there wasn't enough space for all of us, not unless we huddled. I thought of Mary, 'observing the lightning play among the clouds in various parts of the heavens, and dart in jagged figures upon the piny heights of Jura, dark with the shadow of the overhanging clouds'. I wanted to see the lightning, every flash of it, I wanted to hear the thunder.

The mouette glided towards the Quai du Mont-Blanc, and the passengers scrambled onto the jetty. The rain wasn't just falling on us — it was collapsing on our heads, as if the gods were trying to knock us down with water bombs. My shoulders were already slippery as I slid the straps of my backpack over them. I splashed through ankle-deep puddles, kicking forward with my sodden boots. At last, I had a connection with Mary. A portal had opened between her world and mine.

'A finer storm than I had ever beheld,' she wrote that summer. 'The lake was lit up, the pines on Jura made visible, and all the scene illuminated for an instant, when a pitchy blackness succeeded, and the thunder came in frightful bursts over our heads amid the darkness.' If I couldn't breach the Romantics' world at Villa Diodati, here at least the heavens had given me a glimpse of it. I clasped my hands together in thanks to whatever spirit presides over such spectacles.

The thunderous drumroll was still audible when a bus mercifully scooped me up. The lake was mist, the road a neon river of liquid light, red and blue from reflected headlights. I was still soaked when I came out at the great square of Plainpalais, but the rain was down to a trickle. Skating slopes and shuttered stalls sparkled with water, and I strode between them, relishing this stormy afternoon that had given me the place to myself. I had nowhere to stay, and several more hours to purge before my night bus. Where else to while the time away? There was no sign of Rousseau's bust, which drew the Shelleys on their visit here two centuries ago. But across the park, near a poster for a music festival, was another famous figure, cast from bronze.

His bones clawed out of his chest, under his neck, out of his wrists and feet. The exposed bones on his belly were plugged with nails, there was a bolt in his left ear, his neck was collared in loops of metal. He was recognisably Frankenstein's creature, yet somehow the artists had avoided a Karloff-like cliché. He looked like a man, a miserable, wretched man, with his deep eye sockets and drawn-down mouth. Installed in 2014 by the KLAT collective, here at the place where the monster commits his first murder in the novel, he is known as 'Frankie', described as a representation of a 'marginal or vagabond figure' and 'an invitation to benevolently consider otherness'. The sculpture conveyed the menace of Frankenstein's creature, but also the poignancy at the heart of the story. Because to be a monster is to be misunderstood, an outsider watching the feast from the fringes. It is to be Grendel howling at the mead-hall in *Beowulf*, or King Kong, peering into the cosy bedroom of a New York apartment. In a sense, this is what a monster means: somebody or something that doesn't belong.

But in the postmodern imagination, monsters are landmarks, meeting venues, backdrops for selfies.

'*Eh, que cosa!*'

Swinging a plastic umbrella, a young woman trotted over. She pressed her back to the creature, while a boy in a denim jacket photographed her in various poses. She checked his screen, making sure of the results, and for the final shot, she lifted herself on her block heels and air-kissed the monster. Isn't that what he always wanted — 'sweet looks directed towards me with affection'? But it was never going to last. A pivot of heels and off they tottered, leaving Frankie to his customary solitude.

THE GULPH OF MELANCHOLY

Having a story isn't enough, however spectacular the vision in which it came. The story must be written, redrafted, edited, published. If the stormy summer of 1816 had been Mary's idyll, her life back in England was anything but. Ensconced in Bath, where she wrote out her original draft of *Frankenstein* and crafted the finished tale, she scribbled out a revealing letter to Percy, who was up in London dealing with his creditors: 'give me a garden & *absentia Clariae* and I will thank my love for many favours.' Poor Claire had her own miseries to deal with — jilted by Byron but heavily pregnant by him, legally bound to give up her child to him (who would die aged six after Byron shoved her off to an Italian convent, prompting Mary to write to Claire that his 'hypocrisy & cruelty rouse one's soul from its depths'). It's a reflection of their tempestuous circle that these two were far from the unhappiest.

In October 1816, Mary's half-sister Fanny (Mary Wollstonecraft's firstborn child) took an overdose of laudanum in Swansea. Two months later, Percy's ex-wife, Harriet, threw herself into the Serpentine. The complexities of human relationships presided over these tragedies, but it must have seemed as if death was haunting the novel Mary was writing. She had lost her firstborn, unnamed baby the previous year, and would lose another in 1817, while she was still working on *Frankenstein* (she gave his name, William, to the monster's first victim in the novel: the boy murdered at Plainpalais). A third would die in 1820.

Predisposed to depression, 'the gulph of melancholy on the edge of which I was & am continually peeping', Mary was pushed deeper into the abyss by the terrible events of her young life. Sometimes her depressions gripped her so hard, even Percy struggled to reach her. 'But thou art fled, gone down the dreary road, / That leads to Sorrow's most obscure abode', he wrote in 'To Mary Shelley', 'Thou sittest on the hearth of pale despair'. Although acquaintances admired Mary's temperate nature, there was something else under the surface. 'She is a torrent of fire under a Hecla snow,' to quote her friend Leigh Hunt. That combination was supercharged by the events of her young life — 'the crucible year in which everything is forged', as Daisy Hay put it to me: 'she's seen post-revolutionary Europe, relatives have died, children are born, everything comes together with an intensity which is mirrored in *Frankenstein*.'

Completed, re-written, and edited with significant help from Percy, the novel was ready at last to go before the public. But a story like *Frankenstein* was never likely to have a smooth run. Being a masterpiece by a débutant — and what's more, a female of the nineteenth century! — it was subjected to the sort of initiation ritual in which the book world has long specialised. 'Poor Mary's book came back with a refusal,' wrote Percy in August 1817, 'which has put me rather in ill spirits. Do any kind friend of yours Marianne [Leigh Hunt's wife] know any bookseller or has any influence with one?' It was turned down by several publishing houses, including Byron's publisher John Murray (despite Byron's very sincere praise of it), before being brought out in January 1818, with flimsy binding and a drab grey cover, by a small concern called Lackington Press, which specialised in niche books about the occult.

Early notices said more about the age than the book. To the *Monthly Review* it was 'uncouth', to *The British Critic*, its 'power is so abused and perverted, that we should almost prefer imbecility', and *The Edinburgh Review*, in a classic of nineteenth-century critical appraisal, raged that 'our taste and our judgement alike revolt at this kind of writing, and the greater the ability with which it may be executed the worse it is — it inculcates no lesson of conduct, manners, or morality.' Well, as Henry Fielding memorably put it in the previous century, most critics are 'Vampyres, being dead and damn'd'.

But Mary did have support among her nearest and dearest. 'It is a most wonderful performance full of genius', wrote Claire in a letter to Byron, 'and the fiction is so contrived and extraordinary a kind as one could imagine would have been written by so young a person ...' So it would prove for the public at large. In the summer of 1818, Thomas Love Peacock told Percy about a day at the Egham Races: 'I met on the course a great number of my old acquaintances, by the reading portion of whom, I was asked a multitude of questions concerning "Frankenstein" and its author. It seems to be universally known and read.'

The snide reviewers were being swept back by a tide of enthusiasm, in which notable authors joined their voices, among them the much-loved novelist Sir Walter Scott. *Frankenstein* was transforming from a rejected oddity into a full-blown literary triumph. But as the newly published novel was crackling with popularity, tragedy was rushing towards poor Mary, as inexorably as her creature to Victor's honeymoon abode.

In 1822, her beloved Percy was drowned at sea, caught in a storm on his way back from visiting Byron in Italy. 'Well, here is my story — the last story I shall have to tell,' wrote Mary, 'all that might have been bright in my life is now despoiled — I shall live to improve myself, to take care of my child, & render myself worthy to join him.' So she became enshrined as the eternal widow, grieving for her husband as his poetic reputation blossomed, never grieving enough. 'I continue to exist,' she told her friend Maria Gisborne, 'to see one day succeed another; to dread night, but more to dread morning & hail another cheerless day.'

In fact, this was not the last story she would tell. She composed new prefaces for reissues of *Frankenstein*, produced and edited new volumes of Shelley's poetry, driving his growing reputation among the public, and wrote more novels of her own, publishing four during her widowhood, as well as several short stories and novellas. The most striking of them is *The Last Man* (1826), which tells of a plague that destroys humanity — a plausible enough scenario for somebody who had lived through so much tragedy.* The doom-laden atmosphere, and the echoes of Mary's acquaintances among her ill-fated characters, make it a chilling book to read. It resonates today, in our age of dystopian fantasies and apocalyptic visions, although it was trashed by critics at the time and failed to capture the feverish attention humming around Mary's debut. It was *Frankenstein* that kept finding new ways to reach the public, bearing out a line in the first theatrical production of 1823: 'It lives!'

---

* 'The last man!' she wrote in May 1823. 'Yes, I may well describe that solitary being's feelings, feeling myself as the last relic of a beloved race, my companions extinct before me.'

In September that year, shortly after her return to England, Mary wrote to her friend Leigh Hunt about a trip to the theatre: 'But lo and behold, I found myself famous — *Frankenstein* had prodigious success as a drama and was about to be repeated for the 23rd night at the English Opera House ...' By 1826, there had been more than a dozen stage versions, including popular performances in New York and Paris.

From creaky Victorian stage adaptations to the beloved 1930s movies and later Hammer Horror versions, to re-imaginings, comic strips, audio dramas, Halloween cosplaying, *Frankenstein* endures. 'It lives', indeed, or as Victor puts it in the 1931 movie classic, 'It's alive!' Which has been the case ever since Mary first dreamed up her tale in 1816. From a story grown out of a particular Romantic sensibility, stoked by the political concerns of a period dealing with new scientific developments, industrialisation, and revolutionary fervour, with the corrupted ideals of the French Revolution (that historic milestone that ended up consuming its own creators) and the Luddites' concerns over mechanisation, not to mention Mary's own personal traumas, *Frankenstein* has become a universal fable. Nineteenth-century writers fed on it with a ravenous appetite.*

And more than two centuries since its publication, the novel remains extraordinarily fresh meat. It can help to dramatise the psychosis of war-wracked Iraq, the complexities of transgenderism, a modern New York romance, to cite a few of its recent progeny (*Frankenstein in Baghdad* by Ahmed Saadawi, Jeanette Winterson's *Frankissstein*, *Cleopatra and Frankenstein* by Coco Mellors). During my travels, I saw the monster not only in the square in Geneva, but in the costume contest in Louisiana, outside a restaurant in Houston, in masks worn during the Day of the Dead parade in Mexico City, in posters for the Japanese 1960s kaiju movie *Frankenstein vs Baragon*.

---

* Stevenson's *The Strange Case of Dr Jekyll and Mr Hyde*, and Wells's *The Island of Dr Moreau* are two of the best-known of the legion of tales unimaginable without the fire lit by *Frankenstein*.

What these later versions have lost is the pathos of the monster. Frankenstein's creature does terrible things, but as he cries out, 'Shall I not then hate them who abhor me?' The novel pits creator and created in a bondage from which neither can be freed, a devastating mirroring of monster and man. 'You accuse me of murder', the creature exclaims, 'and yet you would, with a satisfied conscience, destroy your own creature. Oh, praise the eternal justice of man!' In his agonised speeches, we see a theme that would become ever more intense as the Industrial Revolution shapeshifted the world. Monsters had always been our mirror, but now they were a mirror of our own making. Monsters like Frankenstein's, and so many that would follow — the beastly hybrids created in Doctor Moreau's House of Pain, Doctor Jekyll's murderous alter ego Mr Hyde — would become records of human shame.

By the time Frankenstein's creature was lurching across the floorboards of the English Opera House, the force of his arguments was already diminishing. Visual media put his monstrousness to the fore — *monstrare*, to show — and Frankenstein's creature certainly knows how to put on a show. But what is lost is the consciousness that written texts communicate so powerfully: the poignancy, in the creature's case, of a being 'alone, and miserable'. Cinema has muted the eloquence of Mary Shelley's being to the growls and snarls of Boris Karloff, Christopher Lee, Robert De Niro, and others, so that now it's hard to associate him with such sophisticated rhetoric as: 'Shall I respect man when he contemns me? Let him live with me in the interchange of kindness; and instead of injury, I would bestow every benefit upon him with tears of gratitude at his acceptance.' The monster has been monstered, his humanity diluted in favour of extra doses of beast.

None of this can even scrape away the dead skin from Mary Shelley's ever-living achievement. In telling the story of Frankenstein, she managed to craft a new folk tale, a monster so universal it broke the boundaries of the novel that spawned it, to be reimagined across a multiverse of media. A monster that has become as ubiquitous, and as timeless, as the other monsters that populate this book. It doesn't emanate from another world; it hasn't crossed the threshold of the supernatural. Instead, it's been cobbled together by an ambitious human scientist. This is why *Frankenstein* was revolutionary: it showed we don't need the gods or nature to punish us with evil spirits, we're pretty damn good at tormenting ourselves. The increasingly 'human' monsters of the undead — the vampires, ghosts, and zombies — had shown the way, but it was Mary Shelley who drove this idea to the next level. In doing so, she made two profound points: about the destructive autonomy of humankind, as well as the pathos of the created being. She asked us to consider how our own inventions might backfire against us, but also what it feels like to be the things we invent.

These two key ideas, fused together like body parts attached to a single organism, would form the propulsive force behind the new artificial beings imagined, with increasing anxiety, as the Industrial Revolution gave way to the Machine Age. It would be down to a writer from a wooded hinterland of Eastern Europe to give this new anxiety a name. I visited his hometown a week before my journey to Geneva, laying down my backpack in the forest of the Krkonoše or 'Giant Mountains', falling asleep to the rustling of undergrowth creatures and the mechanical churring of nightjars.

CHAPTER ELEVEN

The Humans Must Die

THE ELEVENTH TALE
On a distant island, Rossum's Factory for Universal Robots is in full flight. Using a secret process, artificial people are manufactured out of living matter known as 'protoplasm'. There is scarcely a task these synthetic labourers cannot perform. They are stronger than human beings, and their brains much quicker. Cargo is being dispatched to Southampton, New York, Hamburg — from the latter, an order has arrived for 15,000 units. They are the most valuable asset in a rapidly changing world.

But a visitor to the factory has concerns. Her name is Helena, and aside from being the daughter of the president, she is also an activist for the League of Humanity. Do these robots have souls, she wonders? Can they feel pain? Harry Domin, the factory manager, insists they are no different from other machines, like car motors or tractors. Only their superior intelligence sets them apart. But can that really be the case, Helena wonders, when they look identical to humans? For Harry, the arrival of a beautiful woman on the island is far more interesting than any of the ethical questions she raises, and he sets out to woo her.

Ten years later, Harry and Helena are married, living in a house near the factory, with robot servants catering to their needs. Except there's a problem: the robots are becoming unstable. Every so often, a robot foams at the mouth and smashes up the furniture. There is talk of unrest overseas — armed robots revolting in America, firing on crowds in Madrid, deployed by governments in war. Rogue workers, at first, their neural connectivity yokes them into bands. They form their own union, with a manifesto and demands. They take over radio stations, railways, ships, and telegraphs. 'Robots throughout the world,' they broadcast, 'we command you to kill all mankind.'

With the robots turning against humanity en masse, outnumbering them a thousand to one, the humans don't stand a chance. Barricaded in their house, Helena, Harry, and a few of the factory employees try to withstand the siege. One of them, the robot psychologist Dr Gall, admits he altered the robots' character to make them more human. This has made them aware of their superiority, and hateful of their former masters. But Helena blames herself for asking Dr Gall to give them souls. The only advantage the humans have is the secret recipe for making the robots, which Helena burns. But the revolt of the robots — stabbing, shooting, electrocuting — is unstoppable. Helena and Harry are among the last to be tracked down. There is no mercy: they are shot dead with the others.

Now only one human remains: a builder called Alquist. The robots demand that he surrender the secret formula, but he cannot find it. Observing two of the robots, he is surprised to hear them laughing. Is there more to these protoplasmic insurgents than he realised? When he suggests experimenting on them, one of the robots weeps, the other steps forward to protect his partner. The robots are changing, Alquist realises. Humanity may be done for, but a new life is underway.

BOHEMIAN IDYLL

Tap, tap, tap ...

The woodpeckers of the Broumov Highlands were like hammers on steel. Wriggling out of my sleeping bag, I brushed off the leaves that had settled overnight, took a swig of water, and spat out the remains of last night's jam-filled loupaček pastry. Dawn was pulsing through the beech leaves, turning the canopies into parasols of light. Deer watched me from behind a fallen fir, and pines soared over a rising pathway. Sandstone boulders billowed over the track, teasing me with the half-hidden prospect beyond. A chain hung from one of the boulders, where the word 'Lotrando' was scrawled into the rock.

I thought of Karel Čapek's story 'Lotrando', or 'The Robber', in which an over-educated highwayman has to give up his family's robbery business and ends up as a toll-collector. Like many of Čapek's tales, it's slyly witty, poking fun at the hypocrisy of modern life, and rooted in the Czech countryside.

'No matter which hill you climb,' he wrote, 'you look north and see Mount Snezka (Snow Mountain), the highest mountain in the country, which used to be snow-covered the greater part of the year, even long after the fruit trees had lost their blossoms.' On a ridge at the top of the slope, an observatory soars above the forest. Metal echoed against my steps, as if my boots had turned to steel. My knees bent at the top, a defence against gravity. I peered over the tree-line, over the ring of villages around the mountain and the pale-blue hills receding in the distance. Bellowing underneath me was a portable sawmill. The electric groan of its log-cutting mingled with the call of cuckoos, the throbbing of wood pigeons, and the tapping of the woodpeckers. The sun was a pink smear on the horizon, a glowing outline traced around the treetops. I stood there, taking in the landscape, fixing the moment. I was high as a dragon, or — to be more period-appropriate — a biplane.

'In the valley between the Metuje and Úpa rivers,' wrote Karel Čapek, 'are peaceful, rolling hills of black sandstone intermingled with silver groves of birches and dark groves of spruce and bogs of peat. The hills are strewn with cottages where, even in the years of our childhood, you could still hear, banging away from morning to night, the hand-built looms of mountain chroniclers, spiritualists and members of unusual sects.'

A couple of miles downhill in Malé Svatoňovice, Karel and his brother, Josef, are immortalised in bronze, facing the old doctor's surgery where they were born, Karel in 1890, Josef three years earlier. It wasn't a lavish home — their father's income reduced by his refusal to charge the poor. But they had a library, and their mother was a gifted storyteller. Now the old surgery is a museum. Vladimira, the manager, gestured to her computer and I sat down beside her, communicating via Google Translate, discussing how Karel was influenced by the area — 'not only in his work for adults,' Vladimira explained, 'in stories like "Lotrando" and his novel *První Parta*, which was about mining life in this area, and also in the fairy tales he wrote.' Considering Karel's most famous story, this mode of communication seemed apt: AI enabling a conversation about the legacy of the man who gave us the word 'robot'.

In the corridors, Cubist paintings by Josef Čapek hung between portraits of villagers and sketches from the end of his life at the concentration camps of Buchenwald and Bergen-Belsen. On the first floor was Karel's output — copies of his books, posters for plays, screenshots from film adaptations. Butterflies hovered — or, at least, people costumed as them — in promotional photographs from the revue show *In the Life of Insects*, written by Karel and Josef together. A peasant girl in a rural headscarf faced a crowded courtroom in a still from a film adaptation of Karel's novel *Hordubal*. Most voluminous was the promotional material from *Rossum's Universal Robots*, first performed in 1920: photos from the early performances at the National Theatre in Prague, playbills from Broadway in 1922, London's West End in 1923, Sydney in 1925, at which it was described as 'The great modern play that lately created much sensational discussion, when it was presented in New York, London, and in all the capitals of Europe.'

Nothing dates like visions of the future, and *R.U.R.* is a curious piece to read today. But we can record its impact from a single word, used to describe the monsters of our own devisings: synthetic beings, manufactured to serve us, which in many of the stories end up destroying us. 'Frankenstein's Monster in Bulk', as *The Illustrated London News* put it. A story that took its spark from Mary Shelley's novel and blew its scale wide open, anticipating the thousands of cyborg, robot, and android insurrections to follow, from Isaac Asimov's *I, Robot* to the Voc robots of *Doctor Who*, the replicants of *Blade Runner*, the automatons of *Westworld*, or the mind-wiped 'dolls' of *Dollhouse* (where the debt is acknowledged in the name behind the mind-wiping technology: 'Rossum').

The roots of this remarkable piece of theatrical history lie in the mountainous forest around Malé Svatoňovice. 'Scattered about the region,' wrote Karel, 'are old farms and estates where peasant rebellions were born, but today there are government factories and kilometres of hand towels and worsted unfold from Úpice to the world.' Those 'peasant rebellions' took place in the nineteenth century, when Karel's grandparents were young. Throughout Bohemia, labourers were rising up, wrestling against the long-running system of exploitation. Others would replace it, but they managed to cast to oblivion one system in particular, through which peasants were obliged to work unpaid for a fixed period (which, in 1800, was set at ninety days per annum), comparable with the villeinage system of mediaeval England or Russian serfdom. By the end of the century, the practice had been overthrown, and a generation later it was ready to be repackaged, like an old-fashioned name put back in circulation. The name for this practice was 'robota'.

ELECTROPOLIS

From the pale-blue hills of the Giant Mountains, bursting out of thick forests onto a level plateau, over the Elbe towards the furred banks of the Vltava. When the Čapek brothers established themselves in Prague, in the 1910s, the city was on the up, and sweeping changes were afoot. A new world was breaking free, powered by emerging technology, with tramlines where horses had previously trudged, gaslights extinguished, and electric hoardings raised above hissing lampposts. Politically, the new age was equally wired. The Austro-Hungarian Empire was crumbling. Czechs were hankering for national independence, official use of their language, and positions in high office. The First World War dealt the killer blow, and from the shattered pieces of the empire emerged a new, native leadership.

The Čapek brothers arrived in Prague at just the right time. With the Czech language proliferating at a rapid pace, there was an explosion of print media, newspapers in search of articulate native-born writers. Country bumpkins they may have seemed, leaping out of the way of the trams in their chocolate-brown suits, with rosy rural complexions glowing under their bowler hats. But over time, thanks to their burgeoning literary skills, the brothers secured work in the newspapers. Karel was taken on by *Národní Listy* (*National Pages*) in 1916, and Josef was employed by the newspaper in 1918. When he was dropped two years later, for protesting against the paper's opposition to Tomáš Masaryk, the first Czechoslovak president, Karel walked out in solidarity. A few months later, they were both working for another daily, *Lidové Noviny* (*The People's Newspaper*), which counted Karel as a regular contributor right up until his death in 1938.

Reading some of the pieces that Karel filed in the years before he wrote *R.U.R.*, what is striking is the importance placed on freedom, personal as well as political. 'Every thought today,' he wrote for *Národní Listy* in 1917, 'must be directed to the freedom of the nation and only to that! To the freedom of the nation, yes, but add to that also the freedom of an educated, free-spirited nation ... If we want the world to be with us, then we must be with the world, at its side, at least wherever in history and in the present the world has striven for freedom and the ideal human condition.'

He would have got on well with the Shelleys. But his was the zeitgeist of the interwar period: an age of revolution that wiped out a gallery of monarchs. It was easy enough to imagine the overthrowing of the old order when you were seeing it in the newspapers every day. It is out of this atmosphere of revolution and upheaval that Karel's game-changing robot tale emerged.

Today's Prague may well be an obstacle course of tourist traps, with black-market traders in the crowded squares and cheap beer frothing out of riverside bars. But in the eastern district of Žižkov, you can glimpse the spirit of Karel's time. People came to Žižkov to work in its many factories and spent their earnings in the pubs that sprouted around them, more per capita than anywhere else in Europe. With its early tramline, Žižkov was an experiment in new technology, its steep hills providing challenges for the emerging industry, from horse-drawn trams to modern electric ones. Karel Čapek was ambivalent about these shiny new forms of transport. After experiencing the 'sewer with rails' of the London Underground, he wrote, 'I felt a blind and furious opposition to modern civilisation. It seemed to me that there is something barbaric and disastrous in this terrible hoarding of people.'

Tramlines still criss-cross Žižkov, and there are still plenty of workmen with shovels on the roadsides, not to mention the pubs, where Karel might have felt more at home. Inside the district's oldest pub, U Slovanské Lípy, the 1920s atmosphere was kept alive with old bottles on the shelves, braids of dried grass on the coving, and paintings of country life. I sat there, nursing a foamy Pilsner and a plate of boiled dumplings, and it was only when I was halfway through my pint that I noticed the name of the painting overhead. It showed women in a field cutting the corn with scythes and bare hands. A mother was nursing her baby, trying to avoid the gangmaster's attention; another was flailing under his stick. These were the rural slaves of the nineteenth-century system, as the painting's title made clear: *Robota*. One of travel's serendipities. You can rush around looking for clues, but sometimes you just need to sit back and wait for the journey to ping you.

AUTOMATONS ACROSS THE AGES

Few monsters can be nailed to a precise birthdate, but some are clearly older than others. And yet, when it comes to robots, well, they may not have been trundling around as long as dragons, but they aren't as brand new as we often assume. 'Čapek's robots were but the latest in a whole line of mechanical men,' wrote Igor Aleksander and Piers Burnett in *Reinventing Man*, 'and all that the concept had hitherto lacked was a label.'

We can plot our way around the ancient world between its mechanical beings — from Greece (Hephaestus's metal servants on Mount Olympus) to the Middle East (the metal warriors in the City of Brass) to India (mechanical figures guarding the relics of the Buddha). In many stories, they are little more than window dressing, adding fantastical glamour to their narrative furnishings, unable to match the emotional depths of nature. But however limited their roles, they act as mirrors, through which we can explore what makes us human.

Stories of artificial beings have been told since at least the Bronze Age, but alongside the stories are real attempts to create automatic beings, which have been happening almost as long. Another whistlestop tour: from Jacques de Vaucanson's automata in eighteenth-century Paris — a flautist, a pipe-player, a duck, among others — via Leonardo da Vinci's designs for a mechanical giant, across the Mediterranean to the Arab scientist al-Jazari's humanoid waitress in thirteenth-century Baghdad, to the walking, winking automaton presented to Emperor Mu of China three millennia ago, which was so flirtatious that its inventor had to pull it apart to show it was nothing more than wood, leather, and paint.

For all these long-ranging curiosities, it wasn't until the age of industrialisation that mechanical beings became a widespread possibility — and therefore a potential threat to the human race. In 1867, Karl Marx wrote about the 'mechanical monster whose body fills whole factories, and whose demon power, at first veiled under the slow and measured motions of his giant limbs, at length breaks out into the fast and furious whirl of his countless working organs'. In the wake of *Frankenstein*, new stories about technological hubris were pouring out of the ever-expanding range of publishing presses, as industrialisation facilitated imaginative exploration of the anxieties it was causing. You could run from the billowing clouds and clanking steps of Edward S. Ellis's *The Steam Man of the Prairies* (1869) or hide from the great metal limbs of H.G. Wells's alien invaders in *The War of the Worlds* (1897). And from a different angle — less menacing but equally eerie — you might wonder at the invention of a female android in Auguste Villiers de l'Isle-Adam's *The Future Eve* (1886) or M.L. Campbell's *The Automatic Maid-of-all-Work: a possible tale of a near future* (1893), an early imagining of an automated workforce.

The industrial revolution was driven, in part, by abolition and the need for a cheap alternative to slavery. As the German physicist Hermann von Helmholtz put it in 1954: 'we no longer aim to build machines which perform the work of one human but one machine performs the work of a thousand humans'. Who needs human slaves when humans can be, as factory manager Harry Domin puts it in *R.U.R.*, 'an aristocracy nourished by milliards of mechanical slaves'? Karel Čapek was drawing on the issue that had been growing in urgency, with the electric revolution following fast on the industrial, with human populations swelling and the capacity of our machinery expanding at the same time. His choice of 'roboti' has an uncanny resonance in this respect, an old form of slavery echoing through the industrialised world.

It's peculiarly apt that a Czech writer should have produced such a defining take on the idea of artificial beings. After all, prior to *R.U.R.*, one of the most famous of all artificial beings was also associated with Prague. In the 1580s, according to legend, the Jewish community was pressurised by a blood libel — accused of killing young Christians and drinking their blood at the Passover feast. In order to fortify the accusation, a priest called Thaddeus coached a convert from Judaism to claim the Jews mixed blood with the matzas they baked for the

Passover. Against a background of violent anti-Semitic attacks, the head rabbi, Judah Loew, marshalled old cabbalistic texts to mould a man out of clay, taking his closest confidants to the Vltava river to help him. According to the story, they took a ritual bath, performed the Chatzot prayer, and collected clay and loam around the banks. Out of this raw material they kneaded a large humanoid figure three ells in length. As they walked, in ritual order, seven times around this inanimate blob, reciting holy words, the figure started warming up, radiating a heat like red-hot metal. So they ordered it onto its feet, and Rabbi Loew gave its instructions: 'Your mission is to protect the Jews from persecution ... you must obey my commands no matter when and where I might send you ...'

The Golem would prove invaluable — fending off Christian attacks, as well as fetching water for the rabbi's wife. But with its relentlessly literal interpretation of instructions, it also anticipated comedy robots of the future. Once, told to fetch water for Passover, the Golem kept filling huge barrels for the rabbi's wife, and didn't stop filling them, thereby causing a flood. As one of the managers puts it in *R.U.R.*, 'Robots don't know when to stop work.'

So the Golem was put to rest in the attic of the Old-New Synagogue, covered in prayer shawls and books. A trace of its legendary presence is still visible on the wall outside the synagogue, where looped nails run behind the tabernacle all the way to the attic door.

The concept of the Golem dates back to biblical times, and during the mediaeval period several cabbalists wrote about Golems, or were credited with making them. But the stories about Rabbi Loew's Golem flourished in the nineteenth century, and around the turn of the twentieth, they were trending once again. A popular variation was the Prague-based Austrian writer Gustav Meyrink's strange and dream-like novel *The Golem* (serialised in 1913–14), set in the Prague ghetto. Around the same time, the expressionist German filmmaker Paul Wegener made three silent movies about the Golem, also set in Prague and released between 1915 and 1920, which played to packed theatres in Europe and the USA. So when Karel Čapek was writing *R.U.R.*, the story of an automatic being in Prague was especially current, resonating for an age dealing with so much new technology and the anxieties that inspired.

Karel eschewed the old-school depiction of artificial beings as divinely or supernaturally animated. No longer a single Golem, or the lone monster of *Frankenstein*, his artificial beings echoed the claustrophobia of a world increasingly aware of its own teeming multitudes.* Here come the monsters, marching en masse. But Karel's robots were more than just a mindless mob. Like Mary Shelley a century earlier, he was asking about the nature of consciousness, a question with which we are wrestling — with undiminishing urgency — today.

ROSSUM CONQUERS THE WORLD

'I was seized by a dreadful fear,' wrote Karel to his future wife Olga, with whom he fell in love while he was writing *R.U.R.* 'I wanted to warn against mass production and dehumanized slogans and, all of a sudden, I became anxious that it could happen, perhaps soon, that I shall not save anything by my warning, that the same way as I, the author, led the power of these dull mechanisms where I wanted, somebody else may lead the ignorant mass man against the world and God.'

R.U.R. was written fast and accepted by the National Theatre in Prague. Shortly before its opening in January 1921, Olga read it with a group of writers, recording later: 'there was extended silence ... a sign of a deep impression having been created.' Still, this was no guarantee that the play would succeed. So the warm reactions of the critics came as a relief. 'This skilful and funny work,' declared one of

---

* This is a regular motif in Fritz Lang's *Metropolis* (1927), as well as in numerous contemporary films such as Lang's *Dr Mabuse* (1922), Karl Grune's *The Street* (1923), and King Vidor's *The Crowd* (1928).

the Czech papers, 'will immediately impress you with the impression of some dramatic, fantastically scientific and social novel by Wells. Only at a distance will you get to know the Czech core of the work, so interesting that it would be spread to a larger scene abroad.'

Among these responses, perhaps the most indicative of the play's popularity is the memory of an audience member called Milla Tiefenbach, just eight years old at the time. She remembered that tickets had to be booked two months in advance, and she recalled playing 'robots' with her friends, inspired by the play. Is there any better way to measure a monster's acceptance by the public? Rockin' robot, robot chopter, Peter Crouch's robot dance — they all started in Prague 1921, when children like Milla dreamed up their own robot games.

Observed from today's perspective, *R.U.R.* is easy to dismiss as a clunky melodrama, a primitive prototype for the Asimovian tale of robot revolution. But for its original audience, it reflected the changing world around them — the effects of industrialisation, urbanisation, and globalisation. It has 'as many social implications as the most heady of Shavian comedies', to quote *The New York Herald*, while the correspondent for *The Call* declared it 'the most brilliant satire on our mechanized civilization; the grimmest yet subtlest arraignment of this strange, mad thing we call the industrial society of today'.

Not only was it compared to the works of George Bernard Shaw, *R.U.R.* even drew the great playwright's attention. In June 1923, Shaw accompanied the novelist G.K. Chesterton in a debate about the themes of *R.U.R.* at St Martin's Theatre in London. 'Mr Shaw, at one point, turned to the audience calling them robots,' it was reported, 'because they read party press and its opinions are imposed on them.' The idea of the robot as a metaphor for psychological dependence, emotional disengagement, herd-thinking, was taking root.

Shaw's point reflects the play's apportioning of blame. Mankind not only creates the very thing that destroys it, but renders itself all the more vulnerable, accelerating the self-destruction its invention has engineered. 'For our own selfishness, for profit, for progress, we have destroyed mankind,' says the builder Alquist. Freed from labour, humans lack the will to survive. Fertility rates drop, then snuff out altogether. In the climactic conflict, the last humans are rounded up. As far as the robots are concerned, they have only one remaining use: to supply the secret recipe for robot manufacture. Alquist, spared because 'he works with his hands like the Robot', is reluctant to help them at first. But the sight of two robots in love makes him relent. Life continues, he realises. In Čapek's radical ending, happiness is centred not on humans but on this new synthetic form of life.

While *R.U.R.* 'set off for a triumphant journey to the present-day theatres of Europe', as the playwright Arnošt Dvořák rather bitterly predicted, the word 'robot' went on a similar journey, building up momentum until it became the undisputed word for an idea with increasing currency. Storytelling took a while to catch up: it was only towards the end of the 1920s that 'robot' was in regular use, in stories such as O.L. Beckwith's 'The Robot Master' and the hugely popular *Buck Rogers 2430 AD* series (a remote-controlled robot, for example, with a swivel neck and caterpillar tracks, appeared in a 1929 instalment). But the word gained speedier traction elsewhere. There were articles imagining 'Robots in Real Life' in the tabloid press, they were deployed to decry dehumanising labour or power dynamics in political speeches, and advertisers used robots for up-to-date slogans and gimmicks.*

At the London exhibition of the Model Engineers Society in September 1928, all eyes were on a six-foot-tall aluminium figure called Eric. He was operated by levers, bolts, and wheels powered by twelve-volt electric motors, and he had 'RUR' printed on his chest

---

* 'Robots in Real Life' appeared in *The Daily Mirror,* 16 May 1923; in the political sphere, the British MP Shapurji Saklatvala argued, on 20 March 1925, for naval ratings 'to cease being a man Robot and become a human being'; and among other examples, they were used in a 1928 ad for Schweppes: 'A Robot is the only type of man who doesn't enjoy Schweppes'.

plate. Bowing to the audience, he delivered a four-minute speech, with sparks of blue electricity swirling between his teeth: 'Ladies and gentlemen, I am Eric the robot, the man without a soul.' By the following year, the word was so entrenched, it could be cited by the travel writer William Seabrook, contrasting the wild vitality he perceived in Haiti against the 'mechanical, soulless robots' of modern civilisation; or by the novelist Richard Aldington to bemoan the treatment of frontline soldiers in World War I: 'a unit, a murder robot, a wisp of cannon fodder'.

In many of those early references, the label appears in inverted commas, or buffered by explicatory phrases; but through the course of the 1930s, it phased out the alternatives. Leading pulp writers like Edmond Hamilton and Eando Binder called their antagonists 'robot', standing out against old-fashioned terms like 'Mech-Men'. One of Binder's stories was 'I, Robot' (published in 1939), in which a robot, falsely accused of killing its creator, fends off its attackers while reading *Frankenstein*. The most influential of all 'robot writers', Isaac Asimov, was inspired by Binder's story to write his own positronic robot series, and his publisher chose *I, Robot* as the title for a collection of his tales, published in 1950. By this time, the word was supreme. Robots might not have conquered the earth, but as far as terminology was concerned, 'robot' certainly had.

It's an extraordinary impact, a rare instance of a Czech word gone global, comparable to the viral effect of the Serbian word 'vampire' two centuries earlier. Travelling through the Czech Republic, I saw people's eyes light up whenever I mentioned my interest in Karel Čapek. 'Oh, we study him at school,' said a woman in a Žižkov pub. On a train to Prague, the ticket collector did a robotic motion with his arms when he saw an image of *R.U.R.* on my Kindle. 'Karel Čapek!' he declared with a grin. And in a converted Jesuit convent, I met a scientist whose life had been shaped by Čapek. He'd even taken 'RUR' as his personal moniker.

THE MAN IN THE STRIPED PYJAMAS

Another Prague drinking hole. As crisp and dark as the cooling chamber under a spaceship's control room. The only chatter across the bar was a faint droning hum and the occasional click. The server was taciturn to the extreme. I swiped my card on a tablet and watched as a pair of robotic arms twitched and rotated, pumping the liquor from dozens of bottles hanging from the ceiling and slid over my cocktail in a plastic container.

So goes an evening in Prague's Robotic Bar ...

All through my travels I'd been gliding through the uncanny valley, running a relay of robot encounters. There was a smiley-faced mechanical figure directing the traffic by an Istrian motorway tunnel. A coffee-serving barista had a screen for a face in Tokyo Station. At the US–Mexican border, the guards operated four-legged cyber-dogs. Grandest of all was Tradinno, the world's largest walking robot, who stomped around Furth im Wald spouting fire. This is the world we live in: the world forecast by Karel Čapek and his ilk. But how close are we to their visions? If anybody could answer that question, surely it was the man who signed himself 'RUR'.

I met Rudolf Rosa at the Computer Science Block of Charles University, a former Jesuit convent with a high wooden gateway and stucco on the walls. Under long brown hair and a thick beard that covered nearly all his neck, Rudolf's black T-shirt was emblazoned with 'Rossum's Universal Robot'. His eyes smiled warmly behind wire-framed specs as he stuck out a hand. He had the air of somebody at ease in his environment, amused to find himself mapping out visions of the future in a building with such a prestigious past.

Under a vaulted stucco ceiling, I peered across the functional desks to the whiteboard, where a few scribbled equations had been nearly wiped clear. This surreal combination was a reminder of the overlap between our modern world and the older one from which it has poured. Rudolf's father is an electrician, his mother a teacher of foreign languages: 'So I feel I've joined these disciplines together with computational linguistics.' He calls himself a 'robot psychologist', a term he traces to Asimov's *I, Robot*. As part of his role, he was enlisted in a project known as 'THEaiTRE', a collaboration between a tech company, a local theatre, and the computational linguistics department of the university, helping with the creation of a play to mark the hundredth anniversary of *R.U.R.*, entitled *AI: When a Robot Writes a Play*.

'The aim was to see if a robot,' said Rudolf, 'or in fact a computer, could write a play.'

Using the language model GPT-2, with editorial prompts and interventions, it was a test of how far computers have come from the time of *R.U.R.*, as well as an experiment in how computers perceive humans. A century earlier, Čapek had written about robots. *When a Robot Writes a Play* was doing it the other way round.

'I think Čapek might be appalled by what we are doing,' said Rudolf. 'A computer writing a play — and many of the ways in which computers are used. He wrote against these kinds of things all through his life. But we're also trying to break down what makes people wary of computers.'

'And did the experiment work?'

He smiled through his beard. 'It wrote a play, sure. But computers aren't very good at things like character. They weren't always consistent, and some of them would just keep repeating the same line over and over. During the rehearsals, the actors talked about how, when a play is good, they feel energised by it. But in this case, they felt like the life was being sucked out of them.'

A blow for the humans, surely? But in the ongoing argy-bargy over artificial intelligence, there are defeats and victories on every side.

'Čapek imagined a future dominated by robots,' said Rudolf, 'but actually the really striking thing is that AI isn't walking about. It's in computers.'

Here was the debate raging around the world — with growing intensity over the months after I met Rudolf. The proliferation of AI through ChatGPT, Anthropic, Google, and many other models was leading to apocalyptic pronouncements, safety summits, and warnings against 'enfeeblement' — the debilitating state of human dependence that empowers the robots in *R.U.R.* In 2014, the scientist Stephen Hawking had warned that 'It's tempting to dismiss the notion of highly intelligent machines as mere science fiction, but this would be a mistake — and potentially our worst mistake ever.' Even more urgently, in May 2023, the neural network specialists Geoffrey Hinton and Yoshua Bengio (considered the 'godfathers' of AI), the CEOs of OpenAI, Google DeepMind, and Anthropic, and leading academics at Oxford, Cambridge, Stanford, the Chinese Academy of Sciences, and a plethora of other prestigious institutions joined more than 350 signatories insisting on the importance of 'Mitigating the risk of extinction from AI'.

As Rudolf had pointed out, the risk doesn't lie in armies of synthetic humanoids. When the end comes, it's more likely to be dealt out by databases, like HAL in Stanley Kubrick's *2001: a space odyssey*. Whether they'll switch everything off, cut us off from the systems on which we depend, or terminate us with weapons embedded in our devices, that's for the future to unfold, and sci-fi writers to imagine. Across my journey, I was struck by the reach of AI (automated docks where there used to be workers, farmland given over to machines), along with less affluent blind spots where it had yet to cast its gaze, such as the villages of the Balkans or rural Morocco. Like so much technological innovation across the ages, it has the potential to ease people's lives, as the robots' advocates argue in *R.U.R.*, and as Rudolf also pointed out ('in my field of language processing,' he said, 'I can see technology greatly helping people who are not fluent in English, as well as people who have various disabilities,' adding that it is 'democratising access to information'). But it also has the potential to stretch existing inequities, atomise communities, and mess around with the life prospects of people who are already struggling. Whatever the future holds, one thing is certain: the Czech word will remain part of the discussion, in its original form or any of the neologisms it's inspired (bot, microbot, nanobot, chatbot, bot herd, bot farm, robocop, robolution, robopocalypse ...).

*

Karel Čapek's name continues to sparkle in the places that celebrate him — the museum in Malé Svatoňovice; a memorial to the brothers near the Vinohrady Theatre in Prague; a panel on the house where they lived in Prague; the house that Karel developed after his marriage, twenty-six miles south of the capital, 'small, yellow and white', in his words, 'like a hard-boiled egg'. I spent a day at Stará Huť, wandering around his old furniture — a hat stand, a record player, the special chair built to support his back against his lifelong affliction of spondyloarthritis of the vertebrae, a condition that led him to various spa towns in search of pain relief. Another reason why he gave so much thought to synthetic beings unaffected by human frailty.

He was a leading figure of Czech literature by the time he was presented with the house as a wedding gift. But the 1930s were on the march. With the Nazis drumming at the border, the Čapek brothers' outspoken defiance of fascism drew ire. Karel was listed by the Gestapo as one of Czechoslovakia's leading 'public enemies'. A press campaign was launched against him, abusive letters sent, stones thrown at his windows. Stará Huť became a refuge, cocooned from the world's tensions. Here is an echo of the themes of *R.U.R.* — the importance of personal liberty, the image of a lonely voice of humanity, looking out from his sanctuary at the relentless approach of a murderous army.

Throughout that bitter winter of 1938, storms attacked the house, tore down the trees, caused the banks of Karel's pond to flood. Even before the Munich Conference of 1938, friends were urging him to flee the country. But with Hitler's army pouring into Czechoslovakia, time was running out. Still, he put off the inevitable, burying himself in fictional fantasies and the repair works on his house. When the house flooded, he waded through the cold to make a telephone call in the village. It was too great a risk for his ever-fragile health. Influenza ensued, followed by pneumonia and an inflammation of the kidneys. After a few days' illness, he died on Christmas Day 1938.

More than just another author's death, this was a sign of the times. 'With a consistency that has no parallel for horribleness,' wrote Erika Mann, daughter of the Nobel laureate Thomas, 'the best, the most spiritual persons, the true representatives of every country, disappear from the scene in that country as soon as the fascist dictatorship comes to power. They flee, they are killed, they kill themselves — or they simply die ... An artist of Čapek's rank and convictions could not breathe in a mutilated, fascist Czechoslovakia subject to Hitler's overlordship.'

This was more than hyperbole: less than three months after Karel's death, on 15 March 1939, Nazi officers marched into the house at Stará Huť. Refusing to believe he was dead, they ransacked the place. Sometimes, a short illness can be a mercy. We know how Karel would have fared under the Nazis. Because we know what happened to his brother.

On 9 September 1939, Josef was dispatched to Dachau, then Buchenwald. He was moved between concentration camps, spending time in Sachsenhausen and finally, in 1945, Bergen-Belsen, where he was snarled by an outbreak of typhus. He had written and drawn throughout the war; he had even been tasked with drawing the family trees of SS officers. Some of the most moving exhibits at the museum in Malé Svatoňovice are the sketches he made in Buchenwald. But only one item was returned to his widow.

'Can you help me pull down this box?' Vladimira the manager asked me when I visited the museum after my night in the forest. Inside the flaps of cardboard were bits and pieces belonging to the Čapek family. One was Karel's father's black leather surgical bag; another was Karel's brown gardening trousers. Everyday items, they brought a lump to my throat, but that was nothing to the impact of the third item. It was Josef's last change of clothes: a pair of striped blue-and-white pyjamas, standard issue uniform for concentration-camp inmates.

Josef wasn't just Karel's brother; he was frequently his creative collaborator and a sounding-board for ideas. In the case of *R.U.R.*, Josef made a particularly significant contribution, because it was he who suggested the all-important word. While Karel was working on the play, he couldn't decide what to call his artificial workers. 'Labori' was the word he'd come up with, but he feared it sounded too bookish. When he expressed his frustration, Josef was working at his easel, quietly painting. It was then that Josef offered his solution: 'Call them robots,' he said.

*

There is a terrible irony here: the man who suggested the term 'robot' spent his last days reduced to a number, a uniform, a pair of striped pyjamas. In the worst possible way, Josef Čapek learned what it means to be a robota — a body at the mercy of his ruthless overlords. Was there any point in monsters anymore? What menace could a vampire, a giant, a dragon pose, when humans were capable of so much worse?

But in the years after the war, new monsters would be invented, driven by new anxieties in a world increasingly alert to our powers of destruction; driven, at the same time, by the expanding potential of our new and developing media — film, television, computers, magazines. The rise in technology, parabled by Karel Čapek's story of Rossum's 'roboti', would be the catalyst for the most intense period of monster-making the world has ever seen.

Not all the best monsters are ancient — not when imaginations and technology are churning out so many new ones, not when there are so many anxieties feeding new visions of terror. Hard to pick a single example — when you can choose a fifty-five foot ape swatting biplanes from the top of the Empire State Building, a half-dead flying ace fused with swamp vegetation into a shaggy beast like a walking bale of peat moss, a nest of giant ants in the storm drains of LA, a screeching army of metal-bound mutants with a racial superiority complex, giant worms swallowing the profiteers who've disturbed their desert, feudal warriors with craggy ridged heads and high brows, a bipedal parasitical extraterrestrial with a blade-tipped tail and acid drooling out of its jaws, an obese, slug-like gangster presiding over a court of prisoners and slaves, a twenty-five-storey-tall quadruped covered in multi-eyed dog-sized parasites, a telekinetic tetrapod from a parallel dimension with black blood and a head that bursts open like a carnivorous flower ...*

But among all the monsters the modern world has conjured, is there any other that can proclaim itself their king?

---

* These are, respectively, *King Kong* (1933), the comic-strip monster known as the Heap (1940), the giant ants from *Them!* (1954), the Daleks in *Doctor Who* (first appeared 1963), the sandworms in *Dune* (1965), the Klingons in *Star Trek* (first appeared in 1967), the alien in *Alien* (1979), Jabba the Hutt in *Star Wars: Return of the Jedi* (1983), the monster in *Cloverfield* (2008), and the Demogorgon in *Stranger Things* (first appeared 2016). Readers will, of course, have their own favourites and alternatives!

CHAPTER TWELVE

King of the Monsters

THE TWELFTH TALE
Over the Pacific Ocean, the sky lights up in a white-hot blaze. One after another, ships go missing, from huge freighters to tiny fishing boats. What is happening in the sea? A dying crewman makes it back to Odo Island and cries out: 'It got us.' To an elder, the message is clear: 'It must be Godzilla!'

Long, long ago, this ancient sea monster was propitiated by human sacrifice. Now, to forestall further attacks, the islanders perform a ritual dance, donning the masks of tengu (goblins), beating drums, and chanting sacred verses. But Godzilla will not be so easily pacified. He tears across the island, crushing houses and stealing away livestock. Nine people die in the rampage, and a cohort of islanders sets off to Tokyo to appeal for help.

The attack of the giant reptile is headline news in the capital. Government ministers, journalists, and scientists gather to hear the islanders' testimony. One of the scientists, the palaeontologist Professor Yamane, sets out for Odo Island. There, he discovers giant radioactive footprints and a trilobite. But his timing is dangerous — the village bell is rung, for the monster has been sighted. Professor Yamane estimates that Godzilla is fifty metres tall, an ancient marine beast disturbed and awakened by hydrogen-bomb testing. Surely, he speculates, this is the last of the dinosaurs.

Despite the professor's desire to study the creature, more hawkish voices win out. Depth charges are dropped in the sea, rousing the monster from Tokyo Bay. Godzilla stomps into the capital, crushing the railway line at Shinagawa and killing the passengers on a train. All of Japan is on high alert, and painful memories of the war resurface as air-raid shelters fill. A thirty-metre-high electrified fence is built to fend off the monster, but his atomic breath obliterates the barrier and once again the capital is subjected to Godzilla's rampage. He smashes the side of the Diet (Parliament) Building, rips down a clock tower, torches the city's most famous department store, knocks down a broadcasting tower, and lasers fleeing pedestrians with his atomic exhalations. Even the blastings of the air force's fighter jets are unable to stifle the monster.

But there is hope. Professor Yamane's daughter Emiko is engaged to a reclusive scientist called Dr Serizawa. She wants to break it off, for she has fallen in love with a ship captain called Ogata. But when she visits Serizawa, he shows her his latest experiment — the Oxygen Destroyer. The effects of this ruthless killing device are so horrific, Emiko runs out of his laboratory, forgetting the reason she came. She is accompanied by Ogata on a return visit, and together they persuade Serizawa to use his weapon. It may be the only way that Japan can be saved.

So one day, Serizawa and Ogata head out to sea. Clad in diving suits, they drop under the surface and find Godzilla slumbering on the ocean floor. Serizawa detonates his weapon beside the beast, and cuts off his own oxygen supply, ensuring the secret of his deadly weapon will die with him.

His sacrifice saves the nation, and leaves his beloved Emiko free to marry her true love. Godzilla surfaces for the last time, roaring in pain, before sinking back to his grave on the seabed. Professor Yamane, watching pensively from the ship's deck, wonders if this is the last they have seen of the monster. As long as nuclear testing continues, there is surely the threat that another Godzilla will rise.

MONSTER MUNCH

If you're going to plunge inside a giant monster's mouth, it's best to wear a hard hat and a harness. I was standing on a scaffold of iron, my ears blasted by a very nearby roar. You could see the giant mouth between the trees: a hundred teeth poking at disorderly angles, sharpened stakes embedded in a battlefield where the mud was the black-and-brown corrugations of the creature's lips.

'Are you ready for Godzilla?'

Behind me were two self-professed otaku — super-fans.

'Which is your favourite?' I asked, as I checked my waistbelt buckle was secure.

'Shin Godzilla!' one of them said, referencing a box-office smash from 2016.

His friend said, 'Godzilla anime,' prompting a change of mind:

'No, no, Godzilla in the pachinko parlours — that's the best!'

I could hear their relish as I was climbing the steps, clenching my fingers around the handlebars. All that separated me from the monster was a hundred metres of zip wire. Another roar and the metal floor peeled away from my feet, replaced by canopies of willow and air. I yowled with excitement — all those monsters I'd shadowed, now I was eyeball to eyeball with a giant, tumbling over his tongue, my legs shaking as I shuddered onto a platform at the back of the monster's head. A hundred dreams wrapped up in one marvellous fairground experience.

They call it the 'National Institute of Godzilla Disaster', so what

I was doing was not — don't be mistaken about this! — for fun. Let's be clear about it: this was a mission!

Once you're through the turnstile, you're briefed with a short film. A gigantic dinosaur-like beast with spiky spinal plates has emerged near Awaji Island, darkening the sea with blood — Godzilla. Fighter planes swoop overhead, subduing the monster with pacifying mines. 'Alert all sections!' 'Detonate mine!' 'Shift to Phase Three!' The otaku knew what to do. Before I'd hit ground level, they were racing past, plastic rifles in their arms, sliding between military barrels and sandbags. Slouching behind them, I kept a more reptilian pace. Slowly hauling myself onto an observation deck, I watched others zip-wire down, legs twisting under their harnesses, screams of delight swallowed by the monster's roar.

Is this what monsters mean today? Has our brave new world lost all its fear of monsters, when we pay to be gobbled up, when we jostle each other in fairground queues and click on ticketing websites for our turn to face the behemoths?

The Institute of Godzilla Disaster is in the pleasure park of Awaji Island, across a narrow suspension bridge from mainland Japan. There's an anime park and an aqua park and the parapeted walls of the Dragon Boy Castle. The martial beat of the *Godzilla* theme tune drums you towards a glow-up Godzilla, parked outside the only museum dedicated to the world's longest-running movie series. Thirty-eight films and counting (all but five of them made in Japan): the series spans so many sites across the country that a map in the museum is arrowed in every direction by the locations of Godzilla's attacks.

There, Godzilla stands in a diorama, man-sized, over the pink rubble of Tokyo Station, a skyscraper smashed by the wrecking ball of his tail. Over here, he's poised to fight his robotic alter ego, Mechagodzilla, framed by another skyline of tower blocks while the god-monster Mothra, a giant blue-eyed moth, flutters overhead. Like Godzilla, Mothra isn't simply a monster. Often depicted as heroic, she is worshipped by the natives of a South Pacific island before spinning a cocoon in Tokyo Tower and causing widespread destruction. But no monster can destroy like Godzilla. Reliving his greatest hits, he bursts out of an ice cap, roars at an army of Samurai warriors, clenches his fists at the towers he's about to topple. Trapped inside rows of glass cases are the numerous monsters that have flexed their talons and claws against him over the decades: the giant beetle-like Megalon; Gigan with his steel horns and metal saw-like arms; the three-headed golden monster known as King Ghidorah, which is based on a beast out of Shinto mythology.

In the original *Godzilla* (1954), there's a scene in which villagers perform a ritual exorcism — a kagura dance, like the one I witnessed in Kyoto during Setsubun. Donning long-nosed tengu masks, they chant from Shinto scriptures to pacify Godzilla. The scene reflects how Japanese kaiju (the movie monsters that Godzilla pioneered) differ from those in the contemporary West. Retrofitted to folklore, they evoke the ancient myths of apocalyptic beasts, dragons, and other giants laying waste to the land. Worshipped as godlike beings in the movie scenarios, propitiated by sacrifice, they are connected to ancient storytelling roots by threads that haven't been completely severed. As the Godzilla memoirist Bill Tsutsui put it to me: 'to root the mythology, it makes the monsters somehow credible and gives them a depth for a Japanese audience.' It also brings us back to the god-monsters with which this book began.

'I was seven when I first saw Godzilla,' said museum director Ryo Kato. 'It was *Godzilla vs Mechagodzilla*. After that, I was hooked!'

Leading me around the museum, Ryo stopped beside the statue of the robot monster. 'I watched all the movies after that, and I got the toys. I loved playing with them, especially Godzilla versus Mechagodzilla.'

'What about the humans?'

A subtle tilt of the head indicated there was nothing to say on this. The *Godzilla* franchise has always been monster-centric. Its most memorable battles, rather than pitting the monster against some muscle-bound alpha male, hurl him into thunderous, sinew-ripping showdowns with other monsters: Godzilla versus Mothra, Godzilla versus King Ghidorah, Godzilla versus King Kong.

'*Godzilla* isn't as popular as it was,' said Ryo, pointing out that Dragon Boy draws a bigger crowd these days. 'But *Godzilla* will always be important in Japan, because it's our first special-effects movie and it has spread around the world. Older people especially are very proud of it. It reminds them of their childhood, it has nostalgia for them.'

Fancy a metallic *Godzilla* keyring, a bottle of hot *Godzilla* sauce, a Godzilla or Mothra to take home and put on your windowsill? Browsing near me in the shop, a boy about eight years old was weighing up a golden Ghidorah and a horned Baragon (which first appeared in the 1965 cult classic *Frankenstein vs Baragon*).

'I like Godzilla a lot!' he announced. I could see no reason to disagree.

The policy is merch, then munch. After you've shopped, you snack Godzilla-style. A clawed soy-sauce footprint colours a mound of rice. Mothra's tail is fashioned out of lettuce, and her wings out of crackerbreads. For dessert, you can gobble up Godzilla's head, with sliced strawberries as bloodied teeth. However steep the competition may be, there's still plenty of yen in the old beast. But Godzilla has always been defined by more than ticket sales. He matters — for Japan, for its complicated post-war history — as no other movie monster has mattered. In the words of Steve Ryfle, cultural historian and Godzilla expert, he is 'a symbol of Japan's post-war regrets and nuclear fears and, ultimately, the nation's rage and retaliation'.

ASHES OF DEATH

'At around 6.50 am, just before dawn, I saw an explosion in the western sky.'

It was 1 March 1954, and Yoshio Misaki was chief fisherman on the *Daigo Fukuryu Maru*, the *Lucky Dragon Number Five*, a Japanese trawler fishing for tuna in the South Pacific.

'Although I thought a volcano had exploded, I knew that the US had been testing atomic bombs, and I was afraid they might find us and sink our ship.'

That day, the US exploded its biggest ever hydrogen bomb at Bikini Atoll. The ensuing mushroom cloud was 34 kilometres high, the device a thousand times more powerful than the atomic bombs that wiped out Hiroshima and Nagasaki nine years before. A crater sank through the atoll's ocean floor, and atomised coral ash swept the sky, raining down what would be known as 'shi no hai' — 'ashes of death' — over an area of a hundred miles.

'Around 10 am,' said Misaki, 'white, strange, small pieces of debris began to fall mixed with rain ... My eyes hurt so badly that I and the rest of the crew all washed them out with fresh water.' At the same time, the chief of a village on the nearby Marshall Islands saw 'many colours: red, green and yellow ... A strong, warm wind blew and we heard a loud sound like an explosion.' White powder sprinkled the island, and his baby son played in it; eighteen years later, he died of myelogenous leukaemia. The effect on the crew of the *Lucky Dragon* was swifter: headaches, nausea, bleeding gums, sore eyes — the symptoms of radiation poisoning. Their skin showed burn signs and their hair fell out. Six months after the explosion, the chief radio operator, Kobayama, died of leukaemia.

'I pray that I am the last victim of an atomic or hydrogen bomb,' he said shortly before his death.

Nearly seventy years later, I was standing under the wooden hull of the *Lucky Dragon*, peering at a stoppered jar containing the crystal-like 'ashes of death'. The trawler lies in permanent dry dock under a metal roof near Tokyo Bay. A minor fishing trawler it might have been, but the effects of the Bikini explosion were long-lasting. It prompted Bertrand Russell and Albert Einstein to launch a manifesto against nuclear testing: 'We appeal, as human beings, to human beings: Remember your humanity, and forget the rest. If you can do so, the way lies open to a new Paradise; if you cannot, there lies before you the risk of universal death.' In Japan, where radiation levels were measured at extremely dangerous levels (80,000 counts per minute per litre of rain in Kyoto, for example), plastic raincoats became a routine part of outdoor-wear and thirty million people — half the nation's adult population — put their signatures to a petition against further testing.

Another, surprising legacy was hinted at by an origami model standing beside the ticket counter opposite the *Lucky Dragon*: a bipedal monster with chunky legs, a long tail, and spikes on his back.

'Gojira?' I asked (as the monster's name is pronounced in Japan). The ticket lady beamed back a smile: 'Yes, yes, Gojira!'

In the spring of 1954, seeking the green light for his new monster-movie idea, producer Tomoyuki Tanaka showed news clippings of the *Lucky Dragon* incident to the executive producer Iwao Mori at Toho Studios. Japan had recently emerged from post-war US military rule. This wasn't just a question of righteous indignation, it was realpolitik. 'If Godzilla had been a big ancient dinosaur or some other animal,' explained Ishiro Honda, the director appointed by Tanaka to bring his vision to life, 'he would have been killed by just one cannonball. But if he were equal to an atomic bomb, we wouldn't know what to do. So I took the characteristics of an atomic bomb and applied them to Godzilla.' It was a way, as Honda put it, of 'making radiation visible'.

The raw creature, with his clawed fists and fiery snarl, echoes several millennia of monster tales. But the atomic power makes him indomitable. Like Frankenstein's creature and Rossum's robots, the 'King of the Monsters' is a civilisation-shredding guilt trip. His ferocious roar, and the carnage it heralds, is one means of measuring the destruction we have wrought on our planet.

A bullet train 500 miles south-west: it hurtled so fast, even Godzilla would have struggled to keep up. I stood in the Peace Memorial Park of Hiroshima, beside the open-air skeleton of a domed building, one of the few surviving structures from the blast. Ice crystals drifted around me, as slow and white as the 'ashes of death' that powdered the crew of the *Lucky Dragon*. I felt them melt against my fingers and seep through my hair, imagining how a different kind of skyfall might be misinterpreted. Hiroshima was low-slung, mountain-ringed, a sombre city of tower blocks and parking lots, with neither the flashing neon of Tokyo nor the brightly painted temples of Kyoto. A city shadowed by absence, like the shadows that darkened the walls and steps where people once stood.

'The Little Boy', the Americans called their bomb. Three metres long, it contained two divided pieces of uranium-235, one forced into the other by a chemical explosion, creating a supercritical mass that sustained a chain reaction, releasing the equivalent of fifteen kilotons of TNT, destroying or damaging 92 per cent of Hiroshima's buildings and slaughtering 140,000 (not including those who died in the months and years afterwards). One of the survivors was Akihiro Takahashi. A schoolboy at the time, he recalled seeing his friends 'lying all around the school yard' and found his clothes 'scorched into tatters by the heat rays'. When he saw his great-uncle and his wife, 'I felt as if I saw Buddha when I saw them in the living hell'.

Heat rays and the hell of ancient scriptures — this surreal dynamic, between super-modern destructive powers and ancient visions of apocalypse — repeats itself around the Peace Memorial Museum. It's there in the testimony of witnesses on multiple video screens and the artwork by survivors that offers another glimpse into the horror of the bomb.

'It burned so fast!' is the title of a painting by Kazuhiro Ishizu, showing a mother and father with two children, the mother holding a baby to her breast, the father leading a child by the hand. They walk naked under an arc of fire and the charred chaos of broken buildings, scattered corpses, scorched trees, the sheared flotsam of everyday life: house beams, broken bicycles. The painting burns with the purity of an ancient picture scroll. It feels timeless: not so much one horrific day in 1945, more like the Day of Judgement. This is the scale by which many survivors interpreted what they saw — scriptural, apocalyptic. One of the paintings, by Eiichi Uchida, shows a boy with an eyeball in his hand, after it's popped out of its socket. In another, discoloured bodies swell in a surreal floating bubble — purple, red, blue — less like humans than yokai, the traditional monsters of Japanese culture. Keloid scars form hideous bumps on a woman's back in a photographic blow-up, recalling the keloid scars on Godzilla's hide.

Between the paintings and video testimony are the flotsam of ordinary life — singed trousers, glass bottles fused into a honeycomb, the squashed remains of a molten clock, iron girders sheared by the blast: the mundane and the monstrous squeezed together by a terrible deed, perpetrated in a time of extraordinary tension.

No story, no movie scenario, can match the apocalypse the people of Hiroshima experienced. But when the American occupation and censorship was over, when the *Lucky Dragon* incident reawakened the terror of the Little Boy's apocalypse, Tanaka and his team chose to stir these ingredients into an adventure movie: a poetic meditation on monsters, manufactured for box office but inspired by a nation's nightmares. Godzilla is a victim of nuclear testing, scarred by the blasts, seething with rage — and with his atomic breath, he is the manifestation of atomic terror. 'Godzilla is the son of the atomic bomb,' as Tanaka proclaimed. 'He is a nightmare created out of the darkness of the human soul. He is the sacred beast of the apocalypse.' The thread begun with Frankenstein's creature reaches its apex in Godzilla's nuclear blasts. Humans, it turns out, have outstripped nature, God, and the devil, establishing ourselves as monster-makers supreme.

HOW TO MAKE A MONSTER HIT

Monsters come to us in visions. It was through the sorcerer Abe no Seimei's second sight that the great ogre Shutendoji was tracked down; it was in a dream that Mary Shelley imagined Frankenstein's creature.

And, according to Tanaka, Godzilla was the fruit of another vision, turning up in the movie mogul's head on a flight over the Pacific when he had a slot in the schedule to fill: 'What if a dinosaur sleeping in the Southern hemisphere had been awakened and transformed into a giant by the bomb?'

Within weeks, helped by news clippings of the *Lucky Dragon* crew and growing agitation over the effects of nuclear testing, Tanaka had marshalled a crew, among them director Ishiro Honda, who channelled his experience as a prisoner of war in China and observation of Hiroshima on his return home, and mystery writer Shigeru Kayama, who jotted a storyline about 'a cross between a whale and a gorilla' — the Japanese words crushed together to make 'Gojira'. The previous year, the US box office had been lit up by *The Beast from 20,000 Fathoms*, about a dinosaur awakened by an atomic blast and the US military's battle to destroy it with a radioactive grenade. *Godzilla* may be important, but it's hardly original.

So why is *Godzilla* the one that's endured? Where the Beast evoked a particular moment in time, the Japanese monster captured something broader — toppling tower blocks throughout the nation's economic resurgence and its rapid development in the 1960s, a ghost from the past warning of what was being lost in the relentless pursuit of profit, a spectre that continues to chime with Japanese anxieties and to thrill new generations of otaku.

Godzilla was, from the start, a curious hybrid — a beast from the ocean wilds, amplified and awakened by human (more specifically: American) activity; but a hybrid in another sense — inspired by Hollywood's emerging monster-movie genre, while drawing on Japanese sensibilities and folklore: the dragons that coil around the pillars under the torii gates of Shinto shrines, laying waste to villages in ancient folk tales. This traditional element is evoked in the early scene when an elder recalls the old way of appeasing the monster by sacrificing an innocent maiden, a ritual of propitiation followed for millennia around the world.

Tanaka might have had the first 'vision' of Godzilla, but the man who brought the monster to bodily life was special effects supremo Eiji Tsuburaya. Combining the upright ferocity of a T-rex with the dorsal fins of a stegosaurus and evoking the bomb through keloid scars, Tsuburaya eschewed the stop-motion wizardry of the US films for a suit — made with a frame of bamboo sticks and wire, with a metal mesh, cushioning, and a coating of latex on top. (Impressive as it may have been, it was still a man in a suit, stomping over a toy-sized Tokyo. There was only one way for the studio to avoid ridicule: keeping the suit a secret for years.) Tsuburaya was also in charge of recreating the sites of destruction, at a scale of 1:25, with streets made of plaster and buildings constructed out of wood, stuffed with kerosene-soaked rags and sprayed in gasoline to burn under the monster's atomic blaze.

We can watch the film now and look for glitches in its effects, but the success of Tsuburaya's work is clear in the movie's popularity and the enduring appeal of the monster design. *Godzilla* broke box-office records for opening-day ticket sales and generated so much interest that a dubbed version was commissioned for the US market, with inserted scenes incorporating a US actor. The monster, in the original movie, may exist in a one-nation bubble, with no mention of soliciting help from anywhere else, but he would spread around the world.

The legacy of Tsuburaya's design is apparent at the studio where it all began: a sprawling compound of white and grey walls, barriers lifting for cars with tinted windows bringing in talent, and vast murals celebrating Toho's two great hits from 1954. On an outer wall is Godzilla, arms gripped over the blue lettering of the studio sign, mouth wide open in a silent roar at the passing traffic. Beside the reception are the Seven Samurai: spears at their sides, swords over their shoulders, scouting for their enemies in thick grass. Their leader was played by Takashi Shimura, who also took on the role of the palaeontologist Professor Yamane in *Godzilla* — the movie's conscience, deploring the thirst to destroy the beast rather than study it. Yamane delivers the movie's pointed closing line: 'If they keep experimenting with deadly weapons, another Godzilla may appear somewhere in the world.' No mural celebrates the movie's human characters, but there is Shimura, in his alternative guise as the shrewd samurai, his face wrinkly with wisdom, looking over a statue of *Godzilla*. Together, they embody the golden age of Japanese cinema, and specifically the year 1954, when martial artists and a raging monster created movie magic that people are still enjoying seven decades later.

THE TRAIL OF DESTRUCTION

Tokyo is the original Godzilla's target. For an ancient beast from under the sea, could there be any more perfect foil than an ultra-modern sky-rise Alpha City? Sprawling out of the bay that shares its name, originally known as Edo (a compound of 'cove' and 'gate', because it was the gateway to the sea), the city had long replaced Kyoto as Japan's most populous and prosperous metropolis when the emperor moved his court there, between 1868 and 1889, rebranding it 'Tokyo' — 'Eastern Capital'. With railway stations installed across the city in the early twentieth century, its vast royal compound and government buildings, department stores flashing their fascia boards across the fashionable Ginza district, Tokyo was the perfect bull's-eye for a monster's bedlam.

Nowhere takes you back to the original movie's Tokyo like Shinagawa Station. It's there on the map-boards, near the red 'you are here' sign at Shinagawa East: Godzilla breathing fire under the railway bridge. Drills are screeching, sparks flying from welders' tools. Divided vertically by bridges, the railway lines overlap like a restless child's toy constructions, raising a roar of approaching trains under a confluence of cables and green-painted iron beams. Shinagawa is a transport hub, as it's been for the best part of a century. It's also close to Tokyo Bay, which made it a logical early stomping site for the monster. In one of the movie's most iconic set pieces, he tramples the track, tears down cables, smashes the bridge, and seizes a hurtling carriage in his jaws, delivering death to the terrified passengers. The scale of the multiple tracks, the speed of the trains, the sparks on the lines — what giant monster wouldn't relish such a challenge? In tearing up the transport hub, Godzilla smashes into a symbol of modern Japan: its rapidly accelerating communications network.

What was it like to see the monster at the time — to see this groundbreaking movie when it was being wrought at the furnace? I found out from an eyewitness, then an eleven-year-old schoolboy, now a silver-haired musician and Japanese translator living in New Orleans.

'I was just looking out of the window of the bus,' explained Rich Look.

The son of a US intelligence officer who'd been posted in Japan to keep an eye on China, Rich was sitting with his schoolmates, in his blazer and peaked cap, eyes wide open as he took in what was happening on the Shinagawa tracks:

'There were Klieg lights and film equipment, and a man in a lizard suit with a huge, long tail. He only had the bottom half on — it must have been a break in the filming, on his head was a hachimaki headband.'

For Rich, it was an eye-opening moment that would come back to him when he saw the movie months later, and over the subsequent years:

'*Godzilla* looms large in my mind. It was in the air in Japan. The effects of the war. You'd see veterans on the commuter trains, begging for money or playing the accordion. There were people living in tin huts next to the sewage sluices, and you'd hear stories from friends' dads who'd been prisoners of war, eating lizards in the prison camps. And at the shrines at festivals, there were Hiroshima babies — fetuses from the blast preserved in formaldehyde and put on display for a few yen.'

When Rich saw the movie, he felt for the monster. 'It was the horror of the war and horror of the atomic bomb, all that testing. In my mind, the monster was on the side of righteousness. It couldn't help itself. It was seeking a kind of revenge. It was a hero of sorts. I'd never seen anything like it before, it was astounding.'

Seven decades have wrought all kinds of change across Tokyo. Now it's the world's most populated city: a tropical jungle of skyscrapers, where steel and glass soar above the concrete ribbons of spiralling flyovers, five times the height of the original Godzilla. Reflected aeroplanes skim the mirrored walls like buzzing insects, elevators glide up and down from vine-like cables, doors hiss and squawk to the sounds of motion safety sensors, floor pads, and scanners.

And yet ... the same targets toppled by Godzilla remain intact. Along with transport is commerce, in the Ginza district, the media in the towers of the Akasaka TV village, pulled down at the climax of his rampage, political power in the Diet Building. The first of these, Ginza, remains the city's consumer heartland, where hoardings and billboards advertise wellness salons, Italian gelati, or cheese from Neal's Yard. Hugo Boss suits and Baccarat Crystal gleam below an escalator gliding up to the terrace rooftop of the Matsuya Department Store, where the sun is eclipsed by a forest of tower blocks — giant glass trunks emblazoned with brand names — Mikimoto, Bulgari, Cartier.

In 1954, the brands were humbler, but the point stood. Godzilla was serving a lesson in humility, a reminder that chasing yen won't save you when disaster erupts. It was here, on the rooftop, that Eiji Tsuburaya and his team plotted Godzilla's rampage, tracing his route between Tokyo Bay and the department stores of Ginza. So immersed were they, they didn't notice a security guard, who figured they must be anarchists planning an attack. At the doors of the store, they were accosted by a police officer and only released when they showed their Toho Studio cards. It's one of many stories that remind us how Godzilla's rampage overlapped with real-world anxieties.

Uphill from Ginza, along the walls of Old Edo, beyond the imperial castle and a park with a heart-shaped moat, the road flows past the Diet Building — a stepped cube framed by iron gates. Security guards swing the hinges for limousines with tinted windows, then swing them shut again. You can keep out the plebs, but you can't keep out a giant reptile with atomic breath. In the movie, Godzilla bashes into the building and tears a chunk out of it. According to reports from the time, members of the audience cheered at this moment. Like a child stomping on a playset, Godzilla moves with unbridled freedom. In tearing down the symbols of the city's power, the monster fulfils the fantasy of the disenfranchised, the outsiders, the overworked, and underpaid — the majority. It's telling that Godzilla steers clear of the imperial palace and the city's many Shinto and Buddhist shrines and temples. Modern secular power is his target. After all, he's an ancient monster, a god-monster, at heart.

And what happens to gods? They are idolised, carved in stone and bronze, raised on pedestals. Tokyo is a city of screens rather than statues. But Godzilla is a rare sculpted icon. I saw the monster bronze-cast at Toho. I saw him in, and out of, a department store in Osaka; beside the museum at Awaji Island; in front of a restaurant near Shinagawa Station; with his back to a branch of Toho Cinema in the Ginza district, snarling in the direction of Wendy's Burgers (well, wouldn't you?). Nowhere on my journey had a monster been so publicly visible (the dragon of Furth im Wald, perhaps, but that's confined to one town, not an entire country). Godzilla really is King of the Monsters — 'monstrat', to quote the Latin etymology, he 'shows' more than any other; 'monet', he 'warns' us of the hubris of modern life.

There are so many Godzillas around Tokyo, but the most arresting is in the red-light district of Shinjuku. Dancing to its own hyperreal clichés, here is where Tokyo bombards the senses with its 24-7 sound and light show. J-pop stars croon from multilevel screens, neon signs advertise stand-up sushi bars, ramen parlours, pachinko halls, karaoke bars, and 'girls, girls, girls'. Lights flash in all directions, glistening on the sleek hairdos of bar-hoppers half-cut on Asahi beer, their features glowing in the reflected headlamps from the swoosh of traffic. Some of them disappear down shadowy alleyways where the intense lighting dims to alluring darkness. Others rattle down the pavements, under another branch of Toho, multiple screens advertising the latest movie hits, and the tower block of the Hotel Gracery, where a familiar crusty head peers over the rooftop like a fox waiting for its turn in the farmyard. On the hour, the *Godzilla* theme tune drills out its low-pitched brass and strings from the lampposts, the sombre beat that's been sounding out doom in Japanese picture houses since 1954. The head flashes, blue light swirls out of his jaws. Godzilla is awake!

Shinjuku is the kind of place Karel Čapek warned about; the endpoint of Mary Shelley's nightmares: exactly the place an ancient monster would want to trash. But destructive as he may be, in the topsy-turvy world of monster consciousness, Godzilla emerges as a force — a snarling, atomic-breathed brute force — for celebration. As the starring figure in an enduring franchise, he represents something for a wounded nation to be proud of. Godzilla chides the Japanese, and he cheers them.

'When Americans thought of Japan, they thought of Pearl Harbor,' said Bill Tsutsui, son of a Japanese father, who grew up in the post-war USA and developed into one of the most vocal otaku around the world, author of a memoir entitled *Godzilla on my Mind*. For Bill, *Godzilla* was the bridge into his Japanese heritage.

'*Godzilla*,' he told me, 'was the first time I encountered Japan in a positive light. I could play Godzilla versus King Kong and I'd always be Godzilla.'

In third grade, Bill dressed up as Godzilla for Halloween, relishing his costume with its foam rubber and rayon, a pair of dyed-green gloves and a snout made from a tin teacup. The costume didn't last — it fell apart in the haunted house — and to dash it all, somebody stepped on his tail. But still, Bill was living the dream. Who wants to be Professor Yamane or sea captain Ogata when they can be the King of the Monsters? For Bill, to look back on that moment — after a career of researching and writing about Japanese economic history and serving as chancellor of Ottawa University, filling his study with Godzilla figures — is to recall 'a world that was small and simple'.

Which brings us to the nostalgic dreams that feed so much monster love today.

INSIDE THE MONSTER
'Let's walk!'

Norman England is the man who got inside Godzilla, and he's waiting for me outside Nakano Station. Oh, I might have been swallowed up by Godzilla on Awaji Island, like thousands of others, but Norman did it for real: he got himself strapped inside the monster suit at Toho Studios. Wide-jawed and brown-haired, with a thick New York accent and the sharp gaze of an expat who's made a living out of observation, he's not hard to spot in a crowd. But he's a perfect guide into the closed-off world of the kaiju. After all, he's the author of a book about it, *Behind the Kaiju Curtain*.

Light swells as the space around us narrows. We're squeezing through the tunnel of a shotengai, one of the market labyrinths that burrow through Tokyo. Monsters flash from movie posters, banners, and balloons; they appear as mini-figures in the ubiquitous vending machines or manifest as cuddly toys. In a steamy diner, okonomiyaki (a pancake-like dish made with cabbage, dried seaweed, and tempura scraps) is grilled on the hotplate between us, and Norman splatters it with something that tastes like a sweeter version of Worcestershire sauce, while he trots out his tales:

'The other day, I was drinking with Kaneko [director of the 2001 release *Godzilla, Mothra, and King Ghidorah: Giant Monsters All-Out Attack*] and Takahashi [who helmed a 2021 Godzilla anime series]. And Kaneko didn't even realise Takahashi had done a Godzilla!'

It's a rarefied world. Through the connections he made, Norman established himself as a regular on the set of Kaneko's 2001 *Godzilla* movie, the first foreign observer to stay for a full *Godzilla* shoot. He not only observed, he was given the opportunity to get inside Godzilla, for *Giant Monsters All-Out Attack* was one of the last instalments of a dying form: when Godzilla was still a man in a rubber suit. The book Norman produced, *Behind the Kaiju Curtain*, is a dive down the rabbit hole — *Alice in Wonderland* with rubber suits and movie-set mandarins, a tour through Japanese filmmaking from Shinto prayer sessions to canteen protocols. Norman doesn't shy away from the problems he encountered — aggressive studio executives and crew members who never let him forget he was a foreigner. But this is part of his forensic examination of what makes Godzilla — and Japan — tick:

'So for Kaneko — we talked about this a lot — he sees Godzilla as a ghost, influenced by the spirits of the victims of World War II ... those who suffered: Japanese, Chinese, British, American. Godzilla is the manifestation of their pain and anguish; he's the embodiment of their wrath.'

Walk around Nakano with Norman and you're never far from a visual representation of Godzilla. The monster appears in original posters from the sixties, in an otaku store, and in figures in the collectors' stores. Here's a fifty-centimetre remote-controlled Bio-Godzilla, with a six-channel remote control to swing its arms and tail, make it walk and roar. Here's a game board featuring Godzilla and Mothra; there's the three-headed King Ghidorah; here's the bat-like Rodan.

Fans squeeze around us, studying the labels, browsing in the narrow aisles. Monsters are no longer the beast from outside the home — they *are* the home; they take people back to the time when life was 'small and simple', as Bill Tsutsui put it. I think of the monster figures that line the shelves in my study; of the monsters I collected as a child, painted, and played with, or made out of yogurt pots and egg cartons and an awful lot of sticky tape. Forget about Proust's madeleines, they've been gobbled up by the monsters. Now it's the dragons, the ogres, the giant bipedal spiky-tailed reptiles that guide us down memory lane.

Sitting in the diner, wrestling with my chopsticks over chunks of batter and dried seaweed, I ask Norman about 'the suit'.

He compares the experience to being 'jumped by a wild bear', strapped into 'a harness jury-rigged from steel pipes, clamps, and chains'. 'I experienced it very vividly,' he says. 'I can still remember being in the darkness of the suit, just seeing through these pinholes, the light coming through them, looking at my hands and they're Godzilla's hands. That's what I remember: it's not me anymore. I completely lost sense of who I was.'

Isn't that the pull of transformation? I think back to the tales of the rougarou — to experience oblivion, to abandon your respectable self and feel the thrill of the wild. The freedom the kuker had talked about in the Bulgarian mountains. But these days you don't transform by putting on a suit. Godzilla no longer haunts the movie sets. Instead of trembling at a man in a rubber suit, now the actors gurn at strategically placed sticks and chromakey screens. If you want to press flesh with Godzilla, these days you have to follow the fans.

In the Godzilla store in Osaka, among tape dispensers and desktop lights, saké bottles and chopsticks, I meet one of them. With short cropped hair and specs, Hideki beams over a *Hamtaro* T-shirt — a hamster-child zipped inside a super-cute Godzilla suit. He shows me the most popular items — 'the humidifier, that one's selling well ... oh, and this jacket here,' the leather one with Godzilla framed by Mount Fuji, with a 27,000 yen price-tag (£150), 'that one's really popular.' He's seen all the movies, but still rates the original as the best:

'There's two reasons why *Godzilla* is still popular, in my opinion. Firstly, the form: it's unique, but you know instantly who it is. Secondly, the political context. We don't talk about it, but it's there, especially for older fans. The nuclear message, that is important.'

Godzilla tracks the changes in Japanese society and its relationship with the world. Commercial exploitation, industrial pollution, gerontocracy: the 164-foot-going-on-400 scowler provides a lens through which Japanese filmmakers (and occasionally, when they've reached agreement with Toho's lawyers, outsiders) can wrestle with these themes. But there's another reason for the monster's abiding popularity. I've been hearing it ever since I first met the otaku at the zip wire, and it's emphasised again in the pachinko parlours. I've circled these places all through my time in Japan. On my last day in Tokyo, I pop into one.

The signs fill the windows in gaudy gold and menacing black — Godzilla versus the demonic Evangelion, the prickly silhouette versus his coruscating nemesis. Under flashing lights, against the rattling of joysticks, glazed eyes are locked to the screens. Men, all of them, gaze at an underwater world, their avatar a nubile mermaid with a turquoise tail. Others channel bikini-clad Mitaya, who stretches her legs on sun loungers by the pool and drives around in an open-top sports car; or they shoot down adversaries in violent splatter games; or defend a mediaeval castle from a dragon. But the most popular game is the one with the dinosaur-like head moulded over the screen, the monster's tail curling into the joystick.

I scan my QR code and pinballs clatter, like the rattling of a skeleton's teeth. I try to work out what on earth I'm supposed to do with the industrial tower complex on the screen. My nubile avatar rides her car between the towers, skidding out of the way of Godzilla and Evangelion as the monsters wrestle between the towers. My avatar may be human, but the plot is all about the monsters. Girders fly overhead, walls collapse, towers topple, and I'm out of lives. No chance of tips from my fellow players, they're all zombie-tied to their screens, but there's a smoking room at the back where a few of them go to decompress.

'You like Gojira? Which ones have you seen?'

'Well, the original, a bunch of the others.'

'You like anime Gojira — *Singular Point*?'

One of them has been down the zip wire at Awaji Island. Another suggests I check out *Godzilla: Tokyo SOS*.

'You need to see it!'

What is it about this giant reptile with his swinging tail, glowing spinal plates, and really bad breath? There are so many other monsters. I want to reach out for all of them, somehow. I want to spy on the mysterious imbunche, who guards a sorcerer's cave on an island off the coast of Chile. I want to scout the seas for the kraken and wander the Nordic hills in the footsteps of trolls, seek out the mischievous kalikantzari in the fields of Cyprus and shadow the bunyip in the Australian bush. But for these otaku, there's no point looking anywhere else when you've got the King of the Monsters louring over you.

'Gojira's the best.' One of them stubs out his cigarette. 'Nobody messes with Gojira.'

He cracks his knuckles together and steps out for another bout.

The best.

The greatest.

The ultimate.

Raaaaaaaaaaaaaaaaaa!

There are other monsters you could say that about: the dragon of Furth, with its fiery breath and roar; Bolster with his huge stride; the human-guzzling Shutendoji. Monsters take our fears and desires and drag them to the brink. In a world where it's easy to feel trodden-down and reduced, to recognise the appalling brevity of our lives, the narrowness of our reach, there is something inspiring about the size and scope of these magnificent chimeras. When they become our avatars, they make us indomitable.

During the year leading up to my trip to Japan, I had travelled across a dozen countries in three continents. Tokyo's flashing lights kept my senses zipping about like pinballs, but I could feel the weariness of the journey in my bones, the frayed nerves of tight budgeting, the nights on long-haul transport, the daily struggle with languages I was never going to master. After sealing myself inside a pod for the night, a honeycomb of hundreds of sleeping capsules slotted together in a high-rise in the Shinjuku district, I closed my eyes dreaming of home, a raised bed, the faces of my loved ones, the warmth of their hugs. A journey is like a monster, wild and unwieldy, throwing you about with strange weather patterns, dazzling you with addictively unpredictable experiences. But unlike the monsters, a journey has its end. After all, we're only human, and we need our finishing lines. But the monsters carry on: rising from every defeat, roaring again, refusing to ever be truly vanquished. We can try, in our all-too-human way, to impose our endings on them. But the best of the monsters break free, as they've been doing ever since we first started seeing them, through the mists, between the trees, under the rivers' murky skin, all those millennia ago.

Epilogue

It was the end of summer. I had nearly finished the first draft of this book, and I was walking with my family in the remnant of temperate rainforest that runs a mile from our home in Dorset. Among oaks tangled in creepers and sweet-smelling hawthorns fizzing with bugs, giant ferns swoop beside the narrow streams dissecting the woodland like the veins of some mysterious creature. We clambered over the logs that straddle the streams, chasing dragonflies and butterflies, swinging from a rope looped over the branch of an oak.

'There's a wood goblin over there! No, you're looking in the wrong direction — it's over there behind the bridge.'

'I bet there's a dragon under all these trees, just waiting for someone to wake it up.'

'One thing — there's definitely a troll under the bridge. And it's very sensitive to trip-trapping ...'

Sticks were pried from the forest floor, war cries hullabalooed, and we slip-slid across the hills of the forest, twisting against our invisible spectres.

One of the joys of delving among monsters, over the many years it took me to write this book, was the growing fascination of the children with whom I've been lucky enough to share my life.

'Can a Gorgon turn a blind person to stone?'

'How many giants standing on each other's shoulders would it take to reach the moon?'

'Can monsters cry?'

There are questions I could never have asked — could never have imagined — without the wondering minds around me. Bedtime stories were infiltrated by 'rock wraiths', 'lava beasts', 'storm bats', the 'lightning bull', and a twenty-headed marine beast called Quarridus. Among the reams of paper floating around my feet in the play area, I came across the 'blingo' (a bat-like creature with the head of a flamingo), the Toxic Swamp Lord, and a red imp-like villain with gnashing teeth known as 'Putin':

'It's very angry,' the seven-year-old artist explained, wagging a finger in earnest, 'and it attacks Ukraine ALL THE TIME. Oh, and one more thing: if you steal its chips then it tries to blow you up with a massive bomb.'

A reminder of how events in the real world can inspire the magical tales that flourish in children's imaginations. And also that there are people in the world far more terrifying than monsters.

The downside to all this interest (well, let's just say: challenge) was a gnawing scepticism around my choices. Why, I was asked one day, was I not writing a chapter about the manticore?

'But it's got an extra row of teeth and a giant tail with a sting like a scorpion!'

'And, Daddy' — another afternoon — 'what about the basilisk? You know how it can shine its eyes and stop anyone?'

What about the Hydra, the Gorgons, the Cyclops (we were in a *Percy Jackson* phase), the Sphinx, or the Kraken? What about trolls, the Power Phoenix, or the Glarbergastling (*Monster Loving Maniacs* had taken over our airwaves)? Or the yeti? Or the Iron Golem? Well, at least I had some zombies (now we were all about Minecraft). And what about mummies? Or the bogart? Or unicorns (and do they even count)? And was I really, truly planning to put out a book about monsters without a single chapter on the Loch Ness Monster?

*

This book tells a tale of monsters, their history in different places around the world, and the patterns that have developed across the ages. It's about the roots binding them to particular locations, but across the chapters we see the connections that join our monsters — and our different communities — together. There are many others, of course, but the story told in this book needed these twelve monsters. Many are connected to significant events in world history — imaginative renderings of the moments when history turned on its hinge: the Spanish Conquest of the Americas, for example, the Haitian Revolution, the explosion of the atomic and hydrogen bombs. Others shone a light on places that have drifted out of the global spotlight but played significant roles in the past, such as mediaeval Orkney, Cornwall, and eastern Bavaria. Some of the monsters have come to define particular nations, and have become embedded in their national story, from the role of giants in mediaeval British mythmaking to Godzilla's iconic status in modern Japan. Together, they show that history isn't only recorded in the details of events, but also in the emotions that linger long after the dead have been buried. From indigenous Mexicans' feelings of loss — expressed through the story of a ghost — to anxieties around emerging technology — dramatised in robots and other artificial beings — we see again and again how monsters register the emotional states of their epochs. Shadow figures on an individual level, as Jung and Freud so memorably deduced, they amount to something greater on the level of societies: shadows of history, reflecting the fears and furies, desires and anxieties that bind communities together.

I set out on this journey with the aim of organising the monsters somehow, dividing them between periods of history in order to distinguish between them and better understand them. Quixotic this may have been, but it's hardly unprecedented. Monsters defy categorisation, but that hasn't stopped people from making the effort (the mediaeval author of the *Liber Monstrorum*, for example, or the eighteenth-century Japanese artist Toriyama Sekien, whose *Night Parade of a Hundred Demons* I had perused in Japan). As I wrestled with my own monster categories, I learned how they refute these chains, furiously twisting against single-layered interpretations. But it's when we enclose our wild beasts that we can study them. Put a monster in a cage and it will break out soon enough — and in the process, show you its powers.

Can monsters ever be truly fathomed? One of the leading theorists of monster lore, Jeffrey Jerome Cohen, refers to 'a genetic uncertainty principle' that keeps us from pinning them down. Still, even if the monsters elude us, they can operate as lanterns shining illumination back at humanity. 'Monsters are one of the primary vehicles,' Cohen suggested, talking over zoom one evening, 'through which we think about the limits and possibilities of what it means to be human.' In mediaeval Christian dragon-slaying stories, we can identify the violent insecurity of communities afraid of what might lurk beyond the tree-line. In the robot stories of the 1920s, we can read anxieties about emerging technology and political tumult. These are historically specific responses. But the same monsters also express universal fears. The robot, as we have seen, has inspired stories as far back as ancient China; the dragon has a history even richer.

But if monsters resist categorisation, patterns do manifest, and most striking of these is the change in how we see the monsters. Arguably, we have come full circle. If monsters and gods were indistinguishable at the dawn of civilisation, that veneration for monsters is rematerialising, in its own way, as we switch on our TVs to gaze upon the latest giant scaly beings, as we queue en masse for opening nights in the multiplexes, for fan conventions and cosplay events, and as communal gatherings around totemic monsters replace the old religious festivals that are increasingly sidelined. Monsters brought people together in the past, and they are bringing people together, in their own extraordinary way, today.

What is strikingly different is our identification. Think of the Incredible Hulk, Hellboy, Chewbacca in *Star Wars*, the lovable ogre Shrek, the vampires of the *Twilight* saga, the steel-clawed Wolverine, the giant blue Na'vi of *Avatar*. As often as not, it is the humans who are the enemy — the men in suits who run the boardrooms. The traditional monster-slayers, like Saint George or Raiko or Hercules, attract less interest today; while the monsters are more visible than ever, and now they are avatars for the instinctive, creative, screw-the-establishment qualities we admire.

This is a recent trend, but not entirely new. Monsters weren't always the villains in the past, as we have seen in some of the long-ago stories of werewolves and other shapeshifters. But it is in the modern stories, from *Frankenstein* onwards, that our identification with monsters intensifies, as the damage we have done to our world obliges us to consider what it might feel like to be the things we destroy. From recognising the monsters within ourselves, we moved a step further: becoming the monsters the monsters fear.

So monsters are the things we cannot control, cannot understand; they are the lingering remains of the things we have destroyed. And they are, increasingly, a ragged moral compass, illuminating what is cruel, exploitative, or unkind in humanity. They have become, in this sense, a record of human shame. And maybe that's not such a bad thing. After all, is the world so very terrible, when we can cheer on a vampire, or laugh with an ogre, or shed tears for an armour-plated, four-eyed, six-flippered, 300-foot-long whale from the planet Pandora? Monsters register our shame, but they also challenge our empathy.

Society has multiple layers, of course, and humanity has its different stripes. But for many, it can be hard to feel included, or accepted. Stories about monsters help us to reflect on some of these issues — on whom we exclude, and on how we feel excluded ourselves. Perhaps it was my fascination for the monsters, or perhaps it was my own struggles, the long-standing battle with my own demon within, but the further I travelled on this journey, the closer I felt to the monsters. We all perceive reality through the distortion of our own senses, wincing at a world that can feel cruel sometimes, strange, and often hostile. Sometimes it's easier to empathise with a monster's bitterness than it is with the bravado of a hero.

Like vampires being invited over a threshold, many of us need a way in. Stories have been my calling card, in many places around the world, helping me to connect with people to whom I might otherwise have remained a stranger. Thanks to the monsters, I held a collection tin during a giant's pageant in Cornwall, helped to run a costume contest at a werewolf festival in Louisiana, mingled with the cast of the Drachenstich in Germany, stood in the crowd waiting for the oni at a temple in Japan. I met many fascinating people, and it was the monsters that shattered the barriers between us. I'll never forget listening to Hilario and Liliana's tales of ghosts and shapeshifters in Tepoztlán, talking about the risen dead with Mirjana Novaković in a café in Novi Sad, discussing the classifications of jinn with Abdel-Wahed on his couch in Meknes, listening to Barry Ancelet as he turned into the poet and musician Jean Arceneaux, drinking whiskey in Tom Muir's house in Orkney while the rain rattled against the windowpanes and splashed against the puddles outside. The monsters gave me these encounters — and for that I will never stop loving them. And, flipping the thought around, it was those experiences — as much as my research in libraries or the stories I read — that helped me to better understand the monsters. They united me with far-flung communities, and they showed how much those communities have in common — not only within themselves, but with other communities, all around the world.

Imagining monsters is one of the things that makes us human. Which is why the earliest representations of monsters coincide with the dawn of civilisation. The end of monsters will be similarly enlightening about the human journey, because it will show that our species no longer exists, at least not as far as we understand it today. The vampire may not be able to see its reflection — but we can see ours in the vampire. For humans and monsters, truly and beautifully, are mirrors to each other. Take one away, and the other will shrivel and fade, to be lost in the void of eternity.

Acknowledgements

I am grateful to all the people I met in the course of the many journeys that formed the basis for this book. I would like to thank, in particular: Brian Hart, Soozie Tinn, and all the community of St Agnes; Anna Chorlton and Sue Field (thank you Sue for all the pictures and the introduction to the droll-teller!); with thanks to Barbara and Bob Griggs for hospitality in Launceston, and thank you to Mike O'Connor for many hours of conversation in Padstow and inviting me to the storytelling meet-up in Liskeard, and thank you to all the storytellers there; Elisabeth Kager, Werner Perlinger, Ulrike Eder, and Alexander Etzel-Ragusa in Furth im Wald; Matt Alt, Hiroko Yoda, Yuki Fushima, and Norman England in Japan; and thanks to William Tsutsui for discussion and advice; Tom Muir and Lynn Barbour in Orkney; Mike Richardson, Roderick Grierson, Fatima Zahra Salih, and Abdel-Wahed in Morocco; a big thank you to Richard Hamilton for various contacts; thank you to Tahir Shah for a lovely evening in Casablanca; thanks to Professor Rashid Skinner and the organisers of the Muslim Literary Festival in Manchester; and to Jill and Colin Reynolds for their hospitality in Stockport. In the USA, thanks to Jonathan Foret, Lanor Curole, and everybody at the Rougaroufest in Houma; Glen and Michelle Pitre, Rachel Doherty, and Barry Ancelet;

to Peter Dillon and his family for wonderful hospitality in Texas; Fernanda Nuñez Becerra and Viviana García Besné in Mexico; Boris Perić in Croatia and Mirjana Novaković in Serbia, and thank you to Terence McEneny for putting me in touch with Mirjana; Guilaine Brutus and the Haitian Heritage Foundation, Aurelie Gerbier, and Professor Kaiama L. Glover; to René Depestre for responding to my letter; Daisy Hay for discussions on Mary Shelley; in Prague, thank you to Rudolf Rosa and to Benedict Allen for a refreshing mid-journey drink. I'm also grateful to Mary Ann Miranda and the organisers of the Dubai Literary Festival for arranging my flight from Japan, and to Anna Zacharias for discussion about the jinn in the UAE (although sadly this didn't make it into the book).

For taking a look at various chapters of the book and advising me on many nuances that had escaped me, I am hugely grateful to the following people:

Anna Chorlton, Soozie Tinn, and Brian Hart (Chapter One), Alexander Etzel-Ragusa (Chapter Two), Hiroko Yoda, Matt Alt, and Professor Michael Dylan Foster (Chapter Three), Tom Muir (Chapter Four), Safia Lamrani and Roderick Grierson (Chapter Five), Glen Pitre, Barry Ancelet, and Rachel Doherty (Chapter Six), Viviana García Besné (Chapter Seven), Boris Perić and Mirjana Novaković (Chapter Eight), Aurelie Gerbier and Kaiama L. Glover (Chapter Nine), Daisy Hay (Chapter Ten), Rudolf Rosa (Chapter Eleven), Norman England and William Tsutsui (Chapter Twelve).

With thanks to Boris Perić and Glen Pitre for permission to quote from their novels, *Vampir* and *Advice from the Wicked*, and thanks to Jean Arceneaux for permission to quote his lyrics from *Broken Promised Land*.

This book required huge amounts of research, and I am grateful to the staff of the British Library (all the more given the many challenges the library was facing during the research period of this book) as well as the Wellcome Collection and my local libraries in Poole and Bournemouth. Libraries are so valuable, and long may they survive.

On the publishing side, I am grateful to my agent, Carrie Plitt, for helping to shape the proposal, and especially for suggesting Godzilla as a chapter subject, and for her feedback and support throughout this project; and to everybody at the Felicity Bryan Agency. My thanks to everybody at Scribe, including Simon Wright for commissioning and editing the book; Laura Ali, who took on editorial duties from Simon; David Golding for his diligence as copy editor; publisher Molly Slight; publicist Adam Howard; Joe McLaren for his wonderful designs, including the cover; and everybody else who's been working on the book behind the scenes.

Delving into archaic and niche subjects can be baffling to one's friends, but I am grateful to all those who have given me moral support during the course of writing this project, and to friends who've put me up on visits to London. I am most grateful of all to my family, especially my beloved children, Milo and Rafe, who challenge me with such interesting questions, and whose enthusiasm for monsters dovetailed perfectly with the writing of this book. Above all, I'm grateful to my wife, Poppy, who apart from putting up with me is such a boundless source of support, inspiration, and resilience, and who helps me to keep going even when the writing challenges seem insurmountable.

Bibliography

A Great Wonder in Heaven: shewing the late Apparitions and prodigious noyses of war and battels, seen on Edge-Hill neere Keinton in Northamptonshire (London: Thomas Jackson, 1642)

Contes et Légendes d'Haïti, presented by Le Centre de Recherches Littéraires et Sociales (Port-au-Prince: Editions Christophe, 1993)

The Bible: new international version (London: Hodder & Stoughton, 1984)

The Epic of Gilgamesh, translated by Andrew George (London: Allen Lane, 1999)

The Hymns of the Rig Veda, translated by Ralph T.H. Griffith, edited by Professor J.L. Shastri (New Delhi: Motilal Banarsidass, 1973)

The Sagas of Icelanders (London: Penguin, 2001)

Abun-Nasr, Jamil, *History of the Maghrib in the Islamic Period* (Cambridge, England: Cambridge University Press, 1987)

Al-Maari, *The Epistle of Forgiveness*, edited and translated by Geert Jan van Gelder & Gregor Schoeler (New York: New York University Press, 2014)

Aldington, Richard, *Death of a Hero* (London: Chatto & Windus, 1929)

Aleksander, Igor & Burnett, Piers, *Reinventing Man* (London: Kogan Page, 1983)

Ali, Abdullah Yusuf, *The Meaning of the Holy Quran* (Beirut: Alaalami Library, 2001)

Almqvist, Bo, *Viking Ale: studies on folklore contacts between the Northern and the Western Worlds* (Aberystwyth: Boethius Press, 1991)

Arceneaux, Jean, *Suite du Loup: poèmes, chansons et autres textes* (Moncton, New Brunswick: Éditions Perce-Neige, 2003)

Aristotle, *Aristotle in 23 Volumes, Vol. 23*, translated by W.H. Fyfe (London: William Heinemann, 1932)

Asma, Stephen T., *On Monsters* (New York: Oxford University Press, 2011)

Baldick, Chris, *In Frankenstein's Shadow* (Oxford: Oxford University Press, 1987)

Baring-Gould, Sabine, *The Book of Werewolves* (London: Smith, Elder & Co, 1865)

Becerra, Fernanda Nuñez, *La Malinche: de la historia al mito* (Mexico City: Instituto Nacional de Antropología e Historia, 1996)

Bloch, Chayim, *The Golem: legends of the ghetto of Prague*, translated by Harry Schniederman (Vienna: 1925)

Borlase, William, *Observations on the Antiquities, Historical and Monumental, of the County of Cornwall* (Oxford: Jackson, 1754)

Bottrell, William, *Traditions and Hearth-side Stories of West Cornwall* (Penzance: Beare & Son, 1873)

Bradbrook, Bohuslava R., *Karel Čapek: in pursuit of truth, tolerance, and trust* (Brighton: Sussex Academic Press, 1998)

Brand, John, *A New Description of Orkney, Zetland, Pightland, Firth and Caithness, wherein, after a short journal of the author's voyage thither, these northern places are first more generally described* (Edinburgh: printed by G. M. and sold in London by J. Taylor at the Ship in St Paul's Church-Yard, 1703)

Brandes, Stanley, 'Iconography in Mexico's Day of the Dead: origins and meaning', in *Ethnohistory* Vol. 45, No. 2 (Durham, North Carolina: Duke University Press, 1998)

Braünlein, Peter J., 'The Frightening Borderlands of Enlightenment: the vampire problem', in *Studies in History and Philosophy of Biological and Biomedical Sciences* Vol. 43, No. 3 (2012)

Breuil, Henri, *Four Hundred Centuries of Cave Art*, translated by Mary E. Boyle (Paris: Centre D'Études et de Documentation Préhistoriques, 1952)

Brightman, Robert A., 'The Windigo in the Material World', in *Ethnohistory* Vol. 35, No. 4 (Durham, North Carolina: Duke University Press, 1988)

Byron, Lord, *The Major Works*, ed. Jerome J. McGann (Oxford: Oxford University Press, 1986)

Calmet, Augustine, *Phantom World: the history and philosophy of spirits, apparitions, &c.*, edited by Rev. Henry Christmas (Philadelphia: A. Hart, 1850)

Čapek, Karel, *Hordubal* (London: Allen & Unwin, 1934)

Čapek, Karel, *Letters from England*, translated by Geoffrey Newsome (Brinkworth, England: Claridge Press, 2001)

Čapek, Karel, *R.U.R.: Rossum's Universal Robots: a fantastic melodrama*, translated by Paul Selver & Nigel Playfair (London: 1923)

Čapek, Karel, *War with the Newts*, translated by Ewald Osers (London: Unwin, 1965)

Carew, Richard, *Survey of Cornwall* (London: 'Printed by S. S. for Iohn Iaggard, and are to bee sold neere Temple-barre, at the signe of the Hand and Starre', 1602)

Carpio, Manuel, *Poesias del Sr Dr Don Manuel Carpio* (Mexico: Librería de la Enseñanza, 1883)

Chorlton, Anna, *Cornish Folk Tales of Place* (Stroud, England: History Press, 2019)

Christie, Deborah & Lauro, Sarah Juliet, *Better off Dead: the evolution of the zombie as post-human* (Ashland, Ohio: Fordham University Press, 2011)

Clairmont, Claire, *The Clairmont Correspondence* (Baltimore & London: John Hopkins Press, 1995)

Clairmont, Claire, *The Journals of Claire Clairmont* (Cambridge, Massachusetts: Harvard University Press, 1967)

Cohen, Jeffrey Jerome, *Monster Theory: reading culture* (Minneapolis: Minneapolis University Press, 1996)

Cortes, Hernan, *Letters from Mexico*, translated by Anthony Pagden (London: Oxford University Press, 1972)

Crapanzano, Vincent, *The Hamadsha: a study in Moroccan ethnopsychiatry* (Berkeley: University of California Press, 1973)

D'Arcy, Uriah Derick, *The Black Vampyre* (New York: 1819)

Daut, Marlene, *Tropics of Haiti: race and the literary history of the Haitian Revolution in the Atlantic world, 1789–1865* (Liverpool: Liverpool University Press, 2015)

Davis, Wade, *Passage of Darkness: the ethnobiology of the Haitian zombie* (Chapel Hill: University of North Carolina Press, 1988)

Dayan, Joan, *Haiti, History, and the Gods* (Berkeley: University of California Press, 1995)

de Beer, Gavin, 'Iktin', in *Geographical Journal*, Vol. 126, No. 2 (1960)

de Lancre, Pierre, *On the Inconstancy of Witches: Pierre de Lancre's de l'inconstance des mauvais anges et demons (1612)* (Tempe: Arizona Center for Medieval and Renaissance Studies, 2006)

Dennison, Walter Traill, in *The Scottish Antiquary, or Northern Notes and Queries, Vol. 7 & 8*, edited by A.W. Cornelius Halben (Edinburgh: T & A Constable at the University Press, 1893/1894)

Depestre, René, *Change* (Paris: Editions du Seuil, 1971)

Depestre, René, *Hadriana in All My Dreams*, translated by Kaiama L. Glover (London: Jacaranda Books, 2020)

Descourtilz, M.E., *Voyages d'un Naturaliste, et ses Observations, Vol. 3* (Paris: Dufart, Père, Libraire-Éditeur, 1809)

Doherty, Rachel, 'Le Loup-Garou en Louisiane: de la légende à la littérature contemporaine', in *Rabaska Revue d'Ethnologie de l'Amérique Française* Vol. 17 (Société Québécoise d'Ethnologie, 2019)

Dougill, John, *Kyoto: a cultural and literary history* (New York: Oxford University Press, 2006)

Douthwaite Viglione, Julia, *The Frankenstein of 1790 and How It Lives On Today* (UW Seattle, published online, 27 Oct 2018)

Dundes, Alan, *The Vampire: a casebook* (Madison: University of Wisconsin Press, 1998)

Durand, A. & Pedone-Lauriel, G. (editors), *Les Codes Haïtiens Annotés* (Paris: Libraires de la Cour d'Appel et de l'Ordre des Avocats, 1883)

Dylan Foster, Michael, *Pandemonium and Parade: Japanese monsters and the culture of Yokai* (Berkeley: University of California Press, 2009)

Dylan Foster, Michael, *The Book of Yokai: mysterious creatures of Japanese folklore* (Oakland: University of California Press, 2015)

El-Zein, Amira, *Islam, Arabs, and the Intelligent World of the Jinn* (Syracuse, New York: Syracuse University Press, 2009)

England, Norman, *Behind the Kaiju Curtain: a journey onto Japan's biggest film sets* (Tokyo: Awai Books, 2021)

Esquivel, Laura, *Malinche* (London: Pocket Books, 2006)

Fleming, Chris, *Rene Girard: violence and mimesis* (Cambridge, England: Polity, 2004)

Florescu, Radu, *In Search of Frankenstein* (London: Robson Books, 1996)

Frankétienne, *Dézafi*, translated by Charles Asselin (Charlottesville: University of Virginia Press, 2018)

Geoffrey of Monmouth, *History of the Kings of Britain*, translated by Aaron Thompson (Cambridge, Ontario: In Parentheses Publications, 1999)

Gilbert, Davies, *A Parochial History of Cornwall, found on the manuscript histories of Mr Hals & Mr Tonkin, Vol. 1* (London: J.B. Nichols and Son, 1838)

Glisić, Milovan, *After Ninety Years*, translated by James Lyons (Middletown, Delaware: J. Lyons, 2015)

Goodman, Lenn E. & McGregor, Richard (translators & editors), *The Case of the Animals versus Man before the King of the Jinn* (Oxford: Oxford University Press in association with the Institute of Ismaili Studies, 2009)

Gordon, Charlotte, *Romantic Outlaws: the extraordinary life of Mary Wollstonecraft and her daughter Mary Shelley* (London: Hutchinson, 2015)

Groom, Nick, *The Vampire: a new history* (New Haven, Connecticut & London: Yale University Press, 2018)

Hall, Simon W., *History of Orkney Literature* (Edinburgh: John Donald, 2010)

Halliwell-Phillips, James, *Rambles in Western Cornwall in the Footsteps of Giants* (London: John Russell Smith, 1861)

Hamberger, Klaus, *Mortuus non Mordet: dokumentation zum vampirismus 1689–1791* (Vienna: Turia und Kant, 1992)

Hamilton, Richard, *The Last Storytellers: tales from the heart of Morocco* (London: I.B. Tauris, 2011)

Hay, Daisy, *Young Romantics: the Shelleys, Byron, and other tangled lives* (London: Bloomsbury, 2011)

Hazareesingh, Sudhir, *Black Spartacus: the epic life of Toussaint Louverture* (London: Penguin, 2020)

Herodotus, *The Histories*, translated by George Rawlinson (London: Orion Publishing Group, 1992)

Herskovits, Melville Jean, *Life in a Haitian Valley* (New York: Octagon, 1964)

Hoermann, Raphael, 'A Very Hell of Horrors: the Haitian Revolution and the early transatlantic Haitian gothic', in *Slavery and Abolition: a journal of slave and post-slave studies* (published online, 24 Sep 2015)

Honegger, Thomas, *Introducing the Medieval Dragon* (Cardiff: University of Wales Press, 2019)

Hunt, Leigh, *Lord Byron and Some of His Contemporaries* (Philadelphia: Carey, Lea and Carey, 1828)

Hunt, Robert, *Popular Romances of the West of England, or, the Drolls, Traditions and Superstitions of Old Cornwall* (London: John Camden Hotton, 1864)

Hurbon, Laënnec, *Voodoo: truth and fantasy* (London: Thames and Hudson, 1995)

Hurston, Zora Neale, *Tell My Horse* (Philadelphia: JB Lippincott Co, 1938)

James, Ronald, *The Folklore of Cornwall: the oral tradition of a Celtic nation* (Exeter, England: University of Exeter Press, 2019)

Jamous, Raymond, 'Le Saint et le Possédé', in *Gradhiva: revue d'histoire et d'archives de l'anthropologie*, No. 17 (Paris: Éditions Jean-Michel Place, 1995)

Janvier, Thomas, *Legends of the City of Mexico* (New York: Harper & Brothers, 1910)

Jobb, Dean, *The Cajuns: a people's story of exile and triumph* (New York: John Wiley & Sons, 2005)

Jung, Carl, *Memories, Dreams, Reflections*, translated by Richard and Clara Winston (London: Fontana Press, 1983)

Kachuba, John, *Shapeshifters: a history* (London: Reaktion Books, 2019)

Kalat, David, *A Critical History & Filmography of Toho's Godzilla* (Jefferson, North Carolina: MacFarland & Co, 2010)

Katz-Harris, Felicia (editor), *Yokai: ghosts, demons & monsters of Japan* (Santa Fe: Museum of New Mexico Press, 2019)

Kazuhiko, Komatsu, *An Introduction to Yokai Culture: monsters, ghosts and outsiders in Japanese history* (Tokyo: Japan Publishing Industry Foundation for Culture, 2017)

Kleindorfer-Marx, Dr Bärbel, *Oberpfalz und Böhmen* (Regensburg, Bavaria: Oberpfälzer Kulturbund, 1996)

Klima, Ivan, *Karel Čapek: life & work* (North Haven, Connecticut: Catbird Press, 2002)

Knight, Alan, *Mexico: from the beginning to the Spanish Conquest* (Cambridge, England: Cambridge University Press, 2002)

Kriss, Marika, *Werewolves, Shapeshifters and Skinwalkers* (Los Angeles: Sherbourne Press, 1972)

Lauro, Sarah J., *The Transatlantic Zombie: slavery, rebellion and living death* (London: Rutgers University Press, 2015)

Lebling, Robert, *Legends of the Fire Spirits: jinn and genies from Arabia to Zanzibar* (London & New York: IB Tauris, 2010)

Le Fanu, Sheridan, *Carmilla* (London: Hesperus Books, 2013)

Leon-Portilla, Miguel (editor), *The Broken Spears* (London: Constable, 1962)

Lionarons, Joyce Tally, *The Medieval Dragon: the nature of the beast in Germanic literature* (Middlesex, England: Hisarlik Press, 1998)

Luckhurst, Roger, *Zombies: a cultural history* (London: Reaktion Books, 2015)

Lützow, Count, *Hussite Wars* (London: JM Dent & Sons, 1914)

Maarouf, Mohammed, *Jinn Eviction as a Discourse of Power* (Leiden & Boston: Brill, 2007)

Mackay Brown, George, *An Orkney Tapestry* (Edinburgh: Birlinn, 2021)

Madiou, Thomas, *Histoire d'Haiti* (Port-au-Prince: JH Courtois, 1848)

Malchow, H.L., 'Frankenstein's Monster and Images of Race in Nineteenth-Century Britain', in *Past and Present*, Vol. 139, No. 1 (May 1993)

Mantel, Hilary, *Wolf Hall* (London: Fourth Estate, 2009)

Marešová, Soňa, *The Prague Golem: Jewish Stories of the Ghetto* (Prague: Vitalis, 2000)

Marwick, Ernest, *An Orkney Anthology* (Edinburgh: Scottish Academic Press, 1991)

Marwick, Ernest, *Folklore of Orkney and Shetland* (London: Origin, 2020)

Masincup, Emily, 'La Llorona and the First Cries of Mexican Horror', in *La Llorona* DVD booklet (Bordon: Powerhouse Films, 2022)

Massey, Irving (editor), *Posthumous Poems of Shelley: Mary Shelley's Fair Copy Book* (Montreal: McGill-Queen's University Press, 1969)

Metraux, Alfred, *Voodoo in Haiti*, translated by Hugo Charteris (New York: Oxford University Press, 1959)

Mittman, Asa Simon (editor), *The Ashgate Research Companion to Monsters and the Monstrous* (London: Routledge, 2017)

Muir, Tom, *The Mermaid Bride and Other Orkney Folk Tales* (Kirkwall: The Orcadian Limited/Kirkwall Press, 1998)

Nérette Louis, Liliane, *When Night Falls, Kric! Krac!* (1999) (Englewood, Colorado: Libraries Unlimited, 1999)

Nietzsche, Friedrich, *Beyond Good and Evil: prelude to a philosophy of the future*, translated by Helen Zimmern (Edinburgh: T.N. Foulis, 1907)

Novaković, Mirjana, *Fear and His Servant*, translated by Terene McEneny (London: Peter Owen Publishers, 2009)

O'Connor, Mike, *Cornish Folk Tales* (Stroud, England: History Press, 2010)

Orwell, George, *1984* (London: Penguin, 2004)

Ovid, *Metamorphoses*, translated by Frank Justus Miller (Cambridge, Massachusetts: Harvard University Press, 1977)

Owens, Susan, *The Ghost: a cultural history* (London: Tate Publishing, 2017)

Paravisini-Gebert, Lizabeth & Fernández Olmos, Margarite (editors), *Sacred Possessions: vodou, santería, obeah and the Caribbean* (New Brunswick, New Jersey: Rutgers University Press, 1997)

Paz, Octavio, *The Labyrinth of Solitude*, translated by Lysander Kemp, Yara Milos & Rachel Phillips Belash (London: Penguin, 1990)

Peake, Richard Brinsley, *Presumption: or, the Fate of Frankenstein*, edited by Stephen Behrendt, https://english.unl.edu/sbehrendt/texts/Presumption/presump.htm (2011)

Perez, Domino Renee, *There Was a Woman: La Llorona from folklore to *popular culture* (Austin: University of Texas Press, 2008)

Perić, Boris, *Vampir* (Zagreb: Naklada Ljevak, 2006)

Perkowski, *Vampire Lore* (Bloomington, Indiana: Slavica Publishers, 2006)

Perlinger, Werner, *Seit Jahrhunderten Drachenkampf in Furth* (Furth im Wald, Bavaria: Historischer Verein, 2007)

Pitre, *Advice from the Wicked* (New Orleans: Cote Blanche Productions, 2020)

Polidori, John, *The Diary of Dr John William Polidori, 1816* (London: Matthews, 1911)

Polidori, John, *The Vampire: a tale* (London: Sherwood, Neely & Jones, 1819)

Reider, Noriko T., *Japanese Demon Lore: oni, from ancient times to the present* (Logan, Utah: Logan State University Press, 2010)

Reider, Noriko T., *Tales of the Supernatural in Early Modern Japan* (Lewiston, New York: Edwin Mellen Press, 2002)

Riches, Samantha, *Saint George: hero, martyr and myth* (Stroud, England: Sutton, 2005)

Roberts, Anthony, *Sowers of Thunder: giants in myth and history* (London: Rider, 1978)

Robinson, Charles G. (editor), *The Frankenstein Notebooks* (London: Routledge, 2021)

Rosenberg, Yudl, *The Golem and the Wondrous Deeds of the Maharal of Prague* (New Haven, Connecticut: Yale University Press, 2007)

Rowse, A.L., *A Cornish Childhood* (London: Jonathan Cape, 1946)

Ryfle, Steve, *Japan's Favorite Mon-Star: the unauthorized biography of 'The Big G'* (Toronto: ECW Press, 1998)

Sampson, Fiona, *In Search of Mary Shelley: the girl who wrote Frankenstein* (London: Profile Books, 2018)

Saxon, Lyle, *Gumbo Ya-Ya: folk tales of Louisiana* (Gretna, Louisiana: Pelican Publishers, 1987)

Scott Fox, David, *Saint George: the saint with three faces* (Windsor, England: Kensal Press, 1983)

Seabrook, William, *The Magic Island* (London: GG Harrap 1999)

Seymour, Miranda, *Mary Shelley* (London: Faber & Faber, 2011)

Shelley, Mary, *Frankenstein*, 1831 edition, edited by M. Joseph (Oxford: Oxford University Press, 1969)

Shelley, Mary, *Frankenstein* (London: Penguin Books, 2003)

Shelley, Mary, *History of a Six Weeks' Tour Through a Part of France, Switzerland, Germany, and Holland* (London: T. Hookham, Jun. and C. and J. Ollier, 1817)

Shelley, Mary, *Mary Shelley's Journal*, edited by Fredrick L. Jones (Norman: University of Oklahoma Press, 1947)

Shelley, Mary, *The Letters of Mary W. Shelley*, edited by Frederick L. Jones (Norman: University of Oklahoma, 1944)

Shelley, Percy Bysshe, *Posthumous Poems of Shelley: Mary Shelley's fair copy book* (Montreal: McGill-Queen's University Press, 1969)

Shelley, Percy Bysshe, *The Prose Works of Percy Bysshe Shelley, Vol. 1*, edited by E.B. Murray (Oxford: Oxford University Press, 1993)

Sherman, Anna, *The Bells of Old Tokyo: travels in Japanese time* (London: Picador, 2019)

Shonagon, Sei, *The Pillow Book*, translated by Ivan Morris (Harmondsworth, England: Penguin, 1970)

Shuker, Karl, *Dragons: a natural history* (London: Aurum Press, 1995)

Summers, Montague, *The Werewolf in Lore and Legend* (Mineola, New York: Dover Publications, 2003)

Taylor, Thomas, *The History of St Michael's Mount* (Cambridge, England: Cambridge University Press, 1932)

Thomas, Hugh, *The Conquest of Mexico* (London: Hutchinson, 1993)

Thomson, David, *The People of the Sea* (Edinburgh: Canongate, 2011)

Tonkin, Thomas, 'The Parish of St Agnes', in *The Journal of the Royal Institution of Cornwall*, Vol. 7, No. 3 (Truro, England: Blackford, 1976)

Tsutsui, Bill, *Godzilla on My Mind* (New York: Palgrave Macmillan, 2004)

Turinne, Gaël, *Voodoo* (Tielt, Belgium: Lannoo Publishers, 2010)

Tyler, Royall, *Japanese Tales* (New York: Pantheon Books, 2002)

Valvasor, Johann Weichard von, *Die Ehre des Herzogthums Krain, Vol. 11* (Rudolfswerth, Slovenia: J. Krajec, 1877)

Verney, Victor, *Warrior of God: Jan Žižka* (Barnsley, England: Frontline, 2009)

Voskuhl, Adelheid, *Androids in the Enlightenment: mechanics, artisans, and cultures of the self* (Chicago: University of Chicago Press, 2013)

Walpole, Horace, *The Letters of Horace Walpole, Earl of Orford, Vol. 1, 1735–1748* (London: 1833)

Westermarck, Edward, *Ritual and Belief in Morocco* (London: Macmillan, 1926)

Westaway, Jonathan, 'The Inuit Discovery of Europe: the Orkney Finnmen, preternatural objects and the re-enchantment of early modern science', in *Atlantic Studies* Vol. 19, No. 2 (published online, 2 Nov 2020)

Williamson, Duncan, *The Land of the Seal People* (Edinburgh: Birlinn, 2017)

Yoda, Hiroko and Alt, Matt, *Yokai Attack!* (Tokyo: Kodansha International, 2008)

Zlatkovskaia, T.D., 'On the Origin of Certain Elements of the Kuker Ritual among the Bulgarians', in *Soviet Anthropology & Archaeology*, Vol. 7, No. 2 (1968)

Endnotes

PROLOGUE

goes back to the ancient Thracians: Kukerovden is 8,000 years old, according to the School for Bulgarian Folk Dance; it can be traced to Thrace, according to Zlatkovskaia.

speech is fire: *The Epic of Gilgamesh*, p. 18

the soaring confidence of human societies: 'When monotheism became the dominant premise of religious culture,' writes Stephen T. Asma in *On Monsters* (p. 63), 'monsters had to be brought under the omnipotent, omniscient, omnibenevolent creator god.' Non-anthropomorphic gods endure, in Hinduism and many folk religions, but on a much-reduced scale compared with the ancient world, in which deities perceived in modern Western culture as 'monsters' were worshipped by Mayans, Babylonians, Celts, Egyptians, Native American tribes, and many other peoples.

multitude of fiends ... the loathsome spirits: 'The Life of Saint Guthlac of Crowland (Guthlac A)', lines 325, pp. 404–5, translated by Aaron Hostetter, https://oldenglishpoetry.camden.rutgers.edu/guthlac-a/

incorporeall souldiers: *A Great Wonder in Heaven*, p. 5

his hair grew like the feathers: The Bible, Daniel 4:33

PART ONE: WHEN THE WILD ROARS
Appear, O Bacchus, to our eyes as a bull: https://sacred-texts.com/cla/eurip/bacchan.htm

CHAPTER ONE: THE GIANT WHO FELL IN LOVE
The First Tale: the story of Bolster and Saint Agnes is narrated in, among others, Gilbert, Bottrell, and Borlase. Since most versions after Gilbert have included the character of Bolster's wife, I have done so as well.
mighty race of Titans: Bottrell, p. 9
People of the northern hills: ibid., p. 122
Students of ancient geometry: for more on Carn Galver and other sites in Penwith, see https://ancientwhisperspenwith.blogspot.com/
Oh my son: Bottrell, p. 123
human skeleton measuring seven feet: among reports of the giant skeleton are those of Canon Thomas Taylor and the 1899 *Journal of the Royal Institution of Cornwall*
the grey rock in the wood: radiocarbon dating suggests the mount was framed by a hazel wood up to 1700 BC; see de Beer, p. 163
The island was then called Albion: Geoffrey of Monmouth, p. 20
promised island: ibid., p. 19
of such prodigious strength: ibid., p. 20
roused up his whole strength: ibid., p. 21.
There giants whilome dwelt: Havillan, in James (digital edition), loc. 320/613
Sten Sen Agnes: Gilbert, p. 11
the country people: Tonkin, pp. 203–4
attempting her chastity: ibid.
intrenchment: Borlase, p. 292

CHAPTER TWO: CITY OF THE DRAGON
The Second Tale: is a retelling of the story in the *Drachenstich* of Furth im Wald, as told by Joseph Martin Bauer and, more recently, Alexander Etzel-Ragusa. In my version, I have nodded to the legend

of Saint George and the Dragon ('let me succour thee') as told in *The Golden Legend* by Jacob de Voragine.
dragon lying on the mountain: *The Hymns of the Rig Veda*, Book 1, Hymn 32
in a deep lake as large as an ocean: Scott Fox, p. 23
in the name of God: ibid., p. 23
This she did: ibid., p. 28
the largest of all serpents: Isidore of Seville, *Etymologies*, quoted in Lionarons, p. 13
payment of two guilders: 'Zöhrung 2 Gulden': Werner Perlinger, 'Der Drachenstich in Furth im Wald', in Kleindorfer-Marx, p. 179
little town: ibid., p. 181
For a long time: Hierstetter, *Bausteine zu einer Geschichte der alten Grenzstadt Furth im Wald* (handwritten manuscript), in Pfarrarchiv Furth im Wald, Fa.361 (in Perlinger, pp. 60–4; my translation, with thanks to Werner Perlinger for sending me this document)
the whole crowd poured in front: ibid.
turned around and showed: ibid.
The howling and yelling: ibid.
foreign stuff: Eugen Hubrich play-text, quoted in Drachenhöhle Museum, Furth im Wald
Nobody further inland: 'niemand weiter drinnen im Lande hält den Drachen auf, wenn es nicht hier geschieht!': Werner Perlinger, 'Der Drachenstich in Furth im Wald' (my translation), in Kleindorfer-Marx, p. 182
Oh what a disgraceful refuge: Lützow, p. 270
The community that was once: Fleming, p. 62

CHAPTER THREE: THE OGRE ON THE PURPLE MOUNTAIN

The Third Tale: is adapted from the tale of Shutendoji as retold in *The Ogres of Oyeyama* (Japanese Fairy Tale Series No 19, translated by T.H. James) and *Japanese Demon Lore* by Noriko Reider.

Purple Hills and Crystal Streams: this phrase, used by the poet and historian Sanyo Rai in the nineteenth century, 'has been taken up as an epithet for the city', according to Dougill, p. 5
undomesticated expressions of nature: Dylan Foster, p. 15
In many of the traditional stories: the story of the bride devoured by the oni is told in *Miraculous Stories from the Buddhist Tradition* (ninth century); the tale of Watanabe and the beautiful woman who turns into an oni is told in *The Epic of the Heike*; the story of the Buddhist monk and his catamite is told in 'The Blue Hood' by Ueda Akinari (in *Ugetsu Monogatari*, 1776).
the faces behind inexplicable phenomena: Yoda and Alt, p. 7
Shuten Doji was originally a robber: Reider, loc. 177
otherness: Noriko Reider, interview with author, 14 Dec 2022
someone or something outside the powerhouse: Katz-Harris, p. 81
Monsters had been disseminated in mediaeval European romances: in the *Ashgate Research Companion to Monsters and the Monstrous*, John Block Friedman points out that monsters (or monstrous races) were recounted by Greek travellers such as Herodotus and Megasthenes, and they appeared en masse in the 'period of the encyclopediae' (roughly the thirteenth century) as well as in Renaissance collections such as Ambroise Paré's *On Monsters and Marvels* (1573). Another notable and remarkably illustrated monster catalogue is Ulise Aldrovandi's *Monstrorum Historia* (1642).
musing on the semiotics of oni colours: these are much-debated terms, with yellow being particularly nuanced; it was chosen as the colour for Buddhist monks' robes due to its association with humility and the separation from worldly attachments; it is also linked with the earth and rootedness in nature. For more on the philosophy of colours in Buddhism, see https://www.buddhaweekly.com/color-in-buddhism-its-importance-and-deep-spirituality/

PART TWO: WHEN THEY BECOME US
Beware that when fighting monsters: Nietzsche, Chapter 4, p. 146

CHAPTER FOUR: SHAPESHIFTERS AT SEA

The Fourth Tale: is adapted from *The Play of the Ladhie Odivere*, recorded by Walter Traill Dennison and printed in *The Scottish Antiquary*, Vol. 8, pp. 54–8

the Goodman of Wastness: this tale was narrated by Dennison, Vol. 7, pp. 171–7

are rather carefully made: Breuil, p. 176

and everyone aboard: *The Sagas of Icelanders*, p. 299

first truly indigenous fragment: Hall, p. 100

dark rounded hills: Mackay Brown, p. 27

rose out of the water to the height of three feet: *The Orcadian*, 13 Sep 1913

The whole of Dennison's life: Marwick, in Hall, p. 43

It is now well-nigh fifty years: Dennison, Vol. 8, p. 53

But how will I my young son ken: Thomson, p. 206

peerie ... skeeted ...: Dennison, Vol. 8, pp. 54–7

had always been open to the possibility: Westaway, p. 216

The selkies are Orkney folks' cousins: Marwick (1991), p. 47

who sprang from union with a seal man: Marwick (2020), p. 51

The Orkney earldom was a formidable naval power: Almqvist, p. 2

CHAPTER FIVE: THE REALM OF THE UNSEEN

The Fifth Tale: is inspired by oral narrations of the legend of Aicha Kandicha as a warrior against the Portuguese. For my telling, I have drawn on accounts of the legend in *Jinn Eviction as a Discourse of Power* by Mohammed Maarouf, 'Deux Mythes Féminins du Maghreb: la Kahina et Aïcha Kandicha' by Samira Douider, *Invisibles of the Everyday* by Abdel-Wahed Alaoui, Safia Lamrani's short play (Pistachio Theatre Company, Out the Shell 01), and oral accounts I heard in Morocco. I have added details about the Portuguese presence in order to recognise the historical context in which many versions of the story are rooted.

the British writer Tahir Shah: these incidents have been recounted, for example, in Tahir Shah's book *In Arabian Nights*, in his introduction to *Legends of the Fire Spirits*, and 'In Search of the White House' by

Jason Webster (*Financial Times*, 23 February 2023).
fire free of smoke: The Quran, sura 55:14
I am better than he: ibid., sura 7:11
each time the two letters: El-Zein, p. xvi
We see them in the eye of the heart: ibid., p. 23
aerial animals, with transparent bodies: Lebling, p. 62
after I'd lived: Al-Maari, p. 133
Anyone of us could be a speckled snake: ibid., p. 131
we have reason to suppose: Westermarck, p. 396
He is to be classed: Crapanzano, p. 23
Many Moroccans, especially Berbers: ibid., p. 7
It has sometimes been suggested: Jamous (my translation), p. 82
comparable to a state: Crapanzano, p. 196
It disciplines them to submit to the centres of distribution: Maarouf, p. 4
At the notorious shrine of Bouya Omar: see, for example, 'The Gates of Hell Are Finally Closed: the secret story of Bouya Omar Mausoleum', https://www.moroccoworldnews.com (19 Jun 2015)
From the Portuguese threat: Abun-Nasr, p. 208
Beni Mellal, an area they never reached: according to Professor Fatima Zahra Salih (in conversation with the author, October 2023)
In one of the most enduring of these tales: summarising the folk tales about Aicha Kandicha, the Moroccan literary scholar Professor Samira Douider writes: 'Originally from El-Jadida, she would have, in the 16th century, contributed to fighting against the Portuguese invaders. Her technique consisted of using her charms to attack soldiers who were then killed by her accomplices.' ('Deux Mythes Féminins du Maghreb: la Kahina et Aïcha Kandicha', in *Recherches Travaux* No. 81, 2012, pp. 75–81.) Mohammed Maarouf identifies the stories with 'the mythic lore of Doukkala. In this region, it is believed that Aicha was a real historical figure who fought against invaders, especially the Portuguese.' (Maarouf, p. 106.)
ecstatic trance, into which: Crapanzano, p. 43

CHAPTER SIX: WHO'S AFRAID OF THE ROUGAROU?

The Sixth Tale: amalgamates features from several rougarou folk tales: those I heard in New Orleans, Houma, and Lafayette, as well as the stories recounted in *Gumbo Ya-Ya* by Lyle Saxon, *Advice for the Wicked* by Glen Pitre, and *Cajun and Creole Folk Tales* collected by Barry Ancelet. In telling this story, I have striven to capture something of the landscape, the atmosphere of Cajun culture, and the details of rougarou stories, such as the rule of silence for a year and a day and blood-shedding as a way to break the curse.

has left his stamp: Baring-Gould, p. 3
he found the flesh of little girls: de Lancre, p. 331
very long and bright teeth: ibid., pp. 329–30
It is during the sixteenth century: Summers, p. 244
The Devil wants me: Brightman, p. 349
They have such a dread and horror: ibid.
The torn clothes: Pitre, pp. 13–14
A dog's life holds certain satisfactions: ibid., p. 351
In a word the Acadian mothers: Jobb, p. 157
good vassals: ibid., p. 190
primitive: *Harper's Weekly*, in ibid., p. 210
held in contempt: Saxon, p. 182
Dans le creux de la nuit: sleeve notes to *Broken Promised Land*: 'Le Loup'
the dark side of his being: Jung, p. 262
It becomes automatic: 'Linguistic Schizophrenia', in *Equinoxes*, No. 2, Autumn/Hiver 2003–04, https://www.brown.edu/Research/Equinoxes/journal/issue2/eqx2_bruce_tr.html
Children of silence: Arceneaux, p. 99
sinister shadow: Jung, p. 262

PART THREE: WHEN THE DEAD RISE

I do not think that all the persons: Percy Bysshe Shelley, *The Prose Works of Percy Bysshe Shelley*, Vol. 1

CHAPTER SEVEN: THE CONQUISTADOR AND THE GHOST

The Seventh Tale: for this telling, I have used the main outline by Vicente Riva Palacio (who wrote one of the oldest known stories of La Llorona in 1885), but in order to reflect the story as it is most commonly told in Mexico, I have depicted Luisa drowning rather than stabbing her children.

The beginning of her: Janvier, p. 135

no more conscience than a dog: Diego de Ordaz, in Thomas, p. 156

If God helps us, far more will be said: Knight, p. 214

And this present was nothing in comparison to twenty women: Bernal, in Becerra, p. 29

good-looking and mettlesome: ibid.

knew the Mexican languages: ibid., p. 26

the bridge over which the words of Cortes passed: ibid., p. 166

The Mexican people have not forgiven La Malinche: Paz, p. 86

La Malinche said to the guards 'Come forward': Leon-Portilla, p. 135

When the Captain and La Malinche saw the gold: ibid., p. 142

the Chingada in person: 'The Chingada is one of the Mexican representations', Paz, pp. 75, 87

a large gold wheel: Cortes, p. 40

My children, where shall I take you: Esquivel, p. 25

newspapers had reported a dog running through the streets: the Zacatecas incident was reported by CBS News and the *New York Post*, among others (29, 31 Oct 2022); the Irapuato incident by the *New York Post* and *Latin Times* (22, 23 Nov 2022). On the disappearances of indigenous Mexicans, see, for example, 'The Disappeared People of Mexico's Drug War' by Sandra Weiss, https://www.dw.com (30 Aug 2021).

Include the artistic and religious legacy ... specific demographic and political circumstances: Brandes, pp. 211, 214

we enjoy looking: Aristotle, section 1448b

as big as Seville ... square twice as big: Cortes, p. 102

They ran in among the dancers: Leon-Portilla, p. 74

I would not abandon this land: Cortes, p. 138

We have chewed dry twigs: Leon-Portilla, p. 138
The cries of the helpless women: ibid., p. 122
We could not but be saddened: Cortes, p. 233
Your ancestors also erred: Janvier, p. 163
Victorian ghosts were shaped: Owens, p. 190
Full of deadly terror for all: 'A todos llena de mortal espanto, / Y junto al rio en la tiniebla espesa / Se va llorando envuelta con su manto': Carpio (my translation), p. 265
many bad things: Janvier, p. 134
Throw off your rebozo: ibid., p. 137
Yo soy La Llorona: Perez, p. 2
She was not a European monster: Masincup, p. 10
spectacular: 'El Universal', in Masincup, pp. 29, 27

CHAPTER EIGHT: THE AGE OF VAMPIRES

The Eighth Tale: is adapted from the popular Serbian novella *After Ninety Years* by Milovan Glisić (published 1880).
There was no doubt about the certainty: Valvasor, p. 319
sitting behind the door: ibid., p. 317
bore an abhorrence: ibid., p. 318
who had more heart: ibid., p. 319
something like this: ibid.
The first recorded case: Perić, *Vampir* (extract shared by the author)
In this century, a new scene: Calmet (translated by M. Cooper), in Perkowski, p. 119
the first occurrences of the term vampire: Dundes, p. 9
they feed in the night: Rycaut, in Groom, p. 27
As they saw that [Paole] was a real vampire: Flückinger, in Hamberger, p. 50
the heads of the vampires: ibid., p. 53
They also add: ibid., p. 50
without having previously had an illness: ibid.
much liquid blood: ibid., pp. 51–2

A magical plague: Glaser Sr, in Groom, p. 36
we have found no traces: Royal Prussian Scientific Society, in Hamberger, p. 112
implicit faith: Walpole, p. 3
all these occurrences: van Swieten, in Braünlein, p. 13
some of our country's inhabitants: Empress Maria Theresa, in Hamberger, p. 85
in Poland, in Hungary: Voltaire, in Hamberger, p. 263
to indulge the luxury: Forman, see Dundes, p. 6
Brokers, Country Bank Directors, and their disciples: D'Arcy, p. 41
universal emancipation: ibid., p. 36
our fetters discandied ... the whole infernal fraternity: ibid., pp. 36, 38
The contribution of this stereotype: Frayling, p. 9
But first, on earth as vampire sent: 'The Giaour', Byron, *The Major Works*, pp. 207–46
With gloating eyes: Le Fanu, p. 110

CHAPTER NINE: REVOLUTION OF THE UNDEAD

The Ninth Tale: recalls the old folk tale about Haitian zombies and their reaction to salt, told by William Seabrook in *The Magic Island* (1929), and reimagined by the Haitian author Frankétienne in his groundbreaking novel *Dézafi* (1975).
The history of colonisation: Depestre (1971), p. 20
The dominant figure of the undead: Luckhurst, p. 8
The sun beat down: Chantrans, in Fick, p. 28
Last night, a slave choked himself to death: ibid., p. 46
savage people: Edwards, p. 67
From morning to night: Herskovits, p. 39
enthusiasm for general liberty: Daut, p. 51
pamphlets printed in France: Hazareesingh, p. 46
Throw away the image of the God of the whites: Hurbon, p. 45
the slaves strove to be reunited: Turine, p. 11
monstrous hybridity: Daut, p. 71

never before has any monster stained himself: ibid., p. 133
Dessalines is coming to the north: Dayan, p. 40
crime for crime, outrage for outrage: Dessalines, 'Liberté ou la Mort', 8 Apr 1804, in Hoermann, p. 19
noted many times for his cruelty: Madiou, p. 133
The dead-alive zombie: Dayan, p. 37
cunning spirits: de Blessebois, p. 56
the dirtiest and deepest ditch: ibid.
He repulsed her in saying: Descourtilz, p. 220
the use that may be made against a person of substances: the original French from Article 246 is: 'Est aussi qualifié attentat à la vie d'une personne, par empoisonnement, l'emploi qui sera fait contre elle de substances qui, sans donner la mort, auront produit un état léthargique plus ou moins prolongé, de quelque manière que ces substances aient été employées et quelles qu'en aient été les suites.' This provision was added in 1864, under General Fabre Nicholas Geffrard, a Catholic Haitian who had risen to power five years earlier and sought to eradicate traditional superstitious practices. In *Les Codes Haïtiens Annotés: Code Penal*, p. 101 (digitised edition, p. 567).
This colony is swarming with slaves: Fick, p. 66
Among the case studies that emerged: the case of Marie M. was reported by Zora Neale Hurston in *Tell My Horse*, and also (among others) by a Haitian doctor called Arthur Holly, in *Les Daïmons du Culte Voudo et Dra-Po*, 1918, who reported, 'The case is not a unique one in our annals' ('Women Possessed: eroticism and exoticism in the representation of woman as zombie' by Lizabeth Paravisini-Gebert, in *Sacred Possessions*, p. 41). The Jacmel zombie was reported by the American journalist and Pulitzer Prize–winning historian Stephen Bonsal in *The American Mediterranean*: 'The victim recognized no one, and his days and nights were spent moaning inarticulate words no one could understand.' The case of Felicia Felix-Mentor was reported by Hurston in *Tell My Horse*. However, the Haitian psychiatrist Louise Price-Mars, who treated Felix-Mentor, debunked Hurston's account

in no uncertain terms: 'This is evidently a case of schizophrenia and gives us an idea of how cases of similar nature are likely to arouse mass hysteria in a culture where the common people do not usually understand the scientific basis of many natural events which occur in their daily life ... Miss Hurston herself, unfortunately, did not go beyond the mass hysteria to verify her information, nor in any way attempt to make a scientific explanation of the case.' ('The Story of Zombies in Haiti', published in *Man: a record of anthropological science*, Vol. 45, No. 22, March–April 1945, pp. 38–40.)

That blank face: Hurston, p. 189

a band of ragged creatures: Seabrook (1999), p. 95

plodding like brutes: ibid.

the fear in Haiti: Davis, p. 9

In one tale, skeletons clamber out: the clambering skeletons appear in 'La Veillée' by Amilcar Duval, in *Contes et légendes d'Haïti*; the taxi driver story is 'Trafic de Morts' told by Christophe Philippe Charles, also in *Contes et légendes d'Haïti*; the zombie thieves are from 'The Last Zonbi in Konpé Pierre's Plantation' told by Liliane Nérette Louis, in *When Night Falls, Kric! Krac!*

full of dead people: Nérette Louis, pp. 115–21

The zombie is a beast of burden: Metraux, p. 405

Blows, knuckle raps: Franketienne, p. 62

Parisian salon rat: ibid., p. 61

tiny bits and pieces: ibid., 160

To me, Zombies were still: Romero, in *Far Out Magazine*, 18 Jul 2021, https://faroutmagazine.co.uk/george-romero-mistake-created-a-new-genre/

lost in the paralysing void: Depestre (2020), p. 194

an old, oversized champagne bottle: ibid.

a privileged marker ... Zombification is Haitian: Christie, pp. 31, 37

it may be valuable to bear in mind: Malchow, pp. 94–5

yellow skin ... black lips: Shelley (1831), p. 45

inordinate physical strength: see for example Malchow, p. 102

PART FOUR: WHEN THE FUTURE BECKONS
He felt as though he were wandering: Orwell, *1984*, Part One, Chapter 2

CHAPTER TEN: MARY SHELLEY'S MONSTER-MAKING CIRCLE
The Tenth Tale: is adapted from *Frankenstein* by Mary Shelley (1831 edition).
A savage inhabitant: ibid., p. 21
uninteresting tract of country: Shelley (1944), p. 9
wasn't able to sleep all night: Clairmont, p. 22
Their immensity staggers the imagination: Shelley (1817), p. 43
spots of verdure: ibid., p. 41
verdant isles: ibid., p. 54
Nothing could be more magnificent: ibid., p. 48
nothing could be more horribly disgusting: ibid., p. 65
Franckensteina: Florescu, p. 62
Dippel's oil: ibid., p. 80
It seems, then, that the impact of the castle: ibid., p. 62
sick as death: Clairmont, p. 41
Mrs Shelley is very clever: Gordon, p. 90
the cadaverous silence: ibid., p. 24
Abhorred monster: Shelley (1831), p. 77
a fund of literary sources: Baldick, p. 34
commune with the creatures of fancy: Shelley (1831), author's introduction, pp. 1–2
prejudiced: *MWSJ*, 14 Dec 1814, in Seymour, p. 138
The alienated condition: Seymour, p. 137
the offspring of happy days: Shelley (1831), author's introduction, p. 5
To the warm sunrise: Shelley (1944), p. 10
An utter stranger: Clairmont, p. 25
with fond affection: ibid., p. 25
passed the house in which Lord Byron lives: John Pye Smith, Journal of a Tour in France, Switzerland and Italy, in the months of July, August, and September 1816 (entry for 9 August, cited in Clairmont, p. 53)

I believe they looked on me: Byron, in Gordon, p. 167
An almost perpetual rain: Shelley (1944), p. 11
animal electricity: Shelley (1831), introduction, p. ix
the effect of any human endeavour: Shelley (1831), author's introduction, p. 4
Everyone is to relate a story of ghosts: *Fantasmagoriana*, quoted in Frayling, p. 13. Frayling also reports the stories told by the participants at Villa Diodati (pp. 13–15).
fit of fantasy: Gordon, p. 190
My imagination, unbidden: Shelley (1831), author's introduction, p. 4
observing the lightning play: Shelley (1944), p. 11
A finer storm than I had ever beheld: ibid.
a marginal or vagabond figure: https://www.artlog.net/en/art/frankie-aka-creature-doctor-frankenstein
give me a garden: Shelley (1944), p. 14
hypocrisy & cruelty: ibid., p. 140
the gulph of melancholy: Hay, p. 275
But thou art fled: Percy Bysshe Shelley (1969), p. 88
She is a torrent of fire: Hunt, in Hay, p. 271
Poor Mary's book: Shelley (1944), p. 29
uncouth: Sampson, p. 164
power is so abused: ibid.
our taste and our judgement alike revolt: Florescu, p. 149
Vampyres, being dead and damn'd: Groom, p. 40
It is a most wonderful performance: Clairmont, p. 111
I met on the course: Florescu, p. 151
Well, here is my story: Shelley (1944), p. 184
I continue to exist: ibid.
The last man! Yes, I may well: Shelley (1947), p. 193
It lives!: Peake, Act 1, Scene 3
But lo and behold: Shelley (1944), p. 259
Shall I not then hate: Shelley (1831), p. 78
You accuse me of murder: ibid.

alone, and miserable: ibid., p. 111
Shall I respect man when he contemns me: ibid.

CHAPTER ELEVEN: THE HUMANS MUST DIE
The Eleventh Tale: is adapted from *Rossum's Universal Robots* by Karel Čapek (published 1920 and first performed 1921).
Robots throughout the world: Čapek (1923), p. 118
No matter which hill you climb: Klima, p. 20
In the valley between the Metuja: ibid.
The great modern play: playbill for *R.U.R.* at the Playhouse Theatre in Sydney, Australia, 1 Jul 1925 (exhibited in Museum of the Čapek Brothers, Malé Svatoňovice)
Frankenstein's monster in bulk: *The Illustrated London News*, 12 May 1923 (exhibited in Karel Čapek Memorial, Stará Huť)
Scattered about the region: Klima, p. 20
Every thought today: Ibid., p. 50
sewer with rails: Čapek, 2001, p. 35
I felt a blind and furious opposition: ibid., p. 36
Čapek's robots were but the latest: Aleksander & Burnett, p. 10
We can plot our way around the ancient world: these stories are told in *The Iliad*, the *1001 Nights*, and the *Lokapannatti* (eleventh century). The latter is a legend about King Ajatashatru, who reigned in northern India in the fifth century BC and was also known for commissioning a mechanised war-chariot.
mechanical monster whose body fills: Marx, *Capital*, Vol. 1, Chapter 15, Section 1, https://www.marxists.org/archive/marx/works/1867-c1/ch15.htm
we no longer aim: Voskuhl, p. 207
an aristocracy nourished by milliards: Čapek (1923), p. 131
Your mission is to protect the Jews: Marešová, p. 45
Robots don't know when to stop work: Čapek (1923), p. 30
I was seized by a dreadful fear: Bradbrook, p. 45
there was extended silence: ibid., p. 49
This skilful and funny work: cited in Karel Čapek Memorial, Stará Huť

robots: reminiscence of Mila Tiefenbach, in Bradbrook, p. 49
as many social implications: Alexander Woolcott, *The New York Herald*, quoted in the introduction to Čapek (1923), p. ix
the most brilliant satire: Maida Castellum, *The Call*, quoted in ibid., p. x
Mr Shaw, at one point: Bradbrook, p. 49
For our own selfishness: Čapek (1923), p. 133
works with his hands: ibid., p. 165
set off for a triumphant journey: Bradbrook, p. 49
Robots in Real Life: *Daily Mirror*, 16 May 1923
to cease being a man Robot: *The Times*, 20 Mar 1925, p. 9
A Robot is the only type of man: *The Times*, 10 Sep 1928, p. 4
Ladies and gentlemen, I am Eric the robot: *Evening Tribune*, 29 Jan 1929, p. 3, in https://cyberneticzoo.com/robots/1928-eric-robot-capt-richards-english/
mechanical, soulless robots: Seabrook, p. 48
a unit, a murder robot: Aldington, p. 228
It's tempting to dismiss the notion: *The Independent*, 1 May 2014: Stephen Hawking: 'Transcendence looks at the implications of artificial intelligence — but are we taking AI seriously enough?'
Mitigating the risk of extinction: Center for AI Safety, https://www.safe.ai/statement-on-ai-risk
small, yellow and white: *The New York Times*, 16 May 1926, section SM, p. 1
With a consistency that has no parallel: Erika Mann, *The Nation*: 'A Last Conversation with Karel Čapek', 14 Jan 1939 (displayed at Karel Čapek Memorial, Stará Hut')
Call them robots: see Čapek's article in *Lidove Noviny*, 24 Dec 1933, https://web.archive.org/web/20130727132806/http://capek.misto.cz/english/robot.html

CHAPTER TWELVE: KING OF THE MONSTERS

The Twelfth Tale: is adapted from the original *Godzilla* movie (1954, storyline by Shigeru Kayama, screenplay by Ishiro Honda and Takeo Murata).
a symbol of Japan's post-war regrets: Ryfle, p. 14

At around 6.50 am: exhibit in Daigo Fukuryu Maru Museum, Tokyo
I pray that I am the last: ibid. (also see *Japan's Favorite Mon-Star*, p. 20)
We appeal, as human beings: The Russell-Einstein Manifesto, 9 Jul 1955, https://pugwash.org/1955/07/09/statement-manifesto/
If Godzilla had been a big ancient dinosaur: Ryfle, p. 37
making radiation visible: Tsutsui, p. 32
My friends were lying all around the school yard: testimony in Hiroshima Peace Memorial Museum
Godzilla is the son of the atomic bomb: Tsutsui, p. 82
What if a dinosaur sleeping: ibid., p. 14
a cross between a whale and a gorilla: Ryfle, p. 23
If they keep experimenting: *Godzilla,* 3 Nov 1954, screenplay by Takeo Murata & Ishiro Honda
jumped by a wild bear: England, p. 175

EPILOGUE
genetic uncertainty principle: Cohen, p. 3